T0329054

GLOBALISATION

and

AFRICA

Reverse Robin Hoodism

Daniel A. Offiong, Ph.D.
Professor of Sociology
Clark Atlanta University
Atlanta, Georgia, USA

Apex Books Limited

© Daniel Offiong, 2013

APEX BOOKS LIMITED

262, Ipaja Road, Opposite Ipaja Post Office
P. O. Box 2448 Ipaja Post Office, Lagos
Tel: (+ 234) 1 891 5470, 0805 510 5337
E-mail: apexbooks2001@yahoo.com
apexbookslimitedng@gmail.com

ISBN 978-978-922-207-0

First published, 2013

Dedication

To **ARIT**

Thoughtful, caring, loving, magnanimous.

Acknowledgements

I am grateful to all the sponsors and researchers and authors of the various reports that I have drawn freely for this work.

Preface

In his book The Treasure Island, Robert Louis Stevenson shows a pirate landing with a sea chest but ultimately flees without it. In the chest are treasures, gold coins, jewelry and above all, a map which would lead to the discovery of more treasures. The chest is symbolic of a utopian society, which must be found using the key within it. Yet, the discovery of that society has been precluded by the acts of social injustice that were demonstrated by the running away of the pirate. It is still considered that in spite of this barrier, the utopia can still be reached since the framework (the chest) and the strategy (the key) have already been provided. It only requires courageous crusaders to rise up, dare the wrath of the sources of barrier and pick up, on behalf of others, the key to a new and better social order. As crusaders they must be ready to fight on behalf of the oppressed people, against social ills; they as Robin Hood, must be ready to take from the rich exploiter to give to the exploited poor. By taking from the rich and giving to the poor, Robin Hood and his loyal followers fight for the downtrodden and oppressed, Frantz Fanon's the wretched of the earth.

In my opinion, the rich industrialised countries are the ones that have the key and therefore control the chest. They are the ones to act the Robin Hood by sharing the contents of the chest with the poor of the world. Nobody asks them for a fact remains an empty platitude - simply pious baloney. They have been unwilling to use the key they have to open the chest and share the contents with the poor countries. Instead, the biblical statement of taking from the poor and adding to the stupendous riches of the very rich or Karl Marx's notion of the bourgeoisie exploiting the proletariat has become the principle upon which current international economic order operates. This smacks of reverse Robin Hoodism.

This work does not seek to break any new ground in the controversy surrounding the monster known as globalisation and the fact that the poor are not benefiting from its fruits. The goal of this book is a very modest one: It is to use the resources already available in abundance from the United Nations (UN), the World Bank and International Monetary Fund (IMF); reports of advocacy groups; international conferences; and published and unpublished sources to demonstrate the unfairness of the present international economic order; consider the asymmetric global trading system, the role of the World Bank and IMF as tax collectors for Western countries and the role of vulture capitalism, the impact of farm subsidies by Western countries on African farmers and their societies, the forcible liberalisation and deregulation imposed upon poor countries by the World Bank and IMF while the rich countries erect barriers to products from poor countries. In the final analysis, Africa has not benefited from globalisation and this is why the cry for globalisation to be managed in such a way that Africans, particularly the Sub-Saharan region, also benefits from its blessings.

Contents

Dedication, iii
Acknowledgements, iv
Preface, v

Chapter 1: Globalisation: The Triumphalist Juggernaut
Introduction, *3*
The Triumphalist Juggernaut, *5*
The Concept of Globalisation, *12*
The Global Context, *24*

Chapter 2: Globalisation and African Underdevelopment
Africa and Underdevelopment, *28*
Stages of African Subjugation, *30*
Confessions of an Economic Hit Man, *42*
Aid, Poverty and Underdevelopment, *44*

Chapter 3: Globalisation and Poverty
Extent of Global Poverty, *49*
Models of Poverty, *52*
Fluctuating Commodities Prices and Poverty, *65*
Foreign Aid and Poverty, *71*
Foreign Aid and Development, *76*
Poverty and Hazardous Wastes, *81*
The Functions of Poverty, *84*

Chapter 4: Asymmetric Global Trading System
Rigged Rules and Double Standards, *94*
Cotton Subsidies and African Cotton Farmers, *103*
Africa and China, *115*

Chapter 5: Debt, Capital Flight and Poverty
Capital Flight and Poverty, *120*
Nigeria's Foreign Debt Payment and Poverty, *122*
Debt and Poverty, *124*
GNP as a Measure of Progress, *133*
Debt Relief, *136*

Chapter 6: The IMF and World Bank: Enforcers of Dependency
The Scenario, *142*
Post Neo-dependency, *146*
Structural Adjustment Programme, *148*
SAPs and Tightening Dependency, *158*

Chapter 7: Impacts of World Bank and IMF SAPs
Impact of Currency Devaluation in CFA Countries, *171*
UNCTAD Reacts to SAPs, *177*
Impact of SAPs on Education, *179*
Impact of SAPs on Healthcare, *188*
SAPs Intensify Poverty, *195*
Kicking the Habit, *198*
Development Injustice, *200*
Bail-out or Blow-out, *200*
The World Bank and IMF's Reaction to Criticisms, *201*
ECA's Reaction to Failure of SAPs, *213*

Chapter 8: Illicit Financial Flows from Developing Countries
Introduction, *221*
Illicit Financial Flows from Africa:
    Hidden Resources for Development, *223*
Illicit Financial Flows from Developing Countries:
2002-2006, *224*

The Absorption of Illicit Financial Flows from Developing Countries: 2002-2006, *227*
Discussion Paper: Illicit Financial Flows from the Least Developed Countries: 1990-2008, *229*
Privately held, Non-resident Deposits in Secrecy
Jurisdictions, *232*
Illicit Financial Flows from Developing Countries over the Decade ending 2009, *234*
Keeping Foreign Corruption Out of the US:
Four Case Studies, *239*
Stolen Asset Recovery (StAR) Initiative, *245*
Vulture Capitalism and Vulture Funds, *247*

Chapter 9: Taming the Triumphalist Juggernaut
Reforming the IMF and World Bank, *259*
Millennium Development Goals, *265*
The Rich Control the Key to Change, *270*
Thinking Aloud, *272*

Bibliography, *280*

Index, *312*

1

Globalisation: The Triumphalist Juggernaut

Africa has begun the 21st century still plagued with lots of unresolved issues such as poverty, rapid urbanisation, regional integration, food insecurity and violent fratricidal conflicts, among others. The effects of slave trade, colonialism, neocolonialism and the unfair nature of globalisation are still being felt and they have led to the suppression of freedoms, the violation of human rights and dignity of Africans, the looting of human, natural and intellectual resources which have culminated in the perpetual underdevelopment of the continent. Given the present economic condition of various African countries, the Millennium Development Goals (MDGs) can neither be met by the deadline of 2015, nor can one reasonably expect Sub-Saharan Africa to meet them in the near future (if ever).

Sadly enough, the African continent, as observed by Bunwaree (2002:19), remains rather excluded with a marginal role and location in the global system and therefore remains very poorly integrated in this system. This "marginal and mal-integration of the continent in the global capitalist system, goes a long way to illustrate "the unequal power relations as well as the unequal terms of exchange that prevail." These inequalities formed the basis for the call for a new international economic order in the early 1970s. As noted by Arndt (1987), "an international economic order controlled by a few rich countries" does not represent "a just development order." It is important that all participants in the global enterprise "have effective access to resources and share in effective decisions governing their use." As at present the global capitalist enterprise is dominated (may be controlled) by a triad – the United States (US), Western Europe and Japan – although China is making inroads.

Bunwaree (2002:20) has identified "some facts" about the continent of Africa worth noting;

(1) The percentage of African trade in world trade remains quite minimal.

(2) Africa attracts very low level of direct foreign investment (DFI).

(3) Deaths resulting from AIDS are greater in Africa than in any other parts of the world.

(4) The greatest proportion of the poor is found in SSA where millions are subsisting on less than one dollar a day.

(5) Illiteracy levels are very high particularly among women and girls.

(6) The continent is ridden with conflicts and this situation is not conducive to development.

(7) Many countries still remain in a debt trap.

(8) Unemployment levels are quite high.

To these we should add the high levels of corruption, brain drain and political instability. But Bunwaree warns that we must bear in mind that the "intensifying poverty and diminishing viability of African economies and polities" cannot be "attributed to internal dynamics only and to the quality of African leadership and the way that the political systems operate." We must also take cognisance of "a host of external factors including the history that the continent has been subjected to." African history has been one long emancipatory struggle against all manners of oppression: slavery, colonialism, neocolonialism, "home-grown dictators and foreign imperialists." Therefore, in considering the problems of poverty or development/underdevelopment, it is imperative that we bear in mind that both external and internal factors are crucial and no remedy can be exclusive of the other. To reiterate, African problems have both internal and external sources and roots.

Introduction

There are two contending views about globalisation. One view is that globalisation has brought rapid prosperity to underdeveloped countries. The second view is that globalisation serves the needs of the metropolitan countries at the expense of the peripheral countries. But this author recognises that while there is potential for good in the present global capitalist economy, Africa has not benefited from it. Its position has not changed from what it has been since its forcible integration into the system years ago. It still retains its dependency status. The asymmetric relationship between the core and the periphery continues to leave the later in a very weak position of simply relying on the crumbs coming off the tables of the core.

Africa's share of world trade has dwindled, Direct Foreign Investment in most countries has remained at very low levels (as earlier pointed out), and the income gap relative to developed countries has widened. More than 300 million Sub-Saharan Africans survive on less than one dollar per day. Of all the regions in the globe, Sub-Saharan Africa has the largest proportion of people - 48 percent – living in extreme poverty (Nsouli and Gall 2001).

Globalisation in terms of promoting "liberalisation, deregulation and privatisation envisions a market-driven level playing field at a global scale." As noted by Swiss Agency for Development (SADC), as far as Africa (particularly Sub-Saharan

Africa) is concerned, it "is at best a footnote to the world economy.   At worst it is merely considered an object of international charity" (SADC 2002).

In Sub-Saharan Africa, some 650 million people live in 48 countries, corresponding to 11 percent of the world population. Shockingly, their gross domestic product (GDP) equals just the incomes (measured as GDP) of 7 million people living in Switzerland, or 1 percent of the world's wealth. Further, 25 percent of the world's poor living in extreme poverty with less than one dollar per day is found in SSA. The African share in the global trade in general and in raw materials in particular has been declining in the last 50 years. Their foreign direct investment remains marginal while capital flight and brain drain are astronomical. The estimate is that around 30 percent of qualified African manpower lives outside the continent. Further, official development assistance (ODA) to the continent dropped dramatically from US$32 per capita in 1990 to US$9 in 2000. Life expectancy increased from 40 years in 1960 to 52 years in 1990 but then dropped to 49 years by 2000 and continues to decline because of the AIDS pandemic.

Late in 2011 the World Bank and IMF projected that the number of people living on less than $1.25 a day will be 883 million in 2015, compared with 1.4 billion in 2005 and 1.8 billion in 1990. However, much of this progress reflects rapid growth in China and India, while many African countries are lagging behind. The report continues that 17 African countries are far from halving extreme poverty, even as the aggregate goals will be reached.   Regardless of the indices used, Africa lags behind the rest of the world.

Yet, the apostles of globalisation contend that we already live in a global economy that is beneficial to all. In this global economy, flows of trade, capital and knowledge across national boundaries are large and increasing every year. They further note that those unwilling to join risk falling farther behind the rest of the globe in terms of both income and human development (Fischer 2001). Therefore African countries must embrace trade liberalisation and all will be well with them. Unfortunately, the West has always dominated trade relationship with Africa and one wonders how much more Africans can open their countries to global trade in order for them to reap tangible benefits of globalisation. In the final analysis, unless the asymmetric, superordinate-subordinate relationship is altered much will not come out of the present international economic order to the benefit of poor countries and their peoples.

The Triumphalist Juggernaut
The image of globalisation as painted by its apostles is that of triumphalist juggernaut, a massive inexorable force transforming economies, politics and cultures and inevitably vanquishing endemic poverty in poor countries of the world. This is akin to what the arch priests of modernisation had envisaged when they defined modernisation as the "total transformation" of "traditional or pre-modern" societies into the types of technologies and associated social organisations that characterise the advanced, economically prosperous, and politically stable nations of the world (Moore 1963:89). Very much like modernisation, globalisation, as far as Africa is concerned, has been a profound disappointment.

The forces that propel globalisation are not random; globalisation is the culmination of international capitalism that first brought Africa under its hegemony beginning with the work of explorers, missionaries, enslavers, colonialists and neocolonialists. As observed by Madunagu (1999:53), the "concept of globalisation ...was not handed down from heaven

... it did not emerge spontaneously. It was created by dominant social forces in the world today to serve their specific interests. Simultaneously these social forces gave themselves a new ideological name the "international community" – to go with the idea of globalisation.

Globalisation as far as Africa is concerned, and as it will be apparent throughout this book, is a "fundamental project" with the primary objective of "opening up economies" of all countries in the continent "freely and widely to the global market and its forces" (Muyale-Manenji 2010:2).

"Whatever the nature of their economies, their level of development ... their location in the global economy, all countries must pursue a common set of economic policies" (ibid.). These poor countries with very weak economies "must permit the free and indiscriminate operation of transnational corporations." This involves opening their "economies freely and indiscriminately to imports and concentrate on exporting what they are supposed to be good at." They are further required to "reduce the role of governments in the economy" to that of simply supporting the market and private enterprise; the result of this has been massive privatisation of which Westerners have been the primary beneficiaries. These poor countries are required "to leave the determination of prices of goods, currencies, labour, as well as the allocation of resources to the operation of the market" (ibid.).

As already pointed out, globalisation is certainly not an "impersonal process driven by laws and factors of development – such as technology – operating outside human control and agency", instead, it is indeed a conscious programme designed to reconstruct international economic as well as political relations in line with a particular set of interests, by which we mean the profit motivations of the business, especially the transnational corporations of the industrialised countries. Another important goal of globalisation is to reconstruct the "vision," that is, the dogma of the primacy of free market and private enterprise in all processes of human development". African countries have embraced globalisation by deregulating "foreign investment; they have liberalised their imports, removed currency controls, emasculated the direct economic role of the state" and much more. All these have more than undermined "the internal, national productive capacity, social security and democratic integrity" of African countries" (ibid.)

The economies of Sub-Saharan Africa, with a few possible exceptions, have stubbornly refused to respond positively to the medicine administered to them by the World Bank and International Monetary Fund. The situation is so bad that the Swiss Agency for Development and Cooperation (SDC) Workshop *Final Report on Globalisation and Africa* (2002:7) raises the question, "Does globalisation offer more than illusionary benefits to Africa?" This report reminds the world that most of those living in extreme poverty on less than one dollar a day live in Sub-Saharan Africa. In general the African share of global trade has been declining and in particular its share of raw materials trade has been declining in the last 50 years. FDI has been very marginal. Simultaneously, capital flight and brain drain are at record levels.

As already noted, it has been estimated that 30 percent of qualified African manpower, unfortunately, live outside the continent. Official development assistance (ODA) to the continent dropped drastically from US$32 per capita in 1990 to US$9 ten years later. Life expectancy at birth increased to about 52 years in 1990 but since then it has dropped to 49 by 2000 and the prediction remains that it will continue to drop as a result of the HIV/AIDS pandemic. What these suggest is that globalisation has failed to perform its magic or miracle in

Africa. Stanley Fisher, one of those guiding the triumphalist juggernaut, emphasises that countries must "play by the rules of the international system" (Fisher 2001:1). It is important to note that Stanley Fisher was then First Deputy Managing Director of IMF. The captains of the world economy do concede that progress regarding international trade and finance will be measured against "the yardsticks of poverty alleviation and sustainable development" (Rodrik 2002:1).

Most of the developing countries found the 1990s a decade of frustration and disappointment. In SSA most economies never responded to the medicine administered by the international financial institutions. Latin American countries experienced growth rates mostly below their historical averages. Most of the former socialist economies did not fare well as their per capita income rates were significantly lower than they started; even in the rare successful cases of countries such as Poland, poverty rates increased more than under communism. East Asian economies such as South Korea, Thailand and Malaysia, which had been dubbed as "miracles" were humiliated in the financial crisis of 1997 (ibid; Offiong 2001).

However, apostles of globalisation respond in two ways about any criticism of the failure of globalisation. They are comforted by their belief that while most countries have not been doing well, the two largest countries in the world, China and India, have seen accelerated growth. China has seen an average growth rate of 8 percent since the 1970s while India has improved its growth rate from 1.5 percent per capita in the 1980s to 3.7 percent. These two countries contain more than half of the world's poor. Their performance is therefore more than enough to hail the progress of globalisation.

The other argument is that those countries that have experienced the most integration are those that have seen fastest growth and therefore have been able to reduce poverty. China, India and a few other countries like Vietnam and Uganda are often cited as those that have embraced globalisation. The important message here is that in order for the poor countries to catapult themselves out of perennial poverty, they must embrace globalisation, that is, they must open themselves to the world economy which is dominated by the Western world. To emphasise or illustrate their point, they refer to certain statistics from China. For example, in 1960 life expectancy in China was 36 years whereas by 1999 life expectancy there was 70 years. Literacy rate also rose from 50 percent to more than 80 percent. Though China has experienced uneven development, with coastal regions doing much better than the interior, there has been a significant reduction in poverty in the country (Rodrik 2002:2).

One may ask, why has globalisation worked for China that much? The magic is due to exports and foreign investment. China has been able to sell its products on world markets and has also been able to buy capital equipment and inputs that propelled its modernisation. With all these came managerial and technical expertise. But a close examination reveals that China's achievement did not emanate from playing by the rules, which the managers of globalisation require all participants to abide by. As observed by Rodrik, "China's economic policies have violated virtually every rule by which the proselytisers of globalisation would like the game to be played" (ibid.). China does not follow the rules on trade liberalisation and did not join the World Trade Organisation (WTO) until 2001; its economy remains one of the most protected in the world; it did not unify its currency markets until 1994; for a long time China refused to open its financial markets to non-Chinese. China transformed its economy without adopting property rights nor did it privatise its state enterprises. Thus China achieved tremendous success because it ignored the rules of the game. In pursuing their economic development, Chinese policymakers were knowledgeable enough to appreciate that private incentives and markets play critical roles in achieving results while understanding also that "the solution to their problems lay in institutional innovations suited to the local conditions".

As the examples of China, South Korea and Taiwan have demonstrated economic development may call for unconventional strategies that fit awkwardly with the ideology of free trade and free capital flows. South Korea and Taiwan made extensive use of import quotas, local-content requirements, patent infringements, and export subsidies – all of which are currently prohibited by the WTO. These two countries regulated capital flows very heavily well into the 1990s. India chose a path of adopting pro-business policies while remaining one of the most protectionist economies. It allowed a somewhat mild import liberalisation in the 1990s a decade after its economy was showing higher growth in the early 1980s. India has yet to open itself up to world financial markets and this was the reason it was not affected by the Asian financial crisis of 1997.

On the other hand, many of the countries that have enthusiastically opened themselves up to trade and capital flows have experienced financial crises and lackluster performances. Latin America which embraced the globalisation agenda in the 1990s has experienced rising inequality, along with great volatility and economic growth rates far below those of the post-World War 11 decades.

The above experiences in those countries reveal that global markets can be good for poor countries but the rules they have to abide are seldom to their benefit. Poor countries are caught between the agreements they sign with WTO, World

Bank strictures, IMF conditions, and the need to sustain the confidence of financial markets. As a result, they are increasingly "deprived of the room they need to devise their own paths out of poverty. They are being asked to implement an agenda of institutional reform that took today's advanced countries generations to accomplish" (Rodrik 2002:3). The US did not practise free trade while it was trying to catch up with Britain, and not even after it had surpassed Britain. It is important to participate in the world trade, but as examples of successful developing countries have shown, they need to invent their own rule book while taking advantage of what world markets offer. As it will become clear in the pages that follow, and despite the fanfare by advanced industrial countries that they are helping poor countries, they actually impede the progress of developing countries with import barriers.

Such barriers are highest for manufactured products of great importance to poor countries. Prices of essential medicines cost a lot more in poor countries because of intellectual property-rights. Much has to be done to make the rules of globalisation fair to developing countries. The rich nations that sponsor globalisation will have to do a lot to avoid or at least reduce the tendency to dress up policies sponsored by special interests in their respective countries as answers to the problems faced by poor countries. A lot more needs to be done by rich countries in order for poor ones to reap the benefits of globalisation. The poor countries themselves, particularly their leaders, must order their priorities for them to be ready to benefit from globalisation. We now proceed to seek to understand the concept of globalisation.

The Concept of Globalisation

The main force that propelled the world at the end of the 20th century was the all-powerful force called globalisation, the aggregation of "global interconnectedness" (Offiong 2001:1). This phenomenon has gained overriding dominance at the beginning of the 21st century. Globalisation is the consummation of the internalisation of capitalism and its associated institutions and the subjugation of the peoples of the globe, which began several centuries ago. But this phenomenon – globalisation – became a popular term in the 1980s. The interest in the concept of globalisation and its consequences was aroused in part by an interest "to understand the nature of socio-economic changes" which seemed to be consuming all advanced capitalist countries. In part the intellectual interest was also connected with a perception that "the fates of individual national communities" were more and more tied together, a perception underscored by the global economic recession of the early 1980s, the resurfaced threat of "nuclear Armageddon" following the intensification of Soviet-American rivalry and the impending eco-crisis. These, among other developments in the 1980s, emerged as important reference points in a growing literature, which was, after analysing the ways in which daily existence within most nation-states was increasingly becoming entangled in global processes and structures. This extended awareness of global interconnectedness was enhanced by the electronic media, thus creating a sense of a globally shared community or village (McGrew 1996:470). Gradually, the world became villagised and we now talk in terms of a global village.

Globalisation emphasises the "multiplicity of linkages and interconnectedness" that surpasses the nation-states, that together constitute the modern world system. It sets up a process through which events, decisions, and activities in one part of the globe can and does have great consequences for individuals and communities in very distant parts of the world. (Note the sad repercussions of the 2007-2008 financial crisis set in motion by the Wall Street in the United States, to be discussed later). Currently, information, goods, capital, people, knowledge, images, communications, crime, culture, pollutants, drugs, fashion, entertainment, beliefs, among others, all immediately move across territorial boundaries. Global systems of trade, finance and production cement together, in very intricate ways, the prosperity and fate of households, communities and nations across the world. Furthermore, transnational networks, social movements and relationships are quite extensive in every area of human activity, from the academic to the sexual. Increasingly it is becoming crystal clear that territorial boundaries are less significant insofar as social activity and relations no longer cease at "the water edge" (Ibid.).

In the same vein, Haviland *et al* (2011:22-23) see globalisation as a "worldwide interconnectedness," as evidenced in global movements of natural resources, human labour, finance, capital, trade goods, crime, information, and infectious diseases. Certainly, worldwide travel, trade relations, and information flow have been in existence for several centuries; however, the pace and magnitude of these long-distance exchanges have greatly accelerated in recent decades. The birth of the Internet, especially, has significantly promoted information exchange capacities. Haviland *et al* have identified the "forces" driving globalisation to include "technological innovation, cost differences among countries, faster knowledge transfers, and increased trade and financial integration among countries". This phenomenon known as globalisation affects almost everyday life on planet earth; it is about economics as much as it is about politics; it changes human relations and ideas along with the natural environment. Even the most remote geographical communities on planet earth are fast becoming interdependent through globalisation. Thus we have the common notion of a global village.

According to Oman (1994:27), globalisation is often "used in at least two different ways, with rather different implications in terms of their policy focus." In one sense, globalisation is used to mean "multilateralism" in which case "the global trading system, multilateral trade liberalisation and government policies are the focus." Globalisation is thus understood to mean a multilateral lowering of policy impediments to the movement of goods and services across national as well as regional boundaries, and this process is what has been referred to as "multilateralism". In another sense, globalisation is seen as a microeconomic phenomenon, driven by the strategies and behaviour of corporations; here it is the changing dynamics of global competition and international competitiveness – among firms, as well as among countries and regions – that are the main focus of policy debate.

Oman proceeds to add that globalisation can be defined "generally" to mean "the growth of economic activity spanning politically defined national and regional boundaries." Thus conceived, globalisation thrives through increased movement across national and regional boundaries of goods and services, by way of trade and investment, and often of people, through migration. It is propelled by the initiatives of individual economic actors including firms, banks, and people, often in the pursuit of profit, and usually urged on by the pressure of competition. Thus globalisation is characterised by "a centrifugal process," a process of economic outreach, and "a micro-economic phenomenon" (ibid.). Viewed in this sense, globalisation has brought about three crucial effects which are intensified perceptions of increasing "interdependence" or "interconnectedness," reduced national policy sovereignty, and heightened uncertainty and instability.

The definition and analysis of globalisation by the above writers bring us to the contrasting paradigms of globalisation as interdependence and globalisation as the consummation of Western imperialism. ' As observed by Akinboye (2008:3), those who claim globalisation to mean interdependence are of liberal persuasion. Globalisation in this sense represents a "framework of complex and growing interdependence among nations." Those who espouse this paradigm view the "global socio-political and economic integration" in the "context of inter-dependencies which have restructured the world into a new and all inclusive social pattern." They also associate globalisation with "economic liberalisation as a policy option for the development of the south through a process of free trade, investment and capital flows between countries" (ibid.).

These "interdependence scholars" persistently maintain that globalisation remains the "rational end of human development, and that it is capable of impacting positively on the life of state actors that integrate their economies" (ibid.). Extolling the virtues of globalisation, Francis Fukuyama writes in his *The End of History and the Last Man* that the advent of Western liberal democracy was likely the end point of humanity's social and cultural evolution and probably the end of the final form of human government. The end of the Cold War and the intensification of globalisation was not just the passing away of an era as such, but the "end point of mankind's ideological evolution and the universalisation of Western liberal democracy as the final form of human government"

(Fukuyama 1992). As far as Fukuyama is concerned, there are certainly no viable alternatives to Western ideologies as new paradigms in international economic relations which apparently signal the triumph of capitalism on a truly global scale following the end of the cold war, the collapse of the Soviet system and the dissolution of planned economies, particularly in Eastern Europe."

On his part Jan Aart Scholte believes that globalisation has become a buzzword and he goes on to identify five key, broad definitions of globalisation (Scholte 200:15-17). The five definitions are related and overlapping, but the elements they highlight are quite different. The definitions are globalisation as internationalisation, globalisation as liberalisation, globalisation as universalisation, globalisation as westernisation, and globalisation as deterritorialisation or as the spread of supra-territoriality. Of these five definitions, it is the last one that Scholte claims offers the possibility of a clear and specific definition of the phenomenon globalisation. Supra-territoriality means trans-world or trans-border relations and this provides a way into appreciating all that is global about globalisation.

Those supporting the paradigm of globalisation as inter-dependency expect a better world if nation states would embrace the opportunities offered by inter-dependency occasioned by globalisation. Proponents of globalisation as opening up to trade or liberalisation are the ones who goat about interdependency. Trade is one of the manifestations of economic interdependence. To these must be added the flow of factors of production, namely, capital, technology enterprise and various types of labour (Streeten 2001). Economic interdependence involves trade, finance, direct investment, and to these must be added "educational, technological, ideological, and cultural, as well as ecological, environmental, legal, military, strategic, and political impulses" which "are now rapidly propagated throughout the world. Money and goods, images and people, sports and religions, guns, drugs, and diseases and pollution can now be moved quickly across national frontiers".   Thus proponents of globalisation as interdependency should not forget about the negativities associated with it.   Although they advocate free trade and laissez-fair, they do not remember to add "laissez-fair passer," unrestricted travel and migration (ibid.).

On the other hand, advocates of globalisation as imperialism are often seen as being hostile to it and usually referred to as radicals.   While the interdependence school views globalisation as positive development in international affairs, scholars who equate globalisation with imperialism simply see nothing new and different from the ubiquitous rapacious imperialism which has perpetuated the underdevelopment of the underdeveloped world (Offiong 2001, 1980). Further, Ake (1995) concludes that globalisation is a capitalist project designed to perpetuate the underdevelopment of Africa and other Third World countries. In the same vein, Veltmeyer (2005:89) states that globalisation "is a project of world domination and long-standing efforts of the United States to establish its hegemony."

The argument continues that globalisation is international capitalism building "on earlier cultural structures of worldwide trade networks, and it is the successor to a system of colonialism in which a handful of powerful, mainly European, capitalist states ruled and exploited foreign nations inhabiting distant territories" (Haviland et al 2011:393). As a massive inexorable force, globalisation forces individuals, corporations, and political institutions to rearrange as well as restructure the political field to enhance their competitive advantage, competing for increasingly scarce natural resources cheap labour, expanding commercial markets, and more and more profits (ibid.). To achieve all these, they rely on what Eric Wolf calls structural power, which is power that organises and manipulates "the systematic interaction within and among societies, directing economic and political forces on the one hand and ideological forces that shape public ideas, values, and beliefs on the other" (ibid.).

Following up on this point, Joseph Nye (2002) has divided structural power into two: "hard and soft power." Hard power relies on military and economic force. On the other hand, soft power calls for cooperation by appealing for change in ideas, beliefs, values and behaviours. Apart from military and economic hard power in the quest for dominance and profit, states and corporations employ ideological persuasion of soft power "as transmitted through electronic and digital media, communication satellites, and other information technology." Soft power takes up the responsibility to propagate the general concept of globalisation as something quite positive and progressive - bringing or enhancing "freedom," "free" trade, "free" market and more. Soft power powerfully brands "anything that opposes capitalism in negative terms" (Haviland et al 2011:397).

One quick question that arises out of the propaganda is, if globalisation was such a good and a neutral phenomenon, why all the media blitz? Globalisation is just a new form of imperialism. The apostles or apologists of this phenomenon preach the increase in world welfare and social harmony brought about by the lowering of trade and financial barriers and the expansion of world economic interdependence (Ruccio 2003). The international financial institutions have been charged with the responsibility to promote globalisation and whether in Africa or Latin America (and elsewhere) their role is to promote "global competitiveness" by aggressively promoting domestic and foreign investment and incorporating those countries into "global production chain by lowering the cost of operating" in those countries and by reducing the size of the state via accelerated privatisation, while simultaneously strengthening "the public sector's role as facilitator of private sector development" (World Bank 1996). The fact remains that the United States and other rich nations are the beneficiaries of these two major goals (Offiong 2001).

According to John Kay (2001), globalisation often means anything and everything "that people hostile to the modern economy don't like." Petras and Veltmeyer (2002) view globalisation as a sort of euphemism for imperialism. Globalisation has become the centre of "diverse intellectual and political agendas" of "an epoch defining set of changes" that is radically and increasingly "transforming economic relations and institutions in the 21st century." I proceed to draw from Steve McGiffens' review of Petras and Veltmeyer's *Globalisation Unmasked: Imperialism in the 21st Century* (*Spectrezine* 2002).

Globalisation is imperialism in a new form, a new clothe. Petras and Veltmeyer contend that the "inevitability" of globalisation and the subjugation of people in the so-called global society to free market capitalism are contingent upon the capacity of the dominant and ruling classes to get people to believe that their interests are synonymous with the people's interest, a sort of false consciousness. They argue further that "the existing world economic order is in the process of being renovated so as to create optimal conditions for the free play of good, class interest and profit-making." They see globalisation as a "widening and dependency of the international flows of trade, capital, technology and information within a single integrated market." They refute the idea of globalisation as an inevitable process, "the only road available." Globalisation is a form of politics designed to serve a particular vision of economics, and this is a result of a "consciously pursued strategy." Globalisation demands "the liberalisation of national and global markets" and this is central because without liberalisation, the growth of trade would follow an entirely different pattern.

Finally, the two paradigms of imperialism, that is, globalisation as interdependence and globalisation as imperialism, reflect the deep ideological and political preferences of those who espouse them. But whatever the preferences of scholars of development, it must be appreciated that each has its pluses and minuses. As the title of this book states categorically, whatever positive tangibles have so far emanated from globalisation have passed Africa by; they have not been equitably shared. Africa and other poor societies still remain the junior partners in whatever relationships are created by globalisation. The result is that instead of Robin Hood collecting from the rich and powerful nations to distribute among the poor, needy and powerless ones, the reverse is what has taken place. The superordinate-subordinate relationship which characterised imperialism or colonialism and neocolonialism is still the same relationship that characterises the current situation. We talk of interdependence when one society by "unilateral action can inflict harm (or provide benefits) to other countries" (Streeten 2001). And interdependence is measured by the cost of severing the relationship (or the benefits of developing it). It follows that the higher the costs to the country, the greater is the degree of dependence of that country. Should a small or poor country benefit more from the international division of labour than a large or rich country, its dependence is greater. But should both parties to a transaction incur high costs from severing economic links, there would be interdependence (ibid.). As at present, poor societies stand to lose because of the asymmetrical relationship. The relationship is that of dependence and not interdependence.

This takes us to the concept of dependency: a situation in which a certain group of countries have their economy conditioned by the development and expansion of another economy to which the former is subject. The relation of interdependence between two or more economies, and between these and world trade, assumes the form of dependence when some countries (the dominant or core) can expand and give impulse to their own development, while other countries (the dependent, subordinate periphery) can only develop as a reflection of this expansion. This can have positive and/or negative effects on their immediate development. In all cases the basic situation of dependence leads to a global situation in dependent countries that situates them in backwardness and under the exploitation of the dominant countries. The dominant countries have a technological, commercial, capital resources and social-political predominance over the dependent countries (with predominance of some of these aspects in various historical moments). This permits them to impose conditions of exploitation and extract part of the domestically produced surplus (Offiong 1980:73-74; Cockcroft *et al*, 1972).

Viewed as a juggernaut, globalisation is politically disempowering. One wonders the rush to implement neoliberal policies such as liberalisation, deregulation and privatisation all of which are claimed to promote market integration. Globalisation, as we have repeatedly pointed out, is touted as the height of economic rationality, but it has also been portrayed as having a dark side as well. The current form of globalisation is driven by economic power and it promotes the hegemony of Western culture and corporations; it places jobs and communities at risk in the rich countries and exploits cheap labour in the poor countries; it significantly threatens the environment; it undermines the foundations of democracy and social stability by subordinating national political institutions to forces of economic change outside their control (Lerche 1998). As shown in the edited work of Holm and Sorensen (1995), globalisation is uneven in its process as well as its effects. Globalisation has polarised the world into those who see it as beneficial and a key to more opportunities and better living standards around the world, and others who view it as a really malign force that makes inequality worse within and between nations, "disempowers the weak, threatens employment and living standards, and increases poverty." By way of emphasis, we repeat again that globalisation is driven by "technological changes, lower communication and transport costs, increased trade and financial integration among countries" (Ahmed 2000:1).

Probably, similar concerns about globalisation expressed in this chapter prompted Joseph E. Stiglitz to write his book *Making Globalisation Work*, which prompted lots of reviews from which I draw. Stiglitz was chief economist at the World Bank after serving as Chairman of the Council of Economic Advisers to President Bill Clinton and had won the Nobel Prize in economics in 2001. According to Stiglitz, the average European cow enjoys a subsidy of British one pound and two shillings a day, more than what is earned by half the people in the developing world. For much of that world, globalisation is tantamount to "a pact with the devil" (Wavell 2006). *Making Globalisation Work* surveys what Chris Wilson (2006) refers to as "the iniquities of the global economy, and the mechanisms by which developed countries exert an excessive influence over developing countries." Furthermore, through recourse to various measures, such as "overt trade tariffs, subtler subsidies, a patent system that developed countries are far better prepared to navigate, or the damage done to poor countries by global pollution," the world is becoming both economically and politically destabilised, and this brings suffering to all involved. Stiglitz is a critic of free-market fundamentalists and challenges the ideological basis to much of the global economic decision-making. Stiglitz argues that globalisation does not have to increase inequality, destroy cultural diversity, or advance corporate interests at the expense of the well-being of ordinary citizens. Stiglitz raises questions such as the use to developing nations if the G-7 nations open some of their markets but the poor countries have no roads and other infrastructure to get their products there? Why engage them in complex negotiations when many of the poor countries do not have skilled officials to handle them? Why force developing countries to open their financial markets only for big international banks, interested primarily in their multinational clients, drive many local banks out of business, thus depriving the poor of credit? (Garten 2006). Stiglitz reminds us that the responsibility of Western trade negotiators is to get the best trade deal for their respective countries' industries. The United States trade negotiator pushes for intellectual-property rights because he wants Americans paid for what they invent. Simultaneously, "Congress blocks products of poor countries with one-sided anti-dumping laws, an outrageous sugar quota and a ridiculous subsidy to cotton growers" (Ramsey 2006). This is an indictment of the asymmetric global market. Globalisation is improperly managed because of vested interests behind many decisions and the poor prospects for negotiating decisions that are favourable to poor countries. The result is the continued underdevelopment of poor countries. Let me end this chapter by briefly describing the global context under which every society must operate, as a matter of necessity.

The Global Context

Propelled along by innovations in communication and information technology, global economy has attained a level unimaginable not very long ago. By global economy, as it has become clear in the above analysis, we refer to the interconnected nets of economic activity, meaning that economic policies and agendas of nations are significantly influenced by economic activities occurring around the world. The 2007-2008 global economic crisis (which originated in the United States) is a clear example of this interconnectedness; this crisis exemplifies why globalisation has made the world a global village.

The recent housing crisis in the United States was brought about by greedy bankers and financial institutions and this crisis was quick to become a global problem. Between the 1990s and early 2000, inflated housing values enabled a number of people with maxed-out credit cards to continue spending by refinancing their mortgages. Simultaneously there was an increase in subprime mortgages - high-interest on adjustable-rate mortgages that require little money down and are issued to borrowers with real poor credit ratings on very limited credit history. This subprime mortgage lending enabled low wage earners to purchase a house. This brought about increased housing demand which raised home values even more. The housing bubble eventually burst and house values plummeted in 2007-2008 and millions of people became stuck with "upside-down mortgages," in which the amount owed on mortgage is more than the value of the property.

Beginning in 2007, the global economy began to take a downward turn, as banks faltered, credit froze, businesses shut down, unemployment rates accelerated, and investments plunged. This global financial crisis originated in the United States and then spread throughout the world. This explains what is meant by the globalisation of the economic institution. Lack of adequate financial regulatory oversight allowed financial institutions to resort to "predatory and subprime lending during the housing boom in the early 2000s" (Mooney, Knox and Schacht 2011:227). The housing boom eventually turned to bust, and financial institutions reset adjustable rate mortgages to higher rates. The result was that millions of homeowners could not keep up with their mortgage payments and foreclosures accelerated. Homeowners lost their homes, renters lost their leases, and banks in turn owned foreclosed homes often worth much less than the mortgages owed on them. Banks lost revenue and thus had less money to lend and so credit froze. Further, consumer spending took a nosedive, businesses went bust, and investments and retirement accounts plummeted. These events took place in the United States but the reverberations engulfed the entire world, mainly because "those risky subprime and adjustable rate mortgages were packaged and resold as 'mortgage-backed securities' to financial institutions around the world". So we live in a world in which no society is free from the economic policies and agendas of other societies. This is even worse in poor countries that have almost become the neo-dependencies of the rich and powerful countries, as we will see in the chapters and pages that follow.

2

Globalisation and African Underdevelopment

The first issue of *Human Development Report* was published by the United Nations Development Programme (UNDP) in 1990. This publication measured the well-being of populations around the world according to a "human development index" (HDI). HDI measures poverty, literacy, education, life expectancy, and other factors. It is a standard means of measuring well-being, especially child welfare. The index was developed in 1990 by the Pakistani economist Mahbub ul Haq, and has been in use since 1993 by the UNDP in its annual report. The HDI measures the average achievements in a country in three basic dimensions of human development:

1. Longevity, as measured by life expectancy at birth.
2. Knowledge (i.e., literacy, educational attainment), as measured by the adult literacy rate (with two-thirds weight) and the combined primary, secondary and tertiary gross enrollment ratio (with one-third weight).
3. A decent standard of living, as measured by gross domestic product per capita (purchasing parity power in $US).

African countries lag behind in all these measures. In other words, Africa remains an underdeveloped continent. Globalisation is supposed to bring Africa out of its perpetual underdevelopment. However, the notion that globalisation and increasing trade will bring about development and the closing of the gap between rich and poor countries seems to have hit a brick wall. Rather than the gap closing, it has been widening (Mitchell Selignson, 2008). This means that in the 21st century underdevelopment of Africa remains a reality. In 1950, based on 1980 US dollars, the average per capita income of low-income countries was $164, whereas that of the industrialised countries was $3,841, showing an "absolute income gap of $3,677." In 1980, incomes in the poor countries averaged $245, whereas incomes in the industrialised countries averaged $9,648, yielding an absolute gap of $9,403 (p.1). This is a staggering difference, indicating that for each of the 30 years, citizens of poor countries increased their wealth by a paltry $2.70 a year.

This yawning gap continued into the 21st century. According to the World Bank (2003), by 2001 the gap had become wider. In that year the poor countries averaged just $430 in gross national income, while the rich countries averaged $26,710, showing a gap of $26,280. This income disparity goes a long way to sustain the argument that things are not going well in the poor countries in terms of their efforts to get out of underdevelopment and therefore poverty.

Emphasising this dilemma, the UN 2005 *On World Social Situation Report* states emphatically that "poverty remains entrenched, and much of the world is trapped in an inequality predicament." Globalisation carries with it inequalities between and within nations, with the negative consequences in areas of employment, job security and wages. Unemployment is particularly high among the youth. The UN press release, commenting on the 2005 report states that "millions are working but remain poor; nearly a quarter of the world's workers do not earn enough to lift themselves and their families above the $1-per day poverty threshold."

A large majority of the working poor are informal non-agricultural workers. Changing labour markets and increased global competition have spurred an explosion of the informal economy and deterioration in wages, benefits and working conditions, particularly in developing countries.

The press release highlights that in many countries, wage inequalities, particularly between "skilled and unskilled workers, have widened since the mid-1980s, with falling real minimum wages and sharp rises in the highest incomes". These inequalities also adversely affect health and education and this negative effect is worse in Sub-Saharan Africa and parts of Asia. Life expectancy is significantly affected, and this has been made debilitating by HIV/AIDS, particularly in Africa. There are significant gaps in access to immunisation, maternal and childcare, nutrition and education. Such inequalities often invite violence. It is quite revealing that the *World Social Situation Report 2005* recognises that globalisation has brought about "worldwide asymmetries" and then recommends "more equitable distribution of benefits of an increasingly open economy." This leads us to the subject of underdevelopment in Africa.

Africa and Underdevelopment
Underdevelopment means distorted development. There have been two approaches to underdevelopment and these are modernisation and dependency. When we talk about modernisation certain names and works readily come to mind, such as Max Weber's the Protestant Ethic, Daniel Lerner's *The Passing of Traditional Society*, Inkles and Smith's *The Modern Man*, David McClelland's need for achievement, Bert Hoselitz's pattern variables, and Everett Hagen's status withdrawal, among others. However, we are not discussing them here because they have been adequately covered elsewhere. (Please see Offiong 2001: Chapters 2 and 3). Suffice it to say

that modernisation theory generally holds that Africa and other underdeveloped countries remain so because of corruption, inefficiency, inability to part with traditionalism, and general government policies that stand in the way of meaningful development. Dependency on the other hand emphasises the role of the developed and powerful nations as being responsible for underdevelopment through globalisation which forcibly and prematurely integrated the poor nations into the world capitalist economy and therefore forcing them to adapt to an economic system created and maintained by the capitalist leaders.

Whether in Africa, Asia, Oceania or Latin America, underdevelopment is associated with certain characteristics such as poverty, high birthrates, illiteracy, high mortality rates, and economic dependence on the rich and powerful countries of the West. As observed by Gerard Chaliand (n.d.), the underdevelopment of the Third World is marked by a number of common traits which include "distorted and highly dependent economies devoted to producing primary products for the developed world and to provide markets for their finished products." Other traits include "traditional, rural structures," "high population growth" and "widespread poverty."

These conditions are associated with the absorption of these societies into the international capitalist economy either by "conquest" or "indirect domination." The major economic consequence of Western domination was the creation of a world market. Gerard Chaliand notes further that by "setting up throughout the world sub-economies linked to the West, and by introducing other modern institutions, industrial capitalism disrupted traditional economies and, indeed, societies. This disruption led to underdevelopment."

For the simple fact that the economies of African countries have been geared ultimately to the needs of industrialised countries, little wonder that they often comprise only a few modern economic activities such as mining or the cultivation of plantations controlled by large foreign firms. The prices of Third World products are usually determined by the dominant countries of the West, and trade with the West provides the bulk of the Third World's income. During the colonial era "outright exploitation" significantly limited the accumulation of capital in the foreign-dominated countries. Even after the flag or pseudo-independence going back to the 1950s and into the era of neocolonialism (yet to be vanquished), African economies developed slowly, or in some cases not at all, due to deteriorating terms of trade. Only the Organisation of Petroleum Exporting Countries (OPEC) has been able to escape the effects of Western domination of the world economy. Even here, since Western corporations dominate (perhaps control) crude oil exploration and production in Third World countries, they stand to benefit more than the oil producing countries. According to the Ayo Irikefe Crude Oil Sales Tribunal of Inquiry in 1980, foreign oil companies were stealing crude oil while Nigerian workers were looking the other way. For every four oil tankers reported, one was stolen. In many cases Nigerian employees simply lacked the technological expertise or know-how to understand what was going on. On the other hand, they were well taken care off financially and they therefore did not care about what the oil companies were doing.

Stages of African Subjugation

In my book, *Imperialism and Dependency: Obstacles to African Development* (1980), I stated that the subjugation or conquest of Africa was in three stages: slavery, colonialism and neocolonialism. In recent years globalisation has been added as the fourth stage. Here I present the thinking of two such writers. Peter Henriot of Jesuit Centre for Theological Reflection (1998) notes that globalisation represents the fourth stage of foreign penetration of Africa "by forces which have negative social consequences for the African people's integral development." This foreign penetration of the continent has occurred over the past five hundred years in a variety of forms.

The first stage was the period of slavery. During this period, Africa's most precious resources – women and men – were carted away by "global traders, slavers, working for the benefit of Arab, European and North American countries." Estimates of the number of people taken away vary between two and ten million. Some place the number much higher. Regardless of the number taken away, this exercise produced untold economic, social and psychological consequences for the continent (see Offiong 1980).

The second stage was the period of colonialism, during which period British, French, Belgian, Portuguese, Italian and German interests dictated the way that map boundaries were drawn, transportation and communication lines were established, agricultural and mineral resources were exploited, religious and cultural patterns were introduced (Henriot 1998; Offiong 1980). The material benefits that came the way of Africans were "far outweighed by the many negative consequences of economic exploitation, environmental degradation, and social dependencies" (Henriot 1998). Many of the fratricidal wars that continue to plague the continent trace their origins back to colonial stratagems; although often some apostles of the civilising mission of Westerners' colonialism have tried to explain such wars as a result of evolutionary atavism. Whatever benefits may have accrued to Africans and all colonised peoples the world over, were the byproducts of their exploitation after the gastronomic appetite of the colonial oligarchs had been satisfied.

The third stage has been that of "neocolonialism," described by Pope Paul V1 as "the form of political and economic suzerainty aimed at maintaining or acquiring dominance" (cited in ibid.). The political risorgimento of the 1940s and 1950s may have resulted in local governmental rule to many African countries but did not in any way break the tiles – subtle and not so subtle – that bound the continent's future to outside influences. In this asymmetrical relationship, what became obvious was that "trade patterns, investment policies, debt arrangements ... all reinforced earlier conditions that were not beneficial to Africans" (ibid.). During the so-called Cold War, African states, just like other Third World countries, were made "bargaining pawns" as in South Africa. Henriot states emphatically, that "globalisation is not working for the benefit of a majority of Africans today".

In his analysis, Jarle Simersen, Professor Emeritus at University of Oslo begins with internal causes of African underdevelopment. He states that "geographical and demographic conditions are key factors in Africa's development [underdevelopment]" (2011). The agricultural revolution and the use of iron tools" came to Africa south of the Sahara later than to other parts of the world, what some refer to as a "1000-year lag." He notes that the continent is "inhospitable for agriculture and harbours "a number of indigenous diseases that affect both humans and animals." According to him, the disease-carrying tsetse fly is all over the continent and that it can incapacitate draught animals. This explains the traditional low use of ploughs and other animal-drawn farm implements (ibid.).

Turning to demographic conditions, Simensen states that Africa's demographic history has been characterised by low density of population and continuous migration and settlement in new areas. He contends that this migration continues to this day and the result has been that there have been "few tightly-knit stable settlements with established social structures that could form the basis for enduring states and empires of the kind that have fostered advanced civilisations in other parts of the world. Although he acknowledges the medieval kingdoms by the Niger River, the Ethiopian Empire, and the progressive kingdoms in West Africa in the 19th century, he states, however, that "monumental stone constructions and local written traditions like those found in the world are lacking in Africa" (ibid.).

Accounting   for   Africa's   "technological underdevelopment," Simensen notes that the reason for this is "the geographical obstacles to communication both internally and with the rest of the world." The Sahara Desert remains a barrier in the north, and the Atlantic coast never had any contact with the outside world until the arrival of Europeans in about 1500. The Arab world and India could spread the influence only through the Nile Valley and the East African coast, and "little spillover effect further inland." The continent's rivers, with the exception of the Niger and the Nile, are full of waterfalls and have not provided a navigable route to the interior. The problems of the land-locked states only emphasise the crucial importance of communication for economic and cultural development.

Simensen then analyses the contribution of political instability for many of the development problems confronting the continent. He asserts that "the ethnic diversity of the continent is extraordinary" and that linguists have identified

900 different language groups. This is because ethnic loyalty overrides all other forms of loyalty with a ferocity that defies human comprehension. This is contrary to the modernisation theories of the early 1960s which conjectured that ethnicity would disappear as modernisation took roots and one can recall terms like detribalisation, bureaucratisation and so on. But what Simensen fails to point out here is that these ethnic conflicts which have often resulted in fratricidal wars were exacerbated by the intrigues of colonialists and the struggle for satellites during the cold war; many of such conflicts have been direct outcomes of the political arrangements by colonial powers as they were forced to depart. But sure, Africans have added their own dimensions to the problem.

Simensen has raised the question: "Can the slave trade and colonialism be regarded as causes of underdevelopment in Africa?" The integration of Africa into the world capitalist system began in 1500, during the "protoglobalisation era" that this integration "took on a perverted form when slaves became the dominant merchandise from around 1650." He notes "the cruelties" of slave trade which left "deep scars in both the African and the European psyche." Simensen posits that the export of 12 million Africans across the Atlantic, and about the same number to the Arab world in the course of a complete millennium could be a factor in low population growth in Africa compared with that of other continents. In terms of economic, the trade in slaves overshadowed trade in other goods, and although it enabled certain strong kingdoms to increase their power, the trade was quite "devastating for the groups affected by the kidnappings and conflicts that the trade entailed". Politically, the rulers who controlled the slave trade on African side were caught up in a peculiar form of dependence that had profound effects on African political culture.

Simultaneously, African labour was central in building up the "Atlantic system," and thus "a decisive factor in American and European (including Norway's) development." Accordingly, states Simensen, "the foundations were laid for a closely knit web of development and underdevelopment." On this basis, African claims for reparation (see Offiong 2001) are "understandable," but Simensen quickly adds that slavery was widely practised in African societies, that African leaders and their intermediaries were the ones that brought almost all of the slaves to the coast and they are also liable for the blame associated with the odious trade and the evils emanating from it (ibid).   This appears to be an unkind cut by Simensen because he is making a role equivalency between Europeans and Africans.   One does not dispute the participation of Africans in the odious and unconscionable trade but to say that the guilt is proportionally equal is unfair and unkind.

Europeans travelled all the way from their countries in search of cheap labour in the form of slaves to till the lands they had stolen from Native Americans. They were the ones who provided the rum for Africans to drink and become intoxicated in order to fire them up to war against their neighbours. Europeans were the ones who supplied the guns, the gunpowder and bullets. They did not end there. They were masters of intrigues which they carried into the colonial days, and even to this day.   They would go to one neighbouring group and tell them the other group was attacking them in two days and the only way out was for that group to attack their neighbours before being attacked and enslaved.   They instigated those wars from which came slaves. The same intrigues were in force during colonialism when they incited one group against another. And, during the so-called Cold War, the same intrigues were employed which resulted in civil wars which they blamed on tribalism and evolutionary atavism.

Turning to colonial rule, the next phase of Africa's integration into the international economic system, Simensen notes that European policies varied significantly between regions and over time from the brutal period of conquest at the end of the 19th century to active development efforts following World War 11. This was the period of nation-building which was accomplished by imposing European system of competing nation-states onto the continent through the process of conquest that was largely motivated by European strategic interests; the result was a political map that is economically irrational and dysfunctional (ibid.) and a clear example of this is found in West Africa.

In order to make the colonial venture profitable, the colonial powers developed modern export systems, infrastructure and education facilities (a major share of this must go to missionaries, even though they were accomplices in the colonial enterprise). These facilitated rapid integration of the continent into the global market. The colonial system can be criticised for extreme use of violence in the first phase (see Offiong 2001 and 1980); for taking a disproportionate share of the value created; and for failing to use state power to promote broader development until after World War 11. But Simensen argues, using the example of Ethiopia, that the connection between colonisation and underdevelopment is not a straight forward matter. The case of Ethiopia has always been cited by Westerners to make a similar point. But could that be an exception? There is absolutely no gain-saying that colonialism exploited Africa and contributed to its underdevelopment.

Simensen does not say anything about neocolonialism; instead he writes about "post-colonial problems." Given the factors enumerated above, Africa at independence was at a lower general development level. Decolonisation in Africa benefitted from external factors, and most territories were not ready for internal development. Except for European minorities in the southern part of the continent Africa did not have strong, enterprising minority groups with transnational networks of the type found among the Chinese in South Asian countries. Simensen here alludes to Everett Hagen's leaders of innovation in his "Status withdrawal" theory (see Offiong 2001: 35-36).

The main reason for the weak development of African countries after independence remains the "failure of the state." Built upon the legacy of slave trade and colonial period, it led to very fierce competition for control of the state apparatus and whether military or civilian, what manifested were authoritarian regimes beginning in the 1960s. (The reader should bear in mind that colonial regimes were not democratic but authoritarian and the Africans that graduated from that colonial school could not be expected to behave any differently). Both the military and civilian despots concerned themselves with tightening political control, controlling the flow of resources and developing personal networks instead of concerning themselves with building well-functioning public institutions. The nature of governance was "patrimonial rule" or "personal rule" (see Offiong 2001).

The question that arises is to what extent the crisis of African development can be blamed on external factors. Simensen does not seem to blame external factors for the problems of African development. Instead he reminds us of the new system of international development aid following World War 11, which provided significant advantages, enjoying much development assistance, which in some cases amounted to from 30 to 50 percent of the national budget. This aid was central to any development that ever took place in the continent, particularly in the health and education sectors; but it also succeeded in consolidating the regimes in power at the time. Fluctuations in the prices of raw materials were a recurring dilemma and the surge in oil prices after 1973 was a serious blow, accounting in part for the mounting debt problems experienced in the continent of Africa.

Africa and Asia operated in the same international environment. However, Asian countries were able to take significant steps forward by employing a more open, export-oriented strategy and also by placing great emphasis on general and particularly technical education. Paramountly important was "a tight fiscal policy that ensured stable exchange rates and thus won the confidence of foreign investors" (Simensen 2011). On the other hand, African countries were plunged into economic crisis because of artificially high exchange rates, unbridled printing of money and over optimistic loans from overseas. Then the hour of truth came bringing with it "hyperinflation and debt crisis in the mid-1980s. Unfortunately, by this time, African countries were in practice really bankrupt and the international financial institutions then emerged to rescue them by setting up "debt management arrangements" and to assist in reforms (ibid.). As we will discuss briefly here and in subsequent chapters, the international financial institutions were not there to rescue African countries but to further integrate African economies into the global economy and to serve as debt collectors for Western countries and their multinational corporations. Their "remedies" often exacerbated the problem.

Regarding globalisation, the fourth phase of African integration into the world capitalist market, Simensen sees it as starting with the debt negotiations with the IMF and the World Bank. Among the positive effects the intervention of these financial institutions had for Africa were the financial reforms which imposed "reasonable macroeconomic order" through devaluation and deep cuts in public budgets. The cuts mostly affected the general public in terms of reductions in food subsidies and in government spending on schools, healthcare and other public services. But since we intend to examine the impact of the international financial institutions on African problems in more detail later, we simply note here that the World Bank and IMF at least admitted that their policy had been "too rigid" and then proceed to present the conclusions of Eurodad Report (2006) below.

In 2006 Henry Kovach and Yasmina Lansman (authors of the Eurodad Report) examined the conditions that the World Bank and IMF attach to their lending in some of the world's poorest countries. They found that impoverished countries faced "an unacceptably high and rising number of conditions" in order to get development finance. The average conditions are 67. Furthermore, apart from "imposing a massive administrative burden on already over-stretched developing governments," the conditions "often push highly controversial economic policy reforms on poor countries, like trade liberalisation and privatisation of essential services" (Kovach and Lansman 2006:3). These reforms frequently go contrary to the wishes of the poor countries; they also can "have a harmful impact on poor people, increasing their poverty not reducing it, by denying them access to vital services" (ibid.). The authors of the Eurodad Report went on to recommend immediate "radical reforms." With this kind of policy by the international financial institutions, I cannot fathom why Simensen would characterise the involvement of these two banks as positive. They do not have the interest of the poor countries as their concern; their basic interest is serving as debt collectors for their sponsors, the rich countries and their corporations. And, as it has been clear in the analysis of the stages of African integration into the world capitalist system, Africa has been a pawn in the hands of Western countries that have emasculated and exploited her to their (Western) advantage while simultaneously encouraging the underdevelopment of the continent.

Yet another explanation for the underdevelopment of Africa comes from Frederick Cooper's *Africa Since 1940*. I proceed to draw from the reviews of this book by Jeff Grischow of Willfrid University and Wikipedia (both on line, retrieved 5/5/11). Cooper refers to African countries as "gatekeeper states," that is, states that acquired most of their revenue from customs duties, concessions to foreign conglomerates, visas, foreign exchange control, and foreign aid. African governments suffer from a distinctive politico-economic dysfunction that originates from a particular historical sequence. According to Cooper (2002:196-197), "Africa was systematically conquered but not so systematically ruled," which tells us that "colonial states had been gatekeeper states". They had "trouble extending their power and their command of people's interest" internally; however, they were able to control "the interface of national and world economies".

The colonial imperialists wanted some specific things like natural resources from the continent and thus their transformational agenda was limited since extraction could take place in the absence of a strong state. The authority of colonial regimes relied on the superior military forces of the colonial powers, which could easily defeat any organised resistance but was unable to routinise authority or gain legitimacy. The survival of each colony was made possible by external resources and support not on internal or local factors such as established states. The result was that colonial governments established very weak roots in countries nominally controlled by them and thus they could not in real terms govern the social or cultural realms of the subjects under them. Consequently, this external dependence brought about an outward orientation concentrating on "guarding the gate;" that is, the colonies concentrated on collecting most of their revenues from taxes on imports and exports, customs duties, concessions to foreign companies, controlled entry and exit visas, distributed foreign aid, foreign exchange control, and issued licenses regarding who could engage in business activities, and so forth (Cooper 2002).

Cooper tells us that the post-colonial "successor states" unfortunately inherited the mantle of gatekeeper from their erstwhile colonial rulers. The negative consequences of gate-keeping became extraordinarily exacerbated because of competitive communalism (Offiong 1983). Under the colonial tutelage, the gatekeeper was recognised by all but in post-colonial Africa there was no external military force to impose order. Unlike the colonial rulers African rulers really wanted to impose their authority in their respective domains in order to achieve a transformation of the economy and society. The control of the gate had become a zero sum game since whoever controlled it also controlled the resources they could use to fully entrench their rule.

This intensified ethnic rivalry or competitive communalism for control of the gate shortly after independence and this competition culminated in the collectively irrational political upheavals in the continent after independence, as evidenced by cycles of military coups and counter coups and civil wars (Cooper 2002). It takes two to tangle and we see in Cooper's work the fact that Africa continues to feel the impact of colonialism. This does not mean that Africans cannot overcome their obstacles to getting out of underdevelopment. It requires patriotism, political will and good leadership. Africa is yet to be blessed with patriotic, insightful and purposeful leaders. Many of those who parade

parade as leaders are people of doubtful patriotism; they are mostly opportunists who after getting the control of institutions of the country begin to develop their pockets. Mostly, we have thieves in our government houses. No wonder Westerners refer to African governments as kleptocracies (see Offiong 2008a; 2001). It is obvious in Cooper's work that the West played a significant role in the underdevelopment of Africa and the next book to be discussed shows that the West continues to be interested in the underdevelopment of the underdeveloped world.

Confessions of an Economic Hit Man

I consider it appropriate here to discuss a book titled *Confessions of an Economic Hit Man* by John Perkins (2004), because it shows that the West has interest in the underdevelopment of poor countries. Further, it shows how the West continues to devise means to maintain their stranglehold on the poor countries thereby sustaining their hegemony. Poverty is functional (see Offiong 2001 and as we will discuss in this book) to rich nations because it makes poor countries dependent on the rich ones and this enhances the ability of the rich nations to dominate, control and manipulate the poor ones. Perkins describes his previous job as that of an "economic hit man" – a highly paid professional whose duty it was to convince leaders of poor countries to accept huge loans from the World Bank and other international financial institutions, loans that were humongously bigger that the countries could possibly pay back. Such loans were used to develop the country by paying for needed infrastructure, such as roads, airports, industrial plants, electrical plants and shipping ports. A primary requirement (among others) was that the borrowing country had to give 90 percent of the loan back to American companies to build the infrastructure - power grids, industrial parks, harbours, highways; things that actually benefit foreign corporations and a few rich nationals but never really reach the poor at all. The poor are never connected to the power grids. They lack the skills to get jobs in industrial parks. Thus, the wealthiest families in the country are made to enjoy the additional infrastructure and the poor masses are stuck with a debt they cannot possibly pay back. Yes, foreign corporations also benefit from the infrastructure while the nationals have the debt like a millstone around their neck.

What follows is that the United States uses the debt as leverage to ask the indebted country for favours such as oil. If John Perkins is right, how can we in good conscience say that the rich and powerful countries really want poor countries to be free from foreign debts; and how can we really believe that they want globalisation to fairly serve the interest of the poor countries?

We may end this analysis of causes of African underdevelopment by stating that Africa's problems are due to a combination of Western and African factors in addition to the fact that Africa has been integrated into the world capitalist economy on unfavourable terms. Imagine the "doctrine" of export-led growth championed by the World Bank and IMF. This doctrine is based on Ricardian logic of comparative advantage. David Ricardo, a highly successful stock exchange speculator and a member of British Parliament had stated that under a "system of perfectly free commerce," each nation naturally develops its capital labour to such employment as are most beneficial to each." Ricardo continues that this pursuit of individual advantage is admirably tied to the universal good of the whole. And, for Adam Smith, the role of government was to keep the marketplace free and open so that the "invisible hand" might assure the good of all concerned (Lodge and Vogel 1987: 23, 124). As we have demonstrated above, choice in the growing system of interrelationships was rarely free. In the majority of cases more purposeful participants imposed it by force or by constraints stemming from market domination. Coercion or constraint was of the essence of the process; they were not epiphenomena.

The continent of Africa was coerced into the current economic relationships with the West and it is now being constrained through economic domination to continue with the relationship. Africa continues to be the exporter of a few raw materials and importer of manufactured products. The consequence of being exporter of a few raw materials has been quite enormous, especially when we consider the instability of the prices of these raw materials. Africa really needs a reformed, restructured international economic order that will bring a stop to Robin Hood taking from the poor and giving to the rich. Unless the present economic order is reformed to make it possible for poor countries to benefit from its benefits, the hope of reducing poverty will remain an unrealised dream.

Aid, Poverty and Underdevelopment

I consider it germane to briefly examine the belief that foreign aid compounds the problem of poverty and underdevelopment in Africa (we will further discuss this phenomenon in Chapter 3). Africa has been a victim of many uncomplimentary epithets, such as "helpless child," continent of "beggars," "dark continent," land of "gloom, ignorance, and dependency," "land of HIV/AIDS," and more. Despite these epithets, there have been increasing calls for more aid for this poverty-ravaged continent. It is to be recalled that in the 1960s developmental economists believed in what they referred to as the "vicious cycle of poverty." This theory posited that poverty in the developing countries made domestic savings accumulation impossible. According to this perspective, low savings gave rise to low domestic investment and low investment was seen as the key impediment to rapid economic growth. Foreign aid was therefore meant "to fill that apparent gap between insufficient savings and the requisite investment in the economy" (Tupy 2005:1).

Thus from 1960 foreign aid has been pouring into Africa while African GDP per capita failed to improve. In contrast, South Asia performed much better, showing appreciable growth in their GDP per capita growth. In the view of Tupy, "the link between foreign aid and economic development seems quite tenuous" (ibid.). Foreign aid enables government officials to embezzle huge amounts of money and misappropriate a lot on "loss-making projects." In the same vein, after examining foreign aid to Africa as "Hollow Hope," Kwame Akonor (2008:1077) concludes that foreign aid "is no panacea for Africa's development woes." Much of the aid finds its way back into the banks of donor countries through corruption; and those banks are happy to receive the illicit funds. Akonor continues that foreign aid "has created a welfare-continent mentality and has become the hub around which the spokes of most African economies turn." That at the dawn of this century, more than 50 percent of Sub-Saharan African budgets and 70 percent of their public investment came from foreign aid. And yet, the continent is a most resource-rich continent. Dependence on foreign aid compromises the sovereignty of African states. Most aid packages, including those coming from charities, come with stipulations and conditions to which recipient countries must comply before further aid is disbursed (ibid.). Africa cannot develop by relying on external aid, especially when such aid is improperly used. Why should African countries mortgage their independence to the altar of foreign aid? As Kwame Nkrumah preached much of the time, political independence without economic independence is a farce. This is why this author (Offiong 2001) advocates self-reliance, which in no way means autarchy.

There are Africans who have come to the conclusion rightly or wrongly that cooperation with the West has been a boon economically. Foreign aid tends to benefit the ruling elite and enables them to strengthen their grip on power, thereby engendering their underdevelopment. Foreign donors do not care as long as such foreign aid promotes their foreign ideological interest. The receiving government may be authoritarian or a dictatorship; it does not matter. Yes, foreign emergency assistance has enabled Africa's poor to avert hardship, but it has failed to significantly promote economic development.

Providing assistance to Africa's poor is a noble cause but it has turned out to be "a theater of the absurd" (Jallow 2010:1). Between 1960 and 1997 Western aid to Africa amounted to more than $500 billion. In addition to the relief aid and economic development, foreign aid assistance was also given to support reforms and policy adjustment programmes. Between 1981 and 1991, the World Bank provided $20 billion towards Africa's structural adjustment programmes (SAPs). The purpose of SAP was to make public institutions, government agencies, and bureaucracies more transparent, effective, efficient and accountable, so they claimed. Jallow is not surpised that the continent "still suffers from poverty, considering the depth of governments' corruption and missing billions of dollars in export earnings from oil, gas, diamonds and other resources" (ibid.).

The concept of aid was considered as compatible with the central theme of economic development, and was thus accepted as a possible means of helping Africa escape from "the chronic underdevelopment that is characterised by underdeveloped infrastructure and dualistic economies" (ibid.). But this concept or idea has not materialised into development and escape from intractable poverty. Instead Africa has experienced a net decline in the standard of living.

It is not surprising that The Heritage Foundation, a think tank and very conservative organisation in the United States, concluded in 1985 that foreign aid "was contributing to Africa's underdevelopment woes." It has become a popular belief that foreign aid has done more harm so much that Africans have failed to set their own pace and direction of development that is free from external directives or interference. Even the United Nations Conference on Trade and Development admits that foreign aid to Africa has failed to achieve its purpose; despite years of reform no Sub-Saharan African country has completed its adjustment programme or achieved any sustained economic growth (cited in ibid.). In the same way, a Heritage Foundation (another American think tank organisation) study concluded that foreign aid "retards the process of economic growth and the accumulation of wealth." The Foundation then argues that "aid dependency pulls entrepreneurship and intellectual capital into non-productive activities thereby blurring the entrepreneurial spirits of many Africans". The concept of aid is not bad in itself but the problem is how to make it work. In Chapter 7, we shall find out that the amount of aid pouring into Africa is a small fraction of illicit outflows of funds from poor to rich countries.

By way of conclusion, the essential nature of globalisation means a continuation of Western political, economic, intellectual and cultural imposition on the continent through modern technology and the activities of the international conglomerates or multinational corporations and international organisations like the IMF, World Bank and WTO. Their activities do not seem to enhance African development.

Under colonialism, the institutions and the socio-economic arrangements were constructed to enhance Western domination of the people as well as enable them to maximally exploit the people and their natural resources. The political risorgimento following World War 11 and the resultant struggles of the people for decolonisation were based on the hope of ending the long pattern of colonial subjugation, whereby Africa as a free continent, could take control of its own social, political and economic destiny. After independence, however, African countries, very much like the Caribbean, turned to the erstwhile colonial masters for financial, technical and infrastructural assistance, and as observed by RasTyehimba (2006) continue to maintain "the relationships of dependency and exploitation." Thus, it was not surprising that these new and fragile nations continue to be bound to "the values, institutions, paradigms, and economic and political dictates of their former colonial rulers under the guise of 'modernisation' and 'development'..." (ibid.).

Globalisation is an ideological weapon "that makes the mechanisms of hegemony, injustice and control that underlie the neo-liberal globalised world order characterised by free trade instead of fair trade, advanced modern technology, power and wealth and multi-national corporations;" and international organisations such as the IMF, World Bank and WTO are acting as agents of G7 (ibid; also Offiong 2001). Globalisation as at present is characterised by ever-increasing gap around the world between the rich and the poor and destruction of the middle class and small businesses in poor countries.

3

Globalisation and Poverty

Globalisation is supposed to enhance development; and the primary task that development seeks to accomplish is to eliminate poverty. Development is concerned with improving the well-being of people. Raising living standards and improving education, health and equality of opportunity are among the essential components of economic development goal. Insuring political and civil rights is a broader development goal. Economic growth is an essential means for enhancing development, but in itself it is a highly imperfect proxy for progress (World Bank, 1992:29). In 1992 the Bank did say that "substantial progress" had been achieved because average consumption per capita in developing countries had increased by 70 percent in real terms; average life expectancy had gone up from 51 to 63 years; and that primary school enrollment rates jumped to 89 percent. But what must be stated is that these gains were not being evenly spread then, nor have they been evenly spread in the 21st century. Thus poverty has not been meaningfully reduced because more than one-fifth of humanity still languishes in abject penury. Let us now try to describe what poverty entails.

Extent of Global Poverty

The extent of global poverty is alarming. As reported by Shah (2010), not less than 80 percent of humanity lives on less than $10 a day. Over three billion people, that is, more than half the world population, live on less than $2.50 a day; more than 80 percent of the world's population lives in countries where income differentials are widening. The poorest 40 percent of the world's population accounts for 5 percent of global income, while the richest 20 percent accounts for three quarters of world income (HDR 2007:25). UNICEF reports that 22,000 die each day as a result of poverty; and they "die quietly in some of the poorest villages on earth, far removed from the scrutiny and the conscience of the world. Being meek and weak in life makes these dying multitudes even more invisible in death" (cited in Shah 2010). About 27-28 percent of all children in the developing world are estimated to be underweight or stunted. South Asia and Sub-Saharan Africa account for the bulk of the deficit. Over 9 million people die worldwide yearly because of hunger and malnutrition; and 5 million of these are children. According to HDR (2007:5), infectious diseases remain anathema to the lives of the poor across the globe. Some 40 million people are living with HIV/AIDS, with 3 million deaths in 2004. There are 350 – 500 million cases of malaria, with one million casualties. Unfortunately, Africa accounts for 90 percent of all malaria fatalities and African children account for 80 percent of all malaria victims worldwide.

Despite an abundance of resources, natural and human, Africa continues to suffer from widespread and persistent poverty. According to Food 4 Africa (2012), some 315 million people – one in two people in Sub-Saharan Africa – survive on less than $1 per day; 184 million people – 33 percent of the African population – suffer from malnutrition; less than 50 percent of Africa's population has access to hospitals or doctors; in 2000, 300 million Africans did not have access to safe water; the average life expectancy in Africa is about 41 years only; only 57 percent of African children are enrolled in primary education, and a paltry one out of three children complete grade school; one out of six children die before the age of 5, the number being 25 times higher in Sub-Saharan Africa than in the Organisation for Economic Cooperation and

Development (OECD) countries. Water problems affect half of humanity but it is much worse in Africa. About 1.6 billion people live without electricity; in Africa more than half the population lives without electricity. The effects of poverty are disastrous. Poverty engenders diseases, warfare, corruption, and misgovernment. Regardless of the chosen measure for poverty, Africa comes out worse than any other region. The continent has the largest share of people living below $1.25 a day. The tragedy is that while countries in other regions in Asia and Latin America have been slowly moving out of poverty, African countries have been regressing into lower levels of deprivation, with the result that the number of the poor has been increasing instead of decreasing, as it is the case in other regions.

Models of Poverty
There were previously two models of poverty, absolute and relative. In 2008 the World Bank added a third one, extreme poverty. Absolute poverty definitions are concerned with economic deprivation in terms of an objective, fixed standard. It implies a level of income that imposes real physical suffering on people in hunger, disease and the massacre of innocent children. Absolute poverty refers to the inability of people to maintain physical survival on a long-term basis. Following this conceptualization, "poverty can be measured as incomes that fall below the amount of money needed for a minimally adequate supply of material resources such as food, clothing and shelter" (Soroka and Bryjak, 1992:185). Hunger is the target of absolute poverty. Poverty is a form of economic deprivation. Disease is closely associated with it. Both bring physical discomfort and prevent children as well as adults from reaching their physical and mental potential. Those who cannot afford to eat well to provide protection against disease

and productive labour invariably suffer in some other ways as well. Their housing and sanitation are likely to be enough to contribute to disease, their education inadequate to get employment paying enough to properly feed them. All aspects of absolute poverty combine to deny victims a fully, or sometimes even minimally, human existence (Harrison, 1987:406).

Relative poverty on the other hand, can be almost as destructive as absolute poverty "in the sense that it can preoccupy or even obsess one's thoughts and divert him from the enjoyment of his life" (ibid, p.407). The person who is not suffering physically may suffer mentally when he or she compares himself/herself with people significantly better off than he or she and he/she can see no good reason for this discrepancy. Relative poverty definitions compare different groups in order to determine the economic circumstances of one group relative to the others. Thus, "relative poverty is the situation of being economically deprived compared to some other particular groups" (Soroka and Bryjak 1992:185).

People experience relative deprivation when they feel that their legitimate expectations are being blocked. Relative deprivation does not mean envy or dissatisfaction with one's situation in life unless this dissatisfaction is generated by a sentiment or feeling that the inequality is also inequitable. Although there is no consensus on what constitutes legitimate expectations, an expectation is considered to be legitimate when people consider it to be adequate for action. The core of relative deprivation is comparison. Although relative deprivation implies inequalities, it is not solely the outcome of objective conditions; it is created out of an ongoing interpretation of those conditions and their meaning for the individual or group concerned. Relative deprivation is a sentiment that stems from the perception of these inequalities and consequently varies independently of absolute deprivation (Offiong, 1983:7, 8). Thus relative deprivation largely depends on expectations. Poor people compare themselves with the rich and feel they also are entitled to what others have. Relative poverty in Africa invokes shame. Shame because one has a thatched roof while the other has tin, shame that one's children go barefooted to school, shame that he/she cannot entertain mourners well at the burial of a parent, etc. Relative poverty is the suffering that stems from inequality.

On August 26, 2008, the World Bank revised its poverty threshold from \$1 to \$1.25 per day for least developed countries and \$2 per day for middle income countries and regions, including Latin America and Eastern Europe. Those living on less than \$1.25 per day are defined as living in extreme poverty.

According to Adam Parsons (2008:1), this revision of classification placed extra 4300 million people as "absolutely poor." This reclassification contradicted the Bank's celebrated decline in extreme poverty figures in 2007 to less than a billion, the new measurements revealed a far less optimistic outlook – "a total of 1.4 billion poor people in 2005 ... revised from 986 million in 2004 ... a margin of error of 42 percent, defining a quarter of the developing world as living without sufficient means for human survival" (ibid.). Despite this ominous information the World Bank went ahead to stress that poverty eradication was improving as reflected in their rather incongruous report title, "The Developing World is Poorer than We Thought but no less Successful in the Fight against Poverty" (ibid.). Parsons takes the position that the current level of poverty as reported by the World Bank, is a clear testament that globalisation is not beneficial to certain groups and regions. The revised poverty figures say a lot about globalisation which has dominated the world scene in more than a quarter century. The World Bank uses the statistics to back up "its policies of deregulation, privatisation, market liberalisation, and increased economic growth through free trade as the overruling means to combating poverty" (ibid.). But the methodology of the Bank's statistics has been challenged by academics who claim that the figures have been underestimated by up to 40 percent, and may not prove that global poverty is declining. Despite World Bank's optimism, the new poverty figures raise legitimate questions about the success of globalisation.

In the particular case of Africa, the number of the poor almost doubled over the period of globalisation, from 200 million in 1981 to 380 million in 2005, with about half the population of Sub-Saharan Africa living below the poverty line. According to Parsons, India has the largest number of extremely poor people, regardless of the definition adopted by the World Bank. In India more than 4 out of 10 people, that is, 41.6 percent of the entire population, survive on less than $1.25 per day. When compared to the previous estimate of 24 percent of the population, this means that 200 million people struggling under absolute poverty "effectively fell through the cracks of the World Bank's headcount." In addition, "Revisions to China's figures were similarly dramatic, up to 207 million from a previous 130 million people in extreme poverty". We have maintained that globalisation has its merits as well as demerits, prompting people to ask whether it is a boon or bane. The material life of some people and groups has improved but poverty remains endemic – it still looms very high.

Pronounced inequalities make the burden of poverty difficult to tolerate. In many cases one's excess wealth may be the direct cause of another person's poverty. By the same token, it is the contention of the dependency theory that the wealth of the Western industrial countries is responsible for the poverty of much of the Third World. The question we may ask is if poverty is then synonymous with inequality.

Poverty is not synonymous with inequality, although they are related. Whereas poverty is concerned with the absolute standard of living of a part of society, that is, the poor, inequality is the relative living standards across the whole of society. At maximum inequality one person has everything and poverty is therefore high. But minimum inequality (that is, where all are equal) is possible with zero poverty (that is, where no one is poor) as well as with maximum poverty (that is, where all are poor).

Poverty affects physical health as a result of poor nutrition. There is a strong relationship between one's level of income and the nutritional value of diet. Poverty affects both the quality of food and quantity as well. Writing about the superfluity of food in America, David Newman (1997:370) said, "when most of us hear the word *hunger* we are likely to conjure up images of famine-ravaged countries in sub-Saharan Africa or destitute villages in Latin America or Southeast Asia where naked, dusty children, stomachs bloated with the telltale signs of malnutrition, plead for scraps of food." Even though Newman seems to ignore the existence of some forms of poverty (at least among certain groups in the population in the United States) he is right that this phenomenon is the perennial problem of the Third World, with Africa particularly affected. A very large proportion of African children are undernourished; another very large proportion is underweight and very many of these children under the age of five die from hunger-related causes every day. Senator Leahy (Congressional Record, July 25, 1996:S8741) is right when he said that most Americans waste more food in a day than ... the Sub-Saharan countries and others will ever see on their tables.

[Americans] spend more money on diet preparations ... than most of these nations will ever see to feed their new born children or their families." This is a great admission. Senator Leahy also noted that America has less than 5 percent of the world's population but Americans "use more than 50 percent of the world's resources." The world has enough resources to go round, but a number of factors sustain poverty; one such factor is that certain countries, certain individuals claim more than their fair share.

If we define poverty simply as "the inability to attain minimal standard of living" (World Bank, 1990:26), we can appreciate the number of people in the world who are poor. As at 1985 there were 1,115 million people in the Third World countries in poverty and this represents roughly one-third of the total population of the developing world. Out of this number 630 million, that is, 18 percent of the total population of the Third World, were "extremely poor," because their annual consumption was less than $275, the lower poverty line; the upper poverty line is $370 (World Bank, 1990:28). Despite these gigantic figures, the aggregate poverty gap, that is the transfer needed to move everybody above the poverty line, was just 3 percent of developing countries' total consumption, while the transfer needed to move everybody out of extreme poverty was just one percent of developing countries' consumption. The World Bank went on to report that mortality for children under 5 averaged 121 per thousand for all developing countries, aggregate life expectancy was 62 years, and the overall primary school enrollment rate was 83 percent. These figures, however, hide considerable variations within and among countries.

Nearly half of the developing world's poor, and nearly half of those in extreme poverty, live in South Asia. Sub-Saharan Africa has around one-third as many poor, although in relation to the region's overall population, its poverty is just high. Furthermore, both South Asia and Sub-Saharan Africa have low scores on several other indicators: in Sub-Saharan Africa life expectancy and primary school enrollment rates are significantly low, and under-five mortality rates are dangerously high. On the basis of all indicators, the Middle Eastern and North African countries have the next highest poverty. Following them are Latin America and the Caribbean and East Asia. China has an impressive record (World Bank, 1990:29). The number of poor people increased from slightly more than one in 1985 to more than 1.1 billion by 1990. Asia has successfully alleviated poverty because of its supposed economic miracle. South Asia, including India, has had a steady though undramatic decline in poverty, "but all poverty measures worsened in Sub-Saharan Africa..." (World Bank, 1992: 29). On the basis of its projections, the World Bank concluded that the number of poor in Asia would continue to decline, and the adverse trends in Latin America and Eastern Europe would be reversed with economic recovery in these regions. Sub-Saharan Africa is the only region in which the situation is expected to worsen; with increases in the proportion of the population in poverty, the number is expected to increase by about 9 million a year, on average. By the end of the decade, around one-half of the world's poor will live in Asia and one-quarter will live in Sub-Saharan Africa.

In all this African rural population is worst-off. According to International Fund for Agricultural Development (IFAD), a UN agency in its publication, *The State of World Rural Poverty* (1993), about one billion people living in rural areas in Third World countries are facing abject poverty and this represents an increase of 40 percent in the past 20 years. About 204 million of this number lives in Africa. Africa also accounts for 11 of the 15 countries in the world with worst-off rural populations. These troubling revelations prompted the IFAD to conclude that traditional "trickle-down" policies for dealing with poverty have completely failed to adequately address the problem of poverty.

IFAD further states that "the poor are not idle," only that they are poor farmers, poor herders and poor fishermen, and that their incomes come from their work. The answer to this problem lies in "creating the conditions for them to earn more money for their work." The situation of these poor people is similar to those in industrial countries like the United States, who are known as "the working poor." These people work much longer hours than those who make much more money and yet they do not earn enough to support themselves. They cannot feed their families well; they cannot send their children to school; they cannot clothe them; nor can they afford for them basic medical attention. It is difficult to understand why these people could be charged as lacking in motivation to succeed or achieve, as David McClelland (1961) has done. African rural men and women work long hours on their farms, from dawn to dusk. The IFAD report notes that these men and women and even children have the knowledge and skills to increase their production, and must therefore be active participants in their development. As of now, many poor countries, particularly in Sub-Saharan Africa, have per capita real incomes that are much lower than that of the United States at the beginning of the 19th century.

World Bank (1990:3) data confirm that in many countries rural poverty is a critical factor in the overall incidence and depth of poverty. Although urban incomes are generally higher and urban services and facilities much more accessible, poor urban-dwellers may suffer more than rural households from certain aspects of poverty. The urban poor are typically housed in slums or squatter settlements. They often have to contend with appallingly overcrowding, bad sanitation, and contaminated water conditions. The sites are often illegal and dangerous and often governments force them out without any notice. Floods and landslides, and chemical pollution are their constant threats. Some of these people are migrants from the countryside who are seeking better-paid work, which in most cases do not exist. For many, particularly in Latin American countries, migration is permanent. For others, as in some parts of Africa and Southeast Asia, it may be temporary, reflecting, for example, seasonality in agriculture. The effect that migration to urban areas has on poverty depends very much on whether urban employment opportunities are better or worse than in rural areas. Available evidence suggests that urban areas do offer some opportunities for higher-paid work, and this implies that, on balance, urbanisation probably helps to reduce poverty.

The question is often asked as to whether women are poorer than men. Available data on incomes are too weak to clearly give an answer to this vexing question. However, available figures on health, nutrition, education, and labour force participation do indicate that women are often severely disadvantaged. For example, data for 1980 show literacy rate for women was only 61 percent of that for men in Africa; the figures were 52 percent in South Asia, 57 percent in the Middle East, 82 percent in Southeast Asia, and 94 percent in Latin America (World Bank, 1990:31). Women experience all manner of cultural, social, legal and economic obstacles that men, including poor ones, do not have to face. A study in Nepal found that, on average, poor women worked eleven hours a day, men seven-and-a-half. Poor female-headed households are becoming common in Southern Africa and Latin America. In Brazil, female-headed households account for as much as 10 percent of all households but for 15 percent of the poor (ibid.).

What this means is that just as in the United States, Africa and other Third World countries are experiencing the feminisation of poverty. Let me again return to the issue of unclean water that I mentioned previously.

It is common knowledge that unclean water and poor sanitation lead to devastating illnesses in Africa. It is clear that safe water accompanied by improvements in sanitation and personal hygiene, contributes to better health. Quantity of water can also affect health. In many parts of Africa families, particularly women, spend inordinate amounts of time collecting water. In some parts of Africa it takes five hours to collect water. In cities, middle- and upper-income households typically receive subsidised piped water. Households without municipal water service, particularly the poor, are left to buy water from private sellers at high prices.

Unclean water and poor sanitation lead to devastating illnesses in Africa. Polluted drinking water leads to typhoid, and dysentery, and most sources of drinking water in rural areas are contaminated. Concerning the availability of water by region, Africa is one of the regions that contain most of the countries with limited renewable water resources.

A lot can be learned from a comprehensive analysis by US Agency for International Development (USAID) of 100 studies of the health impact of improvements in the quality or availability of water or in the disposal of human waste. The analysis shows great improvements with median reductions ranging from 22 percent for diarrhea to 76 percent for guinea worm. It further shows that environmental improvements have a greater impact on mortality than on illness, with median reduction of up to 60 percent in deaths from diarrheal diseases (World Bank, 1992:49).

Furthermore, an associated analysis by WHO of the largest group of health impact studies – those on the effect of water and sanitation on diarrheal diseases – suggests that the effects of making some improvements at the same time are "roughly additive." Gains are enhanced or reinforced by educating mothers and improving hygiene. If the health risks of the people were reduced by the following margins, 16 percent in quality of water, 25 percent in availability of water, 37 percent in quality and availability of water, and 22 percent in disposal of human waste, then there would be:

a. 2 million fewer cases of deaths from diarrhea each year among children under five years of age (about 10 million infants die each year in developing countries from all causes).

b. 200 million fewer episodes of diarrheal illness annually.

c. 300 million fewer people with roundworm infection.

d. 150 million fewer people with schistomiasis.

e. 2 million fewer people infected with guinea worm (ibid.).

All these emphasise the crucial importance of water. The scarcity of water in various places in Africa is so acute that people, as earlier stated, resort to buying, with their meagre incomes. This situation is worse in rural areas than in the urban centers, where much of government's efforts are expended. Rural areas suffer disadvantages in every dimension. The gap between rural and urban income is wide. For example, in 1975, 68 percent of the urban population had access to safe water supply as against 21 percent of rural. Although one could say that the risk of epidemics may be a little higher in crowded urban areas, this does not explain why most hospitals and clinics are concentrated in the few urban areas whereas rural areas are the centers of African populations. Education, the provision of electricity, roads and other government services are concentrated in cities. And yet, the money used in providing these services is mostly derived from the rural areas. Peter is robbed to pay Paul.

Putting it somewhat differently, much of the money used in providing the amenities in the cities come from foreign loans that must be paid for with foreign exchange that usually comes by exporting farm produce from the rural areas. President Julius Nyerere of Tanzania once said, "if we are not careful, we might get into the position where the real exploitation in Tanzania is that of the town dwellers exploiting the peasants." There is no doubt that African countries have already reached that point. That prophecy has already been fulfilled, because African countries have exploited rural populations to please urbanites. One last observation! The lopsided distribution in amenities goes back to the colonial era. Then, the colonial powers began the process by providing themselves, in their city bases, with the services and salaries they were accustomed to in their home countries. Africans continued these practices after independence (Offiong, 1980a; 1983; 1989).

Apart from government policies that have tended to accelerate the trend from countryside to the city, a pattern that had already begun during colonial times and the consequent exploitation of the rural dwellers to the advantage of the town dwellers, population exploitation has been named as one of the correlates of poverty in Africa. Despite high death rates from poverty and diseases, African populations double every 24 years. Sub-Saharan Africa had a population of 677 million in 1993. In the same year growth rate was 3.0 percent, the same as it was in 1992. This figure is considered high compared with figures for Asia of 2.1 percent, Latin America 1.9 percent, for USSR 0.6 percent, Oceania1.2 percent, and North America 0.8 percent (Population Reference Bureau, 1993). About half the population of Africa comprises teenagers or younger meaning that they are just entering their childbearing years. A much faster growing economy than that of Africa will not be able to support future surges in population. And Africa's population rate between the year 2000 and 2030 will be 2.4 percent, according to the World Bank (1992). It can be assumed that African poverty will persist for a very long time, since any economic growth is going to be overwhelmed by population increase, slowing the rise in living standards. This point is underscored by Ehrlich and Holdre (1988) when they state that "overpopulation contributes to poverty, and poverty breeds overpopulation."

On the other hand, some scholars have resented the old theory of overpopulation, that is, the Malthusian notion of human populations outgrowing their resource base. This theory has been given wide currency by neo-Malthusians who have benefited from the biological concept of "carrying capacity" of local environments. The argument is that many Third World societies have defied their environmental carrying capacity, that is, the natural systems of an entire country. Curtis Skinner (1988) argues that "the difficulty with the carrying capacity argument is that despite the attempts to make it relevant to dynamic social processes it remains an inherently static concept, best suited to looking at traditional, rural societies with a clearly defined impact on the resource base. Even here, changing socioeconomic conditions invariably complicate the picture." That it is rooted in the "Malthusian fallacy" that a surplus population means there are too many people and not enough resources of a faulty inequitable political and economic system. The result is that myth becomes the basis of social policy, and the overpopulation myth is particularly harmful because it tends to preempt deeper probing into intricate causes of underdevelopment. Therefore, while rising population cannot be ignored in the struggle against poverty, the issue of inequitable system of distribution of resources in which certain societies get more than their fair share must be given a critical look. This is important because poverty is at the center of inadequate food security and inadequate nutrition, to which we turn.

Chronic hunger saps energy, decreases productivity and increases vulnerability to disease. Food security in Sub-Saharan Africa has deteriorated since independence and food shortages have been rampant. Agricultural performance directly affects food security at the household level. Generally, malnutrition is seasonal, increasing before harvest when food supplies have decreased. The gap in food intake tends to widen in years of drought, and recurrent famines in 1980s have emphasised the high degree of food insecurity in the continent (World Bank, 1989):72). Energy value food consumption in Sub-Saharan Africa averaged 2,100 calorie per person per day which is 85 percent of recommended requirements. The estimate is that about one-quarter of Sub-Saharan African population obtain, on average good and bad crop years, less than 80 percent of the daily calorie supply recommended by FAO and WHO. Calorie intake in the Sahelian countries and the southern central region consisting of Botswana and surrounding areas, where rainfall is meagre and unreliable, is less than 80 percent of the daily supply recommended by FAO and WHO. This is also the core area of food insecurity. Apart from countries vulnerable to periodic droughts, for example, Ethiopia, there are those in which income distribution is particularly skewed and a part of the population is quite poor, even though the agricultural base and national income levels are strong. Kenya readily qualifies for this category. Food insecurity is also prevalent in countries fighting civil wars, such as Angola, Mozambique, Somalia, Liberia, and Rwanda; those with poor urban populations, such as Uganda and Congo; those with large poor urban populations, such as Zambia and Sudan; and others in which economic management has either stunted growth or not supported equitable distribution of its benefits. From a general perspective on what constitutes poverty, we proceed to examine different phenomena that affect African poverty, beginning with fluctuating commodity prices.

Fluctuating Commodity Prices and Poverty

Numerous studies (for example FAO 2009; UN 2003; Page and Hewitt 2001; UK Department for International Development [DFID]; and South Centre 2005) have all emphasised the negative effect of commodity price volatility on poor countries depending on primary products. Commodity dependence remains quite high in many developing countries, but that of Africa remains a special case. The dependence on primary products enhances vulnerability of these countries to unfavourable market or climate conditions. As observed by South Centre (2005:57), "since low-income countries depend mostly on just a few commodities for the bulk share of their export earnings, commodity price fluctuations directly affect the incidence of poverty, as the vast majority of the poor depend on primary commodities for their livelihoods."

Types of commodities exported by any country are important determinants of a country's vulnerability to exogenous economic factors. As noted earlier, the majority of developing countries are dependent on primary commodities for export revenues. As Brown (2008) has noted, of the 141 developing countries, 95 of them depend on primary commodities for at least 50 percent of their earnings. Volatile commodity prices, when low, reduce government revenues and lead to increase in national debt, thus undermining spending on health and education. When they are high, they tend to distort and undermine fiscal responsibility. They further undermine producers' (and consumers') ability to plan and invest for the future (ibid.). This impact of commodity price fluctuations is greatest in the poorest countries of the developing world, particularly in Africa.

Furthermore, unstable commodity prices bring about macro-economic instabilities and complicate macro-economic management. As underlined by the South Centre (2005:58) report, "erratic price movements generate erratic movements in export revenue, cause instability in foreign exchange reserves and are strongly associated with growth volatility. The more commodity-dependent an economy – that is, the higher the share of primary goods in a country's exports - the more likely it is to be vulnerable to commodity price shocks." For those countries that depend on the export of a few commodities for their earnings, "commodity price fluctuations directly affect the incidence of poverty, since the vast majority of the poor are dependent on the production of primary commodities for their livelihood" (ibid.). As reported by the United Nations (2003: 13) Conference on Trade and Development, African countries depend on two to three main primary commodity exports for most of their foreign exchange earnings, thus they have had to "contend with the problem of short-term instability of primary commodity prices, which is greater than that of prices for non-primary tradable commodities."

Writing about the impact of fluctuating commodity prices on Third World countries, Paul Harrison (1987:336) states, "to the developing countries the great world market place must often seem like a casino where all the wheels, dice and decks are rigged, loaded and marked so that the bankers of the West always win." In the present international division of labour, about three quarters of the Third World's exports are primary products, and about two thirds of its imports are manufactured goods. As we stated earlier, Ricardo had advocated this as a natural and beneficial state of affairs, in which each country specialises in those goods which it produces more cheaply, so everyone benefits by low prices. But the present division of labour originated not in this comparative advantage, but in conquest by force and rule by repression; in the case of non-colonies, it was the premature imposition of free trade by gunboat diplomacy (Harrison 1987: 338).

With very few exceptions, primary products are bad business for everyone aiming for a steady livelihood, but most Third World countries depend on just a few primary commodities. The result is that their balance of payments as well as the foreign exchange they so direly need to buy machinery and other items for their fledging industries, are entirely at the mercy of the fickle commodity trade wins.

By contrast, industrial nations have diversified into many different branches of trade, each one of which provides an insurance policy against setbacks in any of the others. Only very few Third World countries have been able to diversify enough to be less vulnerable to the vagaries of world market. Market fluctuations make it very difficult to plan and budget. Unless a single country dominates a major proportion of the supply of a particular commodity, or is a member of a strong cartel, it cannot predict with certainty the price of its major product. An abrupt windfall can cause inflation and encourage excessive import-buying, which will continue for quite a while even after prices have started falling. This was exactly what happened to Nigeria during the oil boom (or doom?). Nigeria even abandoned agriculture and relied almost exclusively on importing food stuffs, including rice and wheat from abroad, including the United States.

Compounding the problem for poor countries is the fact that "trade in commodities is not a simple matter of the balance between producers' supply and consumers' demand. A whole series of middlemen intervene between the two sides – and it is their curious behaviour that causes much of the fluctuation" (Harrison1987: 341). Export merchants buy up commodities, and in turn sell them to dealers, who themselves sell them to importers, who again sell them to processors or the retail trade. Theoretically, dealers should keep prices steady by evening out supply and demand. When prices go up, they should sell from their stocks, to make profit, thus bringing prices down again. When prices decline, they should buy up supplies while they are cheap and hence raise the price.

However, this rational model of behaviour does not operate in the world of speculation. Harrison (ibid.) asserts that "commodity dealers aggravate price instability. If the price of an item is rising and they think it will go on rising, they buy as much as they can get their hands on in the hope of selling it at a higher price later, and this buying activity pushes the price up even further – a self-fulfilling prophecy. Only when dealers feel downturn is around the corner will they stop buying in as prices rise. A peak is reached, and after it, prices start to fall." When prices start to fall it is very rapid because merchants have generated enough stocks to meet their customers' needs for months ahead and do not need to buy anymore for some time to come. When prices start to fall the speculators do not normally step in to buy up the bargain goods. If they consider that price will go on falling they sell everything they have purchased because they do not want to be stuck with a load of cheap goods, and this act further drags down the price, which is another self-fulfilling prophecy.

Speculators hold off buying as long as possible, in so far as they think the price still has a way to drop. "But then, at the bottom of the abyss, they start buying again with a vengeance. In other words, for most of the time speculators are doing the exact opposite of what most people do. They are buying more when the prices rise, and buying less when they drop. Third World commodity prices would certainly rise and fall anyway as supply and demand changes. But it is the activities of hoarders and speculators that turn the hills and valleys into towering peaks and terrifying abysses" (p.342). The consequences of all this on the lives of the people who depend on these commodities for their survival are too familiar. Africa is the most vulnerable region as far as commodity fluctuation is concerned.

Not even the General Agreement on Tariffs and Trade (GATT) of 1993 could bring solace to Africa. The agreement cut tariffs and brought international trade in agriculture and services under the GATT regime for the first time. But according to a September 1993 study commissioned by the Organisation for Economic Cooperation and Development (OECD) and the World Bank, net losses for Africa resulting from the agreement was around $2.6 billion in the period to 2002 while the leading industrial countries reaped around $135billion, or 64 percent of total annual gains in world income from GATT (Africa Recovery, December 1993-March 1994:9). African export revenues continue to decline as liberalised world trade erodes existing tariff preferences for Africa. The continent's mostly food-importing countries will also be affected by higher world food prices brought about by cuts in agricultural subsidies in developed countries.

Furthermore, African countries will continue to face a further deterioration of their balance of payments situation and worsening of their debt servicing problems unless some measures are taken to offset Uruguay round losses. Although the GATT agreement contains some compensatory provisions, these fail to address erosion of existing tariff preferences such as those in the Lome Convention.   The provisions allow preferential market access to Europe for 69 countries in the African, Carribean and Pacific (ACP) group.   Although the GATT deal allows non-Lome Convention countries to increase their share of European Union (EU) markets, it has been the position of UNCTAD that Africa will lose about 50 percent of its competitive advantage in major European Union, United States and Japanese markets.   So "loss of market and loss of competitive advantage" have been the result of the 1993 GATT agreement. What this means is that this agreement has helped to further depress African economies and intensify poverty.

Apart from the problems arising from commodity fluctuations and unfavourable trade agreements, Africa has got to contend with subsidised agricultural products from Europe. Subsidised European beef exports to West Africa are seriously threatening the livelihood of millions of people in the Sahel region and undermining the economic health of the beef producing countries in the continent. Livestock farmers in countries like Burkina Faso, Niger and Mali are losing markets in coastal West African countries, which until the mid-1980s imported their beef mainly from the Sahel region. Since the mid-1980s, the EU has been subsidising the export of frozen beef to the West African beef markets, "with lower-grade beef in some cases receiving higher rates of subsidy." EU exports account for more than 99 percent of all non-African exports of total EU beef production. This subsidised beef is 30-50 percent cheaper than West African beef. Its export to West Africa increased seven-fold in the 1980s, reaching a peak of 54, 000 tonnes in 1991. Consequently, regional cattle trade in the region shrank at the end of the 1980s by at least 30 percent from its volume in the early 1980s. Apart from undercutting the viability of beef produced in West Africa, the subsidised export of European beef to the region also undermines the EU's own aid programmes designed to improve livestock rearing and beef production in the Sahel. Furthermore, the absence of adequate refrigeration in the importing countries poses a health hazard for Africans who consume the frozen imported beef (ibid.). So economically weak, Africa faces competition everywhere, competition it cannot win and this multiplies its economic woes and poverty.

Foreign Aid and Poverty
We treated this phenomenon in the last chapter and promised to revisit it in this chapter. As we noted earlier, modernisation theory recommends as a panacea to underdevelopment that the rich countries alleviate global poverty or inequality by assisting in population control, increasing food production, introducing industrial technology and by instituting programmes of foreign aid. According to W. W. Rostow (1960; Macionis 1994), investment capital from rich countries would boost the prospects of poor nations striving to reach the so-called take-off stage. Poor countries still striving to develop can use this money to purchase fertilisers and high-technology irrigation projects that increase agricultural productivity as well as building power plants and factories that improve industrial output. This is more of a fantasy. From a purely pragmatic standpoint, improvements in the standard of living of people in the Third World would mean expanded markets for goods produced in the industrialised countries and greater political stability, and morally, "teeming hordes of hungry people are intolerable" (Lewellen 1995; 115). Unfortunately, however, about 50 years since Rostow and his fellow modernisation theorists made the foreign aid prescription which became the foreign policy of America and other Western countries toward the Third World, poverty still remains an

endemic problem. As we discuss the phenomenon of foreign aid, the reasons why it has not been very helpful will become apparent.

In 1988 official development assistance (ODA) was $51 billion, that is, half the net receipts of external capital by developing countries. As for the low-income countries, which harbour most of the world's poor, aid represents about 70 percent of net external finance. In many of these countries aid represents a much more important source of foreign exchange than exports. There may be some benefits derived from foreign aid, especially when it is properly administered, but some of the poorest countries have become trapped in "aid dependency." They must have aid to be able to maintain their present low quality of life, when it should be used to improve their long-term prospects. Thus, aid seems to do much less than have been expected to reduce poverty. According to the report by OECD's Development Assistance Committee (DAC) covering 1960-1985, "Twenty-Five Years of Development Cooperation", "the most troubling shortcoming of development aid has been its limited measurable contribution to the reduction – as distinguished from the relief – of extreme poverty, especially in the rural areas of both middle-income and poor countries" (World Bank, 1990).

There are various motives for giving aid. Three broad groups provide aid. These are bilateral donors, multilateral agencies, and non-governmental organisations. Official aid is disbursed to receiving countries from bilateral and multilateral sources. This consists of grants and loans from official sources that have promotion of economic development and welfare as their primary objectives. Additionally, many non-governmental organisations in industrial countries provide aid. Among DAC members, the US is the largest donor in terms of total volume; it gave $10.1 billion in aid in 1988; Japan ranked second with $9.1 billion. As a proportion of GNP, the US aid was only 0.21 percent, whereas a country like Norway gave 1.10 percent of GNP. Aid from Arab countries in 1988 amounted to $2.3 billion of which $2.1 billion came from Saudi Arabia and $108 million from Kuwait. Saudi Arabia's ratio of aid to GNP equals 2.70 percent, the highest for any donor, and Kuwait's was 0.41, above the average for DAC members (World Bank 1990:129).

Bilateral donors, in particular, provide aid for many reasons, including political, strategic, commercial, and humanitarian. "Reducing poverty is only one motive, and it is usually to countries of key strategic importance such as Egypt and Israel; French and British aid goes disproportionately to former colonies. Some donors – the Nordic countries, for example - have emphasised the reduction of poverty more than others" (ibid.). This practice has several repercussions. One, not all aid goes to low-income countries. In 1988 around 41 percent of it went to middle- and high-income countries. Two, there are certainly wide disparities in the allocation of aid, and the most generous per capita allocations do not go to the poorest countries. Three, many "aid" programmes in donor countries cover an assortment of activities, such as commercial and strategic initiatives, which often have, at least, a tenuous association with development. Only about 8 percent of US aid programme in 1986, for example, could be labeled as "development assistance devoted to low-income countries;" that is to say, recipients are required under the terms to buy goods and services from donor countries. Approximately two-thirds of all aid applied by DAC members are in this category (World Bank 1990:127-28). Thus a significant portion of aid is spent in the donor's country, often on irrationally exorbitant consultancies. Fifth, donors of aid prefer to finance physical capital installations that help their own firms and exporters, and they are quite unwilling to support the operating (recurrent) costs of aid-funded undertakings. But as we know, the bulk of the initiatives required for reducing poverty in the developing countries are in sectors such as health and education that make intensive use of recurrent resources. Not surprisingly, the World Bank (1990:128) concluded that "a substantial proportion of aid is provided at least partly for purposes other than to promote development."

Apart from the World Bank verdict on aid and poverty, there is another view which corroborates the Bank's conclusion. According to Randel and German (1994), aid volumes are declining and donor policies do not give priority to poverty reduction. These authors, writing for Action Aid, contend that "governments do not appear to be making the transition from rhetoric to action." Apart from Japan, which as at 1994 provided one-fifth of all aid by the members of the DAC of the OECD, Denmark, Ireland and New Zealand were the only OECD donors which did not anticipate a reduction in their official development assistance (ODA).

The authors further contend that the volume of resources available for poverty alleviation is threatened both by aid budget cuts as well as by the diversion of funds for other purposes, such as emergency relief and forgiveness of debts arising from commercial export credit agreements. They note that around 7 percent of ODA is currently devoted to spending on emergency relief, compared to 2 percent about five years earlier; they stress the importance of the allocation of adequate resources so that the increased need for relief, peace-making and conflict resolution, although essential as they are, are not met at the expense of those in chronic poverty. Additionally, they call for the establishment of standards to measure the allocation of aid to poverty reduction.

Business interests are significant in donor countries in the awarding of aid. Randel and German (1994) further urge that donors should establish criteria of human development, appropriate technology and sustainable development to be met by companies seeking aid-funded business. Around $15 billion of aid was tied to the purchase of goods and services from donor countries in each of the five years. DAC assistance amounted to $60.4 billion in 1992.

Nigeria's case with the United States clearly demonstrates the significant role of business interests in donor countries in the award of aid. A trade dispute developed because Nigeria decided in 1986 to ban wheat and other basic food imports in an effort aimed at boosting domestic agricultural production. US food aid to Nigeria was tied to Nigeria importing wheat from the US to the tune of over $250 per year, making Nigeria the sixth largest US wheat importer. Agricultural groups in the US demanded US retaliation unless Nigeria reopened its markets to their wheat (Zimmerman, 1993:67). As far as Nigerians were concerned, "the Americans miscalculated how important this issue is to us. They don't seem to understand that our primary objective is economic self-sufficiency, and making money for American wheat farmers pales by comparison" (Noble, December 31, 1989). Nigerians were flabbergasted by the US reaction because the ban affected all countries that had exported wheat, rice and other food items to Nigeria. The rift was ironic because the ban was part of the Structural Adjustment Package imposed by IMF and World Bank and had been encouraged by the US both bilaterally and through the international institutions (ibid., p. 68). As Richard Uku (cited in ibid.) put it, the US "change in stride" resulted from the realisation that its wheat farmers would sustain "substantial losses from a cessation of Nigerian importation" and this suggests "double standard." This action, according to Uku, "called into question the sincerity of purpose behind the professed American commitment to African development. At least this was the underlying sentiment behind Nigerian criticism of American pressure to end the ban." What quickly emerges here is that one, aid allows the political leader to reward those that supported his election and therefore ensure their continuous support; two, or if he was not supported by that constituency, he now can show how hard he has worked for them and therefore deserving of their support at the next opportunity.

Foreign Aid and Development
The purpose of this section is to emphasise that foreign aid is no act of altruism, and that it is a design to promote American economic interest around the globe. I want to also argue that if any benefits accrue to aid recipients at all, they are only the by-products of the manifest intentions of the aid donor. But first, I must recapitulate the relative positions of modernisation and dependency theories with respect to the relationship between the rich and poor countries, particularly as it affects foreign assistance.

According to modernisation theory, the First World (represented by the rich industrialised countries) makes positive contributions to the global economic development. The First World is not the cause of the abject penury that afflicts much of humanity; instead it holds the key to solving global inequality by assisting in population growth, increasing food production, introducing industrial technology and providing foreign aid.

By contrast, dependency theory contends that rich societies have unjustly seized the wealth of the entire world for their selfish purposes. What this means is that the *overdevelopment* of the First World has resulted in the *under-*

development of the Third World. Dependency theorists readily dismiss the claim that First World programmes of agricultural and industrial technology, population control, and foreign aid help the Third World. They contend, instead, that the First World simply acts in pursuit of profit. Selling technology is a means of making money, and foreign aid is money given to the ruling elites, not to the poor majority, in exchange for maintaining a favorable "business climate" for the multinationals (Lappe, Collins, and Kinley 1981).

Furthermore, dependency theory argues that the American capitalist culture encourages people to think and even believe that poverty is natural or inevitable. On the basis of this belief, poverty is the result of "natural" processes including having too many children, and disasters such as droughts. But according to Lappe and Collins (1986), global poverty is far from inevitable; rather it emanates from deliberate policies.   They argue that the world already produces quite enough food to allow everyone in the world to eat and become fat.

The concentration of poverty amid plenty results from a First World policy of producing food for profit, not for people. In other words, the First World cooperates with elites in the Third World to grow and export profitable crops such as coffee while at the same time preventing the production of stables consumed by local population.   Third World governments support this ideology of "growing for export" because they need food profits to try to pay massive debts. Lappe and Collins maintain that at the center of this vicious cycle is the capitalist corporate structure of the First World. Thus foreign assistance is an instrument used to enhance and maintain the capitalist corporate structure of the rich and powerful nations. In other words, even though this analysis is about the United States it applies to all other nations, particularly the G-8.

For Senator Leahy (*Congressional Record*, July 25, 1996:S8743), helping in developing the Third World "is usually the biggest and fastest growing market" for American products; it creates jobs; and "the more exports" Americans create, the more jobs they create and "the fastest growing and biggest potential market is in the Third World." In the same vein, George Burrill in his essay titled "U.S. Foreign Aid Helps Americans at Home" (reprinted in ibid.), notes that as at 1996, exports accounted for 10 percent of the entire US economy, that is, double what it was a decade before. In 1983, 5 million jobs depended on US exports whereas in 1996 it was 12,000,000 jobs. Burrill adds that "the fastest growing markets for U.S. goods and services are in the developing world" (p. S8744). Exports to developing countries increased by nearly $100 billion between 1990 and 1995, creating about 1.9 million jobs in the United States. Foreign assistance goes toward making developing countries "good customers" and the American economy continues to boom mainly because other countries, particularly developing ones, buy the products (ibid.).

Foreign assistance now focuses on promoting certain changes in the developing countries that will enhance American economic expansion and dominance. First, it encourages reform in developing countries' overall economic policy. This aim coincides with that of Structural Adjustment Programme, and it is no surprise. After assisting the Czech Republic to transform its economy from a command to a free-market system, United States exports to that country increased by 11 percent. Second, the US works to dismantle laws and institutions that "prevent free trade." An example of where this succeeded very well is Guatemala which now "exports specialty fruits, vegetables, and flowers." This increased buying power has resulted in a 19 percent increase in exports from the US to Guatemala since 1989. Third, the US helps to privatise state dominated economies. A $3 million assistance to support privatisation in Indonesian energy sector led to a $2 billion award to an American firm for Indonesia's first private power contract. Burrill states rather emphatically that the US "foreign budget has enabled U.S. companies to dominate the global market for private energy" (ibid.). Fourth, foreign assistance encourages developing countries to create business codes and the rule of law, as dictated by the US. Thus foreign assistance helps to create "the stable business environments" that American companies need to operate. Fifth, foreign assistance helps to create a new class of consumers in developing countries. Having developed the appetite for Western products, this very elite class or group are willing to drain their meagre foreign exchange to import those items, an experience that practically every African country has encountered. Sixth, foreign assistance helps to build small businesses. Community-run learning programmes managed by the US government help to expand small businesses and increase per capita income in many developing countries. US companies are the greatest beneficiaries in all this exercise. George Burrill ends his essay by saying that "the relatively small amount of money" the US spends on foreign economic assistance "serves as an engine" for American economic growth (ibid.).

In all this, however, Africa receives the lowest priority and this relates to the marginalisation I mentioned earlier. Senator Jeffords (ibid., p.S772) admits that "traditionally funding for Africa has fallen victim to sudden needs elsewhere in the world." And Senator Simon adds, Africa "has two unfortunate distinctions – it is both the poorest and the most ignored continent" and "aid to Africa" is "considered expendable when resources" are "sought for other purposes" even while Africa "suffers from poverty, pollution, and the scourge of AIDS" (ibid.). Apparently, Africa is not as profitable as the other regions of the world, neither is it of any strategic importance to the West, especially now that the Cold War is over. Another possible explanation is that African-Americans who would lobby for some assistance for Africa are themselves still struggling to establish a firm footing in the American scheme of things. Even the first Black president (black because of the one-drop rule, Barack Obama is multiracial) has not been able to do much for African-Americans, let alone Africa, because the support from the white establishment is missing).

Much of foreign assistance is in the form of arms. In fact, Senator Dorgan admits that "the United States is the largest arms merchant in the world." The United States in 1994 "delivered over $10 billion of the $20 billion worth of arms spread all over the world, " arms used for defense and for killing, in some cases arms provided to both sides of the same conflict by American arms merchants" and by American government (ibid.).   The crisis in Somalia was perhaps encouraged by US arms. Between 1981 and 1991, $154 million of arms were delivered to Somalia from the US. This stimulated an arms race in that country and ultimately the total cost of arms to Somalia was $1.2 billion. And Senator Hatfield's (ibid., S8783) statement is worth quoting at length: "...since the Soviet Union has become unraveled, we [Americans] are now unquestionably the number one merchants of death in this world by our export of arms. We not only export them as a market, we go around promoting it. We go around Ballyhooing the arms that we have, the arms that are exhibited in the Paris Air Show and many international conferences that supposedly are for some international benefit.   It is an arms peddling activity. We even let our embassies be instructed to facilitate arms transfers as part of their duty in the country in which they are representing the United States."

Selling instruments of destruction (and mass destruction) is part of the global trade, particularly in the Third World. In 1993 the US supplied 75 percent of all weapons sold to the Third World, and these are countries who can least afford to buy arms (ibid.) Selling arms to Third World countries has often boomeranged. In the 1980s, the US sent 4, 800 M-16 rifles, 84 106-millimeter recoils rifles, 24 machine guns, 75 81-millimeter mortars and landmines to Somalia. These were the arms that Mohammed Farah Aideed used to ambush and kill 30 American soldiers (ibid.). By the way, in 1996, the US budgeted $628 million of aid for Africa, with a large chunk going to Egypt, for obvious reasons. What is clear here is that countries with meagre coffers drain their treasury to purchase weapons of war while their people are subjected to unconscionable poverty.

Poverty and Hazardous Wastes
African poverty has encouraged industrial nations to pressure them into agreeing to make their countries dumping grounds for hazardous wastes. It is common knowledge that industrial products contain many chemicals and substances that their producers cannot recycle nor dispose of in a simple way. So this has become a major challenge to industrialised countries, especially as they fill up their landfills and as the price of processing the waste materials continues to rise. In about 1987 after the Koko Beach, Nigeria episode in which an Italian ship dumped a load of hazardous waste, the UN drew up plans to regulate such wastes based on the Basel Convention. By 1998, EU had agreed to implement the ban which prohibited industrialised countries from exporting their hazardous wastes

to poor countries; but the US, Canada, Australia and New Zealand opted out. The problem is not limited to industrial wastes. Now there is the threat of dumping electronic waste such as unwanted mobile phones, printers and computers, which are known to contain cadmium, lead, mercury and other poisons.   African countries like Nigeria have become destinations of fairly used items and goods. But a significant number of these almost useless computers cannot be sold and they sit in landfills in Lagos and elsewhere. They do become harmful especially to children.

Industrial countries started early to regulate the movement of toxic and hazardous wastes within their borders. While internal or local disposal has become increasingly difficult and expensive, the absence of similar regulations in the Third World has encouraged the transfer of hazardous wastes to the developing world, and probably Eastern Europe also.   According to *Transnationals* (July 1989:4), "presently, about 20 percent of the hazardous wastes generated in and exported from industrial countries is shipped to developing countries. However, that figure is likely to rise." It is estimated that 10 to 15 percent of industrial wastes are hazardous and they increase at about 2 to 5 percent per year.   As environmental controls in the industrial countries tighten up, producers and brokers of wastes will continue to try to dispose of wastes as expediently as possible by dumping in developing countries with weak regulatory and administrative mechanisms.   They exploit the poverty endemic in poor countries to trick them into accepting toxic wastes. Others are even dumped without the knowledge of the people or with the connivance or cooperation of the gatekeepers. The present hardship attending SAPs has made it easy for people to cooperate with foreign companies or corporations.

Several West African countries have been victims of many recent hazardous wastes dumping. Nigeria discovered 4,000 tons of illegally shipped toxic wastes from Italy in its territory in 1988. In Sierra Leone, 625 bags of hazardous wastes originating from the United Kingdom were abandoned in the capital city's garbage dump. Cases of attempted dumping involve a British company in Liberia, an American firm in Guinea-Bissau and a Belgian firm in Sierra Leone. In Guinea, toxic dumping by a Norwegian company in a coastal town ruined the local fishing economy and brought tourism to an end. In 1984, cascamite was dumped in Senegal causing gases (*Transnationals*, July 1994:4).

In many cases, wastes were illegally dumped in a clandestine manner. "In other cases, private individuals, businesses or governments were paid to accept wastes, especially in countries where economic crisis has created a desperate need for foreign exchange (such as Benin and Guinea-Bissau") (ibid.). Furthermore, proven hazardous industrial processes are increasingly being located in developing countries through transnationals' affiliates. Just as in the case of shipment of hazardous wastes, the incentives range from direct payment to proposals to process imported wastes for energy generation and various other developmental applications. In Senegal and Gambia, European and American companies have attempted to export hazardous wastes as part of proposed manufacturing schemes. As *Transnationals* (ibid.) puts it, "Profit is the major catalyst in the waste. Disposal costs in developed countries run as high as $200 per metric ton but only $3 or less per ton in Africa. This huge differential far exceeds shipping costs and dumping risks."

Many (more than a dozen) African countries have been approached by waste brokers seeking to obtain import permits for hazardous wastes in recent years. This situation prompted the Council of Ministers of the Organisation of African Unity (OAU) to adopt a resolution in May 1988 "calling for a total ban on the export of dangerous wastes to African countries." West African countries have on their own part responded to this threat by enacting national legislation on toxic and hazardous wastes and environmental impact disclosure by *Transnationals*. In all African countries lack the technical and institutional capacity for the safe treatment, disposal and management of hazardous wastes, even those generated by industrial processes within these countries. They often lack the know-how to recognise the toxicity or potential toxicity of these wastes, or even to evaluate their environmental and ecological impact. On every score, African countries are the losers. While still struggling under the pangs of poverty, Africans may have to face the effect of toxic and hazardous wastes which may filter into their sources of drinking water, or get to them through some other means. The exporters of these hazardous wastes do not care, because selling them is just like doing business with any kind of commodity. Hazardous waste is a commodity. This leads to the notion that poverty is functional but the question is functional for whom?

The Functions of Poverty
Poverty, according to H. Gans (1971, 1996), is functional. He identifies several economic, social and political functions of poverty. Gans' functions apply to the American society but I contend that some of them can be extended to include the international scene. America remains the richest country on earth and yet there are pockets of absolute poverty within the same society. Poverty persists because it performs certain functions to certain groups of people. It follows that the existence of poor countries has some positive functions for the

rich and powerful countries of the world. The rich are able to use poor African countries as landfills for their waste products.

Economically, poverty benefits the rich countries. Third World countries provide ready pool of low-wage labourers who are available to perform the "dirty work" that people in rich countries are unwilling to perform. Poor people from Latin America, the Caribbean, Africa and Asia flock to the US every year. These are the people who work at low wages, picking cotton and doing other menial jobs. They do dangerous, undignified jobs that Americans are unwilling to do but that are crucial to keep business operating. It is a common law of economics that when many poor people compete for scarce jobs, businesses resort to paying low wages. Corporations in rich countries are able to move their businesses to poor countries where they pay workers starvation wages. Third World governments are made to guarantee corporations cheap labour before they even move their business there. Many products sold in American markets are produced by cheap labour in Third World countries and then shipped back to the US where they make unconscionable profits. They do not hesitate to exploit child labour as in Pakistan and India, among others, and prison labour, as in China. The case of brain drain is a classic one. The United States and other Western countries receive highly skilled manpower from the Third World. Medical doctors, engineers, among many others, migrate to rich countries because there are facilities for them to practice their profession to the full potentials of their capability, and they are also well paid. At times they are forced out of their countries because of troubling political situations.

In a class discussion on illegal aliens in a race and ethnic relations course, students, both American and foreigners, discussed a pathetic practice which they said is common in Georgia. The practice is that there are people who specialise in recruiting illegal aliens into the state and they are paid, of course. Many employers, according to the students in the class discussion, hire these illegal aliens and promise to pay them, say, in three months. A few days before the promised date, the employers invite immigration officials (apparently privy to the arrangement) to frighten the illegals who run away without receiving their pay. Within a few days another group is brought in to be treated the same way.

In the United States, for example, the welfare system supports a large network of private sector business that makes enormous profits by providing the system with a number of goods and services. Some government assistance programmes provide certain things to the poor that inevitably must be bought from private industry. On the international level, when certain assistance, like disaster relief, is provided to African or other poor countries, the necessary items are purchased from private industry. President John Kennedy once defined foreign aid as money given to friendly countries to keep their leaders (who are American good boys) in power (Offiong, 1980a). Much of the relief money is used to purchase items from the donor's country, even if they could be purchased at considerably cheaper prices elsewhere. This practice benefits the president or prime minister because it allows him or her to show favour or gratitude to those who supported him or her in the last election or to lobby for votes from certain groups in a forthcoming election.

According to George Burrill (*Congressional Record*, July 25, 1996:S8743), "nearly six out of 10 Americans" believe that the US "spends more on foreign aid than on medicare." The truth is that "government collects only about $11 per person each year from income taxes to pay for foreign assistance." Unfortunately, however, few Americans are aware "that 80 percent of the total foreign assistance budget is spent right here in the United States, on American goods and services – more than $10 billion in 1994." Burrill continues that "this translates to about 200,000 American jobs. For example, Cormier Textile Products in Maine provided tarps for disaster relief and temporary housing in Africa."

Poor countries purchase goods and services that would otherwise be destroyed. For example, second hand goods, used clothes, food stuffs, incompetent physicians and others like them who move to poor countries to become experts. Jalopies from rich countries adorn automobile markets in poor countries. Even old and antiquated military hardware that had long become useless or about to be scrapped are sold to poor countries; sometimes they are part of foreign aid. Trade in used items purchased from rich countries constitutes a gigantic industry in Africa. Certain items for export to poor countries are of very poor quality. There is nothing like quality control and even there may be no laws guarding against such dumping; and even if there are laws, officials in charged are bribed to look the other way while the items are moved in. Poverty forces poor countries to allow rich countries to dump toxic and hazardous wastes in their countries for very little amount of money. Poverty enables rich and powerful countries to dictate economic terms with the poor. Most loans are designed to improve those sectors for which foreign firms or corporations will benefit, while the loan is paid back from the sweat of the indigenous people. Poor countries provide jobs for the so-called experts from rich countries. When aid or loan is given, the poor recipient country is required to recruit experts from the donor's country and fees to those experts are often outrageous. When those programmes fail, the experts return to their country of origin to enjoy their fees.

Apart from economic functions, poverty also serves social functions. Poverty is a clear reminder to the Third World of the "legitimacy" of the important values of thrift, honesty, and hard work. In other words, Third World countries, particularly African countries, have not yet adopted the Protestant ethic; they have not yet joined the Calvinist cult that Max Weber credited for the economic development of the West. For this reason, poor countries are responsible for their poverty. This is the position of modernisation theorists. The victim is responsible for his poverty. In addition, "poverty guarantees the status of those who are not poor. The poor provide a reference point against which others compare themselves"(Newman, 1997:375). Responding to disasters in the Third World allows the rich and powerful countries to "symbolically demonstrate their concern and philanthropy and reinforce their feelings of moral superiority" (ibid.). It is not uncommon to hear America announce that they supply disaster assistance on moral ground. This was the reason invoked when the US gave $100,000 to North Korea during their economic disaster. Usually other nations wait for the United States to take the lead before they join in. No matter what one may say about the United States, its leadership role is often essential for any relief success. They have the resources, the technical know-how, among others.

Poverty provides politicians with campaign issues. There are those who claim that immigrants from the Third World are part of their economic problem. Thus stopping immigration and deporting illegal immigrants and denying legal immigrants certain benefits they previously enjoyed have often become great political issues. Pat Buchannan ran for nomination as presidential candidate of the Republican Party mainly on such issues. Lobbyists make millions of dollars from foreign governments who want them to plead their cases with congressmen and other government officials for foreign aid. Poverty allows rich countries to twist the arms of poor countries at the United Nations for their votes to support the positions of rich countries on international matters. They have to vote with the G-8 if they want to receive assistance or loans from the international financial institutions, or to have their onerous debts rescheduled. Those countries that do not "behave" or "fall in line" have their leaders branded "radicals;" and once so labeled, their country is subjected to treatments which unfortunately end up punishing the poor. During the Cold War days, branding a country's leader as a radical was ominous or portentous of serious consequences. For, such a leader was subjected to attacks by the Western press and usually the Central Intelligence Agency (CIA) would undertake some covert actions to overthrow the leader and replace him with someone amenable to Western interests. Russia was not left out in this game of neocolonialism.

In sum, poverty in Africa is very severe and its extent, as has been demonstrated in this chapter is of alarming proportion. I agree that social stratification is a culture universal and poverty exists in all social systems of social inequality. But the concept of poverty incorporates two different forms. Relative poverty is a universal phenomenon and refers to deprivation of resources of others. On the other hand, absolute poverty refers to deprivation of resources considered to be life threatening. And, millions live under $1.25 per day, defined as extreme poverty by the World Bank. All three levels of poverty exist in Africa with absolute and extreme being prevalent. The severity of poverty can be inferred from per-person's income, the quality of life, among others, all of which do not favour Africa.

In rural areas of Africa, where the bulk of the population lives, close to half the population are ill-nourished. In the entire world about 100 million people are without shelter and more than one billion people do not eat enough to allow them to function normally. Among these, millions are at the risk for their lives (Sivard, 1988; Helmuth, 1989). Africans suffer from inadequate nutrition; from diseases (many of which are preventable) and even from lack of safe water. In the entire world about one person dies every minute of every day due to lack of basic nutrition. This means that about 15 million people die each year. This deplorable state of humanity calls for immediate action. But one would be mistaken to expect much to be done other than the usual rhetorical platitudes. The fact of the matter is that the functions of poverty are far outweighed by its dysfunctions which include, for example, suffering, violence and waste of human and material resources. The dysfunctions of poverty could be eliminated by "functional alternatives" such as higher pay for doing dirty work, or by the intentional redistribution of national (Kornblum, 1998) and international wealth commandeered and enjoyed by a few.

Now that the East-West confrontation is history, these two groups that made Africa, indeed, the Third World their battle ground, should remember that the same region remains the battle ground for fighting poverty and gross inequality. The abject penury that Africa finds itself, coupled with the end of the Cold War, which therefore frees Africa from East-West struggle and the proxy wars it entails, the resurgence of Eastern Europe, the developments between Israel and Palestine and other Arab nations, in addition to the belief that it is more profitable (so they claim) to invest in Asia than in Africa, has resulted in the marginalisation of the continent, and made it more dependent on the West than ever before. It is to this asymmetric relationship that we now turn.

4

Asymmetric Global Trading System

As evident in Chapter 2, the rise of a global trading system stemming from the European colonial expansionism had culminated in a "colonial division of labour," in which the colonised (subsequently dubbed developing) countries were sentenced to the role of exporting primary products, agriculture and minerals, while Europe and North America exported manufactured goods. Since then, the former colonial territories have become independent of their erstwhile colonial masters and the structure of trade has been changing, particularly in recent decades. According to Sutcliffe (2001:71-75; UNCTAD 1999), the following represent important recent characteristics of global trade patterns:

(1)   75 percent of the world exports are from developed countries while a paltry 25 percent are from developing countries; developed countries export largely manufactured goods: 83 percent of their total, 62 percent of total world exports; developed countries also export more manufactured goods than primary products: 56 percent of their total, 14 percent of world exports. More primary products are exported by developed than by developing countries: 14 percent of world exports, compared with 11 percent. According to Sutcliffe (p.76), most developing countries increased their volume of trade in the 1990s, but the increase was very uneven. As noted by Sutcliffe;

(2)   From 1950 to 1970, developed countries gained in the share of total world exports, while developing countries lost;

(3)   In the 1980s and 1990s, a group of developing countries in East Asia significantly increased the exports of

their manufactured goods, and this led to their increased share of the world trade;

(4)   Latin America's share fell substantially from 1950 through 1990, and then began to increase slightly;

(5)   Exports from West Asia and North Africa fell since 1980, due to declining petroleum prices;

(6)   That there has been a historic decline in the exports of the Sub-Saharan region; its share of the world total has declined from over 3 percent in 1950 to barely 1 percent in 1996; and the explanation offered for this drastic drop has been that there has not been any change in the products it exports, and that the prices of such products have tended to fall.

As it is clear from the above statistics, even in the volume of trade Africa has lost out; it has been greatly disadvantaged at least partly due to the nature of its products which goes back to its colonial status. International trade has the potential to provide the means by which people could improve their quality of life; unfortunately, however, the prevailing trading practices and policies make it very difficult for some countries, particularly those in Africa, to compete and prosper in the current global market.

There has been an on-going debate regarding global inequality. In 2005 there were two very important reports on the issue and both of them agreed that global income inequality has been increasing. According to the United Nations Development Programme (UNDP) Human Development Report (HDR) 2005, only 9 countries (4 percent of the world's population) have reduced the wealth gap between rich and poor, while 80 percent of the world's population has experienced an increase in wealth inequality. The report noted that the richest 50 individuals in the world had combined income greater than that of the poorest 416 million. The 2.5 billion people living on less than $2 a day, constituting 40 percent of the world's population, received 50 percent of global income, while 54 percent of global income went to the richest 10 percent of the world's population.

The *World Social Situation 2005: The Inequality Predicament Report* identified non economic factors of global inequality such as inequalities in education, health, employment, gender and opportunities for social and political participation, as causing and exacerbating poverty around the globe. These institutionalised inequalities have resulted in greater marginalisation within society. This report cites high unemployment, particularly among youth. Millions are working but remain poor; about a quarter of the world's workers do not earn enough to lift themselves and their families above the $1-per-day poverty threshold. Despite some progress in some contexts, health and education inequalities have widened since the mid-1980s. Such conditions of inequality tend to encourage social disintegration, violence and national and international terrorism (Makwana 2006).

Both the HDR (2005) and UN's *Report on the World's Social Situation 2005*, just like previous reports, lay the blame squarely on the forces of globalisation, deregulation and liberalisation as central to global inequality. The HDR blames the unequal global trade system as a primary cause in increasing global inequality. With symmetrical trade, greater financial benefit would be given to the South by the North. Unfortunately, the nature of the global trade emphasises asymmetry, inequality and the North's agricultural subsidies alone cost developing countries' economies almost the amount they receive in overseas development assistance.

Based on the above findings, the *Report on the World Social Situation 2005* made several recommendations including the following:

·   Worldwide asymmetries resulting from globalisation must be tackled, with emphasis placed on more equitable distribution of the benefits of an increasingly open global economy;

·   That democracy and the rule of law should be promoted while special efforts are made to integrate marginalised groups into society; and

·   Inequalities in access to resources and opportunities should be redressed to prevent global conflict and violence.

Rigged Rules and Double Standards

The asymmetry that characterises the global economic system has been a tremendous concern to poor countries and Oxfam International, an international non-governmental organisation (NGO) has determined to "make trade fair." Oxfam sees a "paradox at the heart of international trade" in the globalised world where trade remains a most powerful instrument affecting people and it is also a source of unprecedented wealth to certain countries. The unfortunate thing is that "millions of the poorest people of the world are left behind. As at present, very significant "increase in prosperity is simultaneous with mass poverty and the widening of unconscionable inequalities between rich and poor."   While there is no doubt that international trade has the potential to reduce poverty and for increasing economic growth, "but that potential seems to have been lost. The problem does not lie in the trade itself but the fact that 'the rules that govern it are rigged in favour of the rich" (Oxfam 2002:3). The WTO is dominated by the rich and powerful countries. In fact we find a situation in which the fox is guarding the hen house. Noting the human costs of unfair trade, Oxfam observes that if Africa, East Asia, South Asia, and Latin America were each to increase their share of world exports by just one percent this would result in gains in income which could lift 128 million people out of poverty. This reduced poverty would lead to improvements in other areas, such as child health and education (ibid.).

In their rhetoric, governments of the rich countries emphasise their concern and commitment to eliminating poverty around the globe. Ironically, those very governments use their "trade policy to conduct what amounts to robbery against the world's poor." Exports to markets in rich countries' "face tariff barriers that are four times higher than those encountered by rich countries in poor countries. Those barriers cost them $100bn a year – twice as much as they receive in aid" (ibid.). What is obvious here is that when the rich countries prevent poor countries from trading in their markets, they are sentencing them to eternal poverty, a problem that the world community claims to be fighting against and to eradicate.

Again, the irony is that when rich countries close their markets, the same rich countries enlist the support of the World Bank and IMF to become their debt collectors and to employ every means possible to pressurise poor countries "to open their markets at breakneck speed, often with damaging consequences for poor communities" (p.4). This has been compounded by low and unstable commodity prices, which consign millions to abject penury. At the same time transnational corporations (TNCs) are free to engage in investment and employment practices which encourage poverty and insecurity, "unencumbered by anything other than weak voluntary guidelines." The WTO has contributed immensely to the problem by protecting the interests of rich countries and powerful TNCs in the areas of intellectual property, investment, and services, while simultaneously imposing huge costs on poor countries (ibid.).

Fair trade directed by equitable rules would enhance reduction in poverty, but this potential has not materialised despite the growing integration through global trade. The inequality between the rich and poor countries has generated ritualist debate between two competing camps – the "globaphiles" and the "globaphobes," as Oxfam refers to them. The globaphiles argue that trade has made globalisation work for the poor, therefore there should be no change in the set up of things. On the other hand, the globaphobes turn this world-view camera obscura (topsy-turvy), by saying that trade is inherently not good for poor countries, as more participation leads to increased inequality and poverty (p.5).

To the contrary, the expansion of trade under globalisation has had some successes, but in the midst of rising wealth generated by global trade, more than one billion people are still struggling to survive on one dollar a day, the same number of people as in the mid-1980s. High income countries constitute 14 percent of the world's population and yet they account for 75 percent of global GDP which is around what it was in 1990 (p.7). Inequalities in global trade help to intensify and perpetuate wider inequalities in poverty. In the 1990s while rich countries increased the per capita value of their exports by $1938, low income countries increased theirs by only $51, and $98 by middle income countries.

While export success in some developing countries have been noted, this has been quite concentrated, with East Asia accounting for more than 75 percent of manufactured exports, and even greater share of high-technology products. South Asia and Sub-Saharan Africa together account for less than two percent, while the share of Latin America is shrinking, with the possible exception of Mexico. Even Mexico reported as a major exporter of high technology goods and services is "trapped in low-value-added ghettoes" and the growth in exports "has little impact on their levels of poverty" (ibid.). Less than two percent of the value of its exports is derived from local inputs. This situation is equally true of a number of countries showing high rates of export growth in the garments sector; this includes Bangladesh and Honduras. What transpires here is that export production consists of simply assembling and re-exporting of imported components under the auspices of TNC, with very little transfer of technology (Oxfam p.8). Those countries that rely on the export of primary commodities have witnessed the shrinking of their shares of world trade and Sub-Saharan Africa bears the brunt of falling prices, which has further worsened its poverty (Offiong 2001). According to trade theory, poor people in developing countries will benefit from integration through trade, but the reality has been quite different. Rapid growth in exports has resulted in rising unemployment and stagnating incomes (Oxfam 2002:8).

As we noted earlier, trade restrictions in rich countries cost developing countries about ($100bn a year – twice the amount they receive in aid. Sub-Saharan Africa remains the world's poorest region and it loses about $2bn a year; India and China are in excess of $3bn. Trade barriers are destructive to the poor because they are targeted at the goods that they produce, and these are usually labour-intensive agricultural and manufactured products in which women constitute a large share of employment.

Oxfam has attempted to determine those countries that damage the interests of developing countries through trade barriers by what it calls "Double Standards Index" (DSI). DSI measures ten important dimensions of rich-country trade policies, such as average tariffs, the sizes of tariffs in textiles and agriculture, and restrictions on imports from the Least Developed Countries (p.9). They call their measurement Double Standards Index because "it measures the gap between the free-trade principles espoused by rich countries and their actual protectionist practices." By this index none of the industrialised countries emerge "with credit, but the European Union emerges as the worst offender beating the United States by a short head" (ibid.). The double standards of industrialised-country governments, is most apparent in agriculture. These countries provide a total of more than $1bn per day to their domestic farmers. These subsidies go mostly to the wealthiest farmers and these are the people who cause environmental damage. They also generate over-production and the resulting "surpluses are dumped on world markets with the help of yet more subsidies financed by taxpayers and consumers".

Oxfam argues that the removal of trade barriers in rich countries would certainly bring benefits for poor countries. In addition, "carefully designed and properly sequenced import liberalisation in developing countries can also benefit the poor, especially when the lowering of trade barriers is part of a coherent poverty-reduction strategy". But rapid import liberalisation in poor countries has often tended to aggravate poverty and inequality. The IMF and World Bank share in this problem because of their loan conditions. The leaders of strong advocates for trade liberalisation are the IMF, the World Bank, and most Northern governments. The IMF and World Bank back their advocacy by loan conditions which require beneficiaries to reduce their trade barriers. Mostly as the result of these conditionalities, poor countries have opened their markets for trade much faster than rich countries. Oxfam notes that average import tariffs have been cut in half in Sub-Saharan Africa and South Asia, and reduced by two-thirds in Latin America and East Asia. The international financial institutions and governments justify their support for liberalisation by relying on World Bank research seeking to establish that trade liberalisation is good for growth and that the poor do share in the benefits of growth on an equitable basis. Oxfam has challenged the findings of the research as unreliable (ibid.).

Liberalisation from every indication seems to have failed to deliver on its development promises and this has led to a growing number of economists questioning whether trade liberalisation helps or hurts the poor. For example, Dr. Thomas Palley, an economist at Yale University, stated that "main-stream policy economics has been gradually lowering its claims about the positive impact of trade in development and poverty reduction... A decade ago, mainstream policy economics argued vigorously that trade promotes development. If this were true, given the massive increase in global trade over the last 25 years, the global economy ought to have experienced accelerated growth. Instead, global economic growth has actually slowed relative to the prior quarter-century," thus suggesting that trade is at best only weakly associated with growth, and as a corollary, even more weakly with poverty reduction (2000:2).

Even granting that a positive association does exist, the question remains rather contentious because positive correlation does not mean causation. Those countries "that discover economic success become successful traders." The implication here is that "trade is an artifact of development rather than a cause of development" (ibid.).

Apart from empirical challenge, there are theoretical challenges to the claim that trade increases growth. Palley argues further that, "standard growth theory decomposes the sources of growth into capital accumulation, labour force growth, and technological advance" (ibid.). As far as developed countries are concerned, there is little reason to believe that "trade impacts any of these factors, and trade is therefore growth-neutral. Since developing countries lag behind in their capital accumulation and technology, "trade may raise both factors if it encourages investment and diffusion of technology from developed countries. Such an outcome should then precipitate a surge in growth" (ibid.). Even though Dr. Palley argues that growth is necessary to reduce poverty in developing countries, this is quite insufficient because "increased welfare rather than growth is the real goal of economic policy." The constant claim that increased trade automatically reduces poverty "is belied by the increasing income ratio of North to South" and "the widening wealth gap is *prima facie* evidence that any beneficial trade effect is at best weak" (ibid.).

According to Tetteh Hormeku of the *Third World Network*, "trade liberalisation has not been beneficial to African economies. Africa has not improved its "location in the global economy." Africa has not moved out of dependency on primary commodities." It has "not moved into more efficient provision of manufactured goods and services." Africa is "on the receiving end of the global economy, which is repatriating our resources and locking in IMF and World Bank conditionalities through trade agreements ... What we have at the moment is a trade paradigm that African countries should open up all sectors of their economy to foreign providers in a context that destroys the basis for domestic production and jobs; it can never lead Africa out of poverty" (cited by Fleshman 2006:16-17).

Evidence continues to mount that Africa cannot trade its way out of poverty without significant changes in the present global economy. The global trading system has not delivered prosperity and economic development for the African poor. According to Fleshman (2006:17), "By most measures, Africa is poor, less industrialised and less of a contributor to world trade than in 1986, when the launch of trade talks in Uruguay marked the beginning of the modern era of trade liberalisation." Also, questioning the link between development and trade and the inequality in the Uruguay agreement, Nobel laureate Joseph Stiglitz, wrote in 2005: "As chief economist of the World Bank, I received the Uruguay Round of 1994 and concluded that both its agenda and outcomes discriminated against developing countries." He continues that "both as it was conceived, and even more as it has evolved, today's development round does not deserve its name ...Many of the issues that it has addressed should never have been on the agenda of a genuine development round, and many issues that should have been on the agenda are not... Those in the developing world who believe that there has been a history of bargaining in bad faith have a strong case" (ibid.).

A study sponsored by the International Fund for Agricultural Development (IFAD) to examine the impact of globalisation and trade liberalisation on rural producers in developing countries, came up with findings which confirm the inequalities in international trade. One of such findings had to do with "imbalanced multilateral trade rules, which enable developed countries to maintain high protection support (mainly domestic and export subsidies) for their agriculture sector" which encourage "continued dumping of the rich countries' farm products into developing countries' markets" (Khor 2006:7). At the same time "the developing countries are required to place restrictions on their subsidies, to prohibit quantitative restrictions of imports; and to progressively reduce their tariffs, thus exposing their farmers to import competition) including from subsidised imported goods" (ibid.).

The study also discovered "a set of policy conditionalities attached to loans from the international financial institutions that are in many ways inappropriate for the promotion of rural development in many developing countries" (ibid.). These requirements involved withdrawal of the state from being involved in agricultural activities such as marketing, subsidy for and supply of production inputs. It also included reduction of agricultural tariffs to low levels, as well as discouraging or even prohibiting "the use of WTO flexibilities of raising the applied import duty rate towards and up to the level of the bound rates, especially when import surges affect local production" (ibid.).

The study further found regional and bilateral agreements that characteristically require developing countries' partners to significantly "reduce their agricultural tariffs, often to zero." There has been absence of international cooperation on the problems involving agricultural export commodities of the developing countries and this has resulted in "a trend, decline in their prices, with dire consequences for the small producers." The study concludes that on the whole the global framework is significantly powerful in determining or influencing national policies and practices. But the problem of trade imbalance is still enormous.

Now, since economists have come to realise that development and poverty reduction are lagging despite extensive trade liberalisation, the claims regarding the benefits of trade liberalisation are being modified. They have adopted a new position that "trade remains good for growth, but to promote development and poverty reduction, trade must also be accompanied by flanking policies that ensure investment in health and education (human capital) and investment in transportation and communications infrastructure to enable distribution and marketing" (ibid.). But until the issue of trade imbalance is addressed, the inequalities between the rich and poor countries will continue and the dream of reducing poverty will ever remain just that, a dream. The subsidy issue has to be addressed.   And, there is a near consensus that Western countries and the United States have severely hurt African cotton farmers. It is to this matter that we now turn.

Cotton Subsidies and African Cotton Farmers

There are several facts about cotton that should be noted before we examine the impact of subsidies on African growers. According to Allen (2004:1) cotton is grown in some 85 countries and exported by 55.   China is said to be the largest producer of cotton in the world but it makes use of most of its production internally. The US is the second largest producer of cotton and by far the largest exporter in the world and regularly ships 40 to 60 percent of its yield abroad. The US accounts for about 50 percent of the world's exported cotton. Also, from 1995 to 2001, 78 percent of the US subsidies for cotton went to only 10 percent of the cotton farmers. More than 11 million bales of US cotton per year were dumped on the world market between 1995 and 2003 "at rock bottom prices." By 1997 the price of cotton had dropped to 48 cents and then bottomed out at 28 cents in 2000. Prior to 2003 the price continued to stay in the 48 cent range.   At this range cotton was being sold at about 30 cents less than the average cost to grow this product and 40 cents less than the average of what US farmers received for it at the cotton gin.

India is another country that grows cotton.   In this country low prices for cotton and high prices for chemicals have sent tens of thousands of farmers into bankruptcy. "As a result, there have been more than 20,000 cotton farmer suicides since 1995. Additional thousands of Indian farmers sold their kidneys into the world organ market to pay for their pesticide and fertiliser to Monsanto, Cargill or multinational banks" (ibid.).

More than a million people in Africa directly depend on cotton exports for their livelihood. Cotton pays for health care and education; it helps build houses and schools where children are educated. It helps feed the family. Mali, Benin, and Burkina Faso have lost twice as much on the drop in cotton prices as they have received in US foreign aid. This has forced more than 4 percent of each country's population into abject penury. Thus the more they produce, the more they export and the poorer they get. There are a number of other facts about cotton, such as the effect of dumping of subsidised surplus American cotton (as well as corn, wheat and other crops in Mexico) but let us turn to examining the impact of cotton subsidies on African farmers.

The major factors affecting the declining price of cotton are varied and complex, the most cited factor is the increase in government subsidies paid to cotton farmers in the US. In the same vein, agricultural subsidies in the EU are often cited as key factors in the decline of the world price of sugar. According to Mutume (2003:18), "rich nations of the Organisation of Economic Cooperation and Development spent about \$360bn on agricultural supports during 2001, for a range of commodities."

The West African nations of Benin, Burkina Faso, Chad and Mali, known as the Cotton-4 (C-4) produce the cheapest cotton in the world but instead of the farmers being able to support themselves and families, they are languishing in abject poverty. Why? A major report from Fairtrade Foundation released on 15th November 2010 reveals that the West African industry is blocked by a wall of free cash dished out by the US and EU to their farmers. Fairtrade reveals that \$47bn subsidies lock West African farmers in poverty.

Fairtrade states further that in nine years (between 2002 and 2010) \$47 billion had been given out by the US, the

EU, China and India to their cotton farmers. More than $24 billion of this $47 billion have been given to US farmers. China subsidised its cotton farmers with more than $15bn and the EU gave almost $7bn to its growers. The most recent figures show that the US accounts for 34 percent of world exports. West Africa produces about 4 percent of world production. The C-4 nations export virtually all their cotton, largely to China.

American cotton growers and, to a lesser extent, Europeans, benefit from subsidies, thus creating a "global price dampening effect." Even considering a recent cotton price spike, cotton has lost much more than half of its value compared with 1975. For the West African C-4, this is tantamount to economic strangulation. Receiving no subsidies like their counterparts in the US and Europe, African farmers face insurmountable odds to compete. As a result of lack of revenue generated by the cotton sector, C-4 governments have been unable to build roads, ports or engage in other infrastructure to catalyse a garment industry that could offer employment to millions of people and thus create greater value in an underdeveloped sector.

The effect of the decline in real terms of cotton prices has disproportionately affected African cotton growers because they are so heavily dependent on cotton exports for their livelihoods. This in part explains why cotton production among 12 main African cotton growers fell by about 50 percent between 2005 and 2009. African cotton growers could not benefit from increase in cotton prices on world markets between the end of 2007 and 2008 because the dollar was weak against the CFA franc.

Global cotton prices depend on both the supply and demand as well as on the level of subsidies to producers and exporters in other countries. Producers receive a subsidy on the basis of the difference between the world price and set support price. EU cotton producers receive subsidies on inputs such as credit to invest in machinery, insurance and publicly financed irrigation; this is in addition to output subsidies they all receive. On the other hand, US farmers receive guaranteed price regardless of whatever befalls cotton prices in the future. This encourages steady cotton production.

Due to guaranteed price product, decisions are not entirely market driven. Subsidies encourage higher levels of production that demand and supply world normally determine in a free market. What happens is that the world price slumps whenever the supply of cotton is artificially increased. Eliminating subsidies would lead to rapid expansion in other countries in response to higher prices. The inevitable result would be that production would move toward lower-cost producing countries like the West African C-4. The experience of this group of countries prompted Michael Nkonu, Director of Fairtrade Africa to write that "the West African Cotton-4 case reveals how the global trade system works against the interest of the world's poorest farmers. Cotton is cheaper to produce from West Africa than anywhere else. But subsidies from rich power blocks stop West African farmers from getting a fair price" (Fairtrade 2010:7).

According to the International Cotton Advisory Committee (ICAC), "subsidies reduce prices by 10%; the World Bank says by 12.9%, amounting to an annual revenue loss to African producers of $147m. Oxfam calculates that removing US cotton subsidies alone would increase world prices by 6-14%, producer prices in West Africa by 5-12%, and average household income in West Africa by 2-9% - enough to support food expenditure for a million people" (Africa Europe Faith and Justice Network – AEFJN 2011:2). The ICAC states further that the US is not only the world's leading exporter of cotton but also the country with some of the highest costs of production.

The average cost of production in the US is $0.80 per pound but in Benin in West Africa it is just $0.35 per pound. Thus the US subsidises its exports to make it competitive with the world's poorest countries which now hold a natural competitive advantage in cotton production. In fact ICAC puts the cost of producing a pound of cotton in Burkina Faso at $0.21. However, state subsidies guarantee a minimum price to US farmers of about $0.52 per pound. The only comparative advantage US cotton farmers have over their African counterparts is their access to subsidies without which they could not compete in the global market.

The US gives the overall highest amount of subsidies while the EU gives out the largest amount of subsidies per pound of cotton. The 2009-2010 average assistance per pound produced in the EU was $2.51 compared to $0.14 in the US. Cotton subsidies in the EU began as part of the Common Agricultural Policy (CAP) in 1981 when Greece, a cotton producing country, joined the European Community. Spain followed shortly and today cotton subsidies are distributed to some 100,000 producers in Europe – 10, 000 in Spain and 90,000 in Greece.

It is the position of Oxfam that production and export subsidies in the US have devastated not just communities in Africa, but entire regions. In a study on the impact of cotton subsidies on Africa, titled *Cultivating Poverty: The Impact of US Cotton Subsidies on Africa*, Oxfam documents the ill effects of the policy. On the very cover of the report, Oxfam states categorically that the "American cotton subsidies are destroying livelihoods in Africa and other developing regions. By encouraging over-production and export dumping, these subsidies are driving down world prices..." US agricultural subsidies are at the centre of a deep crisis in world cotton markets. Their cotton farmers "are first among equals in the harvesting of subsidies, reaping windfall financial gains from government transfers" while rural communities in some of the world's poorest countries suffer the consequences. While the US constantly advocates free trade and open markets in developing countries, the subsidies it doles out are destroying markets for vulnerable farmers. No region is more seriously negatively affected by unfair competition in world cotton markets than Sub-Saharan Africa.

The report states further that the scale of government support to America's 25,000 cotton farmers is really staggering, reflecting the political influence of corporate farm lobbies in key states. Every acre of cotton farmland in America attracts a subsidy of $230, or about five times the transfer for cereals. In 2001-2002 farmers reaped a bumper harvest of subsidies totaling $3.9bn – doubling the level in 1992 (p.2). It is clear that Robin Hood has not been fair to African farmers and this is a case of reverse Robin Hoodism. Oxfam is emphatic that by driving down prices US taxpayers as well as their European counterparts in other product groups, bear a direct responsibility for the endemic poverty in Africa.

Back in May 2002, the US passed legislation to further increase the amount the government pays farmers. The new Farm Act provides an additional $83bn in farm expenditure, above the $100bn spent on existing programmes. Cotton farmers, comprising mostly corporate agricultural companies, are expected to receive an additional $2.5bn annually for about six years.

This legislation inflamed all those developing countries involved in the cotton subsidy controversy. This prompted Brazil to lodge a legal challenge against the US at the WTO, charging that US is in breach of a "peace clause" in the organisation's Agreement on Agriculture.

On May 3, 2009, at a meeting of the WTO's Dispute Settlement Body (DSB) in Geneva, Brazil claimed the right to impose $2.5bn in retaliatory sanctions against the US. According to Schnepf (2009), Brazil's proposed sanctions total comprised three separate components: a one-time countermeasure of $300 million related to the US Step 2 programme, an annual countermeasure of $1.2 billion based on the prohibited subsidies ruling concerning the US export credit guarantee programme, and an annual countermeasure of $1bn based on the actionable subsidies concerning price-contingent programmes. As part of its prohibited subsidy countermeasure, Brazil then sought "cross-retaliation" rights that would permit retaliation in sectors other than just the goods sector (e.g., intellectual property rights and services agreement). The US and Brazil disagreed over the amount and nature of retaliatory trade sanctions and the parties then asked for an arbitration panel to review countermeasure proposals. The DSB did not complete its work within the usual 60 days.

However, in June 2010 the DSB gave its ruling agreeing that the US programmes violated international free trade agreements that the US itself had championed. Thus the WTO authorised Brazil to retaliate by levying tariffs against other American products. Brazil's threat to use that authority against US goods such as wheat and software, "forced the Obama administration to forge a truce with Brazil." The cotton programme was becoming a liability for future trade growth. Instead of reforming the programmes the US government instead opted to pay $147.3 million annually to Brazilian agribusiness so that the US could continue to give $3bn a year to large US agribusiness. This also enabled the US to continue to support American cotton farmers to the tune of $3bn annually.

Oxfam's report, *Cultivating Poverty* (pp.6-7) states categorically that the C-4 has the same legal case as Brazil and could as well lodge a dispute case against the US. Retaliatory measures are applied to inputs. Brazil has different ways to retaliate against the US, but C-4 countries do not import much from the US. Sanctions on this very small amount would not affect the US economy in any significant way. The financial barriers to joining a WTO dispute are quite prohibitive for poor countries especially when such complaints are directed against rich countries able to call out armies of lawyers and economists.

Crucially important is the fact that the WTO itself is not insulated from the imbalances in financial and political power between rich and poor countries. Governments of developing countries are highly vulnerable to retaliatory action by rich countries should they challenge their trade policies in areas regarded as politically sensitive. Oxfam report continues that "Africa is especially vulnerable because of its high level of dependence on aid, debt relief, and trade preferences" (p.7). Examples include the preferences provided by the US under African Growth and Opportunity Act (AGOA) which can be unilaterally withdrawn. US food aid can be withdrawn or limited by the Secretary of Agriculture for any reason, including the filing of a complaint against US farm subsidies. The US occupies dominant positions on the Boards of IMF and World Bank and these international financial institutions play key role as gatekeepers for aid and debt relief. Oxfam does not see the US unwilling to employ the various avenues to exert its influence on any recalcitrant African government. Given this impossible situation, C-4 countries or all of Africa have been rendered impotent. Taking the cotton matter as a case in point, it is clear that all the promises about assisting poor countries to overcome poverty are nothing more than platitude.

Free trade in agricultural products benefits Western countries including the US.   The costs of subsidies and protectionism are great and include higher taxes and much higher food prices. As noted by Antrobus (2001:1), "in the long run Western farmers are also damaged." This is so because barriers to imports disrupt the price signals guiding farmers' business decisions and as a result, they discourage the diversification of production into higher-value-added items. Higher prices of particular products also discourage domestic consumption and may also encourage the use of lower-priced substitutes, thus undermining the protected sector's own domestic market share (ibid.).

There are other related problems to the asymmetric global trading system that can be examined here as well. Africa has suffered under globalisation more than any other region. African countries face heavy debts, unfavourable trade and those problems arising from the conditions imposed by the IMF and the World Bank. Globalisation and trade liberalisation have had disastrous consequences for Africa. The problem and imbalance of unfair trade with developed countries did not begin with the era of globalisation, however. As we have already noted, the problem that predated globalisation is that African countries have remained the producers of mostly agricultural products and importers of manufactured goods. A crucial problem here is that while the prices of African exports have been falling, the value of imports has continued to rise. While markets of the developed countries continue to rise in part because they use global as well as regional trade organisations, the markets for African products continue to shrink because of all kinds of barriers, tariffs and non-tariffs.

As observed by James Mutethia (2000), because of the

low prices of African products and fewer markets, Africans have been "forced to borrow in order to pay for imports." This further compounds their problems because they are already heavily indebted to Western countries. African countries have in most cases borrowed "to pay existing debts with little capital left for development" (ibid.). Agreements with and promises by different developed countries will not likely bring an end to these problems.

Consider, for example, the AGOA signed into law by President Bill Clinton on May 18, 2000 designed to expand US trade and investment with SSA, to stimulate economic growth, to establish the AGOA Forum to promote a high-level dialogue on trade and investment-related issues, to encourage economic integration, and to facilitate SSA's integration into the global capitalist economy. To begin with, the US congressional opposition led to agricultural products that Africa would have a competitive advantage in exporting, such as sugar, tobacco, peanuts, and beef, were not included on the list" (Hanson 2008:1). It did not end there; countries that met separate requirements were allowed to export specific kinds of textiles, such as cloth and other fabrics and from textiles, duty-free.

Reacting to AGOA, Jagolish Bhagwati of Columbia University and Arvin Panagariya of the University of Maryland, both professors of economics, noted that "the Act reads superficially as if it were an 'aid package,' a one-way grant of free trade to the poor countries in Africa. But this gift horse is actually a Trojan horse. The tariff preferences in the Act are contingent on preferential purchase of inputs from the US. For example, for duty-free access, shirts assembled by the qualifying African country must be made from American yarns. This forces on Africa imports from the US displacing cheaper imports from elsewhere." (2000)

In support of their argument regarding the US interest in Africa, the two professors remind their readers of the controversy over AIDS drugs in South Africa. The South African government had wanted to make cheap generic drugs that could limit the effects of the disease and also import cheaper drugs from Botswana. As noted by Mutethia (2000:1), "The US used all types of threats, including the suspension of aid to persuade South Africa from pursuing these policies." Even in the AGOA case, "all interested lobby groups in the US are empowered to challenge the actions of African governments on everything from intellectual property to labour standards. All these are mechanisms used to wrestle economic concessions from poor countries while claiming to maintain standards".

The US is not alone in this game of taking advantage of poor African countries. For example, in the Cotonou Agreement which replaced the Lome Convention, a trade pact between the European Union and nations of Africa, the Caribbean and Pacific, they employed the new global rules to gain much advantage, while in the old agreement they used barriers to block goods from their agreement partners from the Third World. They make use of certain excuses to get economic concessions such as insisting that African, Caribbean and Pacific countries uphold rules of good governance, as defined by European governments. Despite the new agreement, the European governments are unwilling to remove tariffs on Third World goods.

The rules of globalisation are also used in the area of debt to perpetuate underdevelopment. African countries, as argued in this book and elsewhere (Offiong 2001) are forced to embark on stringent austerity measures, to sell their state-owned enterprises at give way prices to foreign multinationals and to give up their political independence. Those that accept the conditions are given more loans which sink them further into debt and are then presented as good examples for others to follow. These practices by the developed countries do not suggest that globalisation is meant to be even-handed or meant to benefit the poor and help catapult them out of underdevelopment and poverty.

The African situation is compounded by the fact that they are at the mercy of the rich and powerful countries. The WTO has some weaknesses of its own, because it allows the United States and other European nations to ignore the rules. For example, the WTO does not enforce the WTO pact that was intended to fairly govern trade in agricultural products. The agreement on Agriculture came into effect in 1995. This agreement requires all member nations to reduce subsidies that negatively affect trade.   Unfortunately, however, "numerous loopholes, and rules weighed in favour of the more dominant members of the WTO, have not only allowed industrial countries, but to continue raising them in some cases" (Mutume 2003:19). There seems to be no way out for Africa. In the final analysis, what is required is for the United States to reform its cotton market and start the process of reducing its subsidies. But this is not likely; it is not politically expedient. Additionally, the European cotton market must be reformed and transition to other crops should be considered. Until rich countries remove the inconsistencies in their dealings with the poor countries, the situation will remain the same indefinitely, especially since the umpire of the global trade, the WTO, is dominated by the rich and powerful nations. This is tantamount to asking the fox to guard the hen house. Finally, because of the growing relationship between Africa and China, I want to briefly examine that relationship.

Africa and China

Much has been said about the relationship between Africa and China. One often hears African and Chinese leaders referring to the growing relationship between the two as "win-win proposition;" but a closer look seems to reveal that the Chinese are there to exploit cheap raw materials and labour. They are in the continent much in the same way the Europeans and Americans are: They are there to promote their self interests and that they very much control the relationship between themselves and Africans. The Chinese are the senior partners in every relationship with Africans, at least implicitly. After all, African countries receive aid from China; the giver and the receiver cannot be on equal footing. China is technologically superior to African countries and China is going to be the presumed senior partner in any relationship.

China has invested in South Africa's manganese mines, Niger's uranium, Sudan's oil, Congo's cobalt, Zambia's copper, among other countries. Simultaneously, China has been exporting to the continent manufactured goods such as radios, socks, flashlights, machinery and numerous other items thus "hampering Africa's ability to make its own products and develop healthy diverse economies" (Polgren and French 2007). The Chinese have a tendency to import fellow Chinese workers rather than recruit the nationals of the country they are doing business with.

Most countries of the continent have supposedly been independent of colonial rule for more than half a century and yet they have failed to develop manufacturing, and this has turned out to be a very huge opportunity for China which has found Africa a huge market for its manufactured goods. This has prompted some Africans to view them as just coming in to replace Europeans and Americans as African exploiters.

The few African manufacturers have not been able to compete with the Chinese despite the relatively low wages because "China's currency policies undervalue the Yuan and give Chinese exporters a huge advantage" (ibid.). In addition to this, many industries in China also benefit from subsidies and free or low-cost government financing, making their costs lower. Compounding African problems, as experienced by manufacturers, are inadequate infrastructure such as inadequate or inaccessible roads and railways, and unreliable and epileptic electricity supplies. Manufacturers have to be able to generate their electricity through generators and they must also augment the unreliable water supply. All these add to the cost of doing business.

It is important to note that China's economic involvement in Africa is fanned by "thousands of individual entrepreneurs, a small number of large, state-owned enterprises, and a host of companies owned by provincial and municipal authorities" (Bosshard 2008:1). Small private enterprises are involved in commerce and manufacturing while state-owned enterprises engage in extractive and infrastructure projects. When it concerns integrated investment packages, government institutions and state-owned companies work closely together. "The Chinese government's active involvement in resource extraction is not fundamentally different from the financial, political and military support granted to oil and mining operations by the US, French or South African governments" (ibid.). It is also worthy of note that the Chinese government, as a matter of policy, does not interfere in the investment decisions of the enterprises it owns, it however, offers diplomatic support as well as financial incentives. Despite the reported positive impact of Chinese investment in Africa, there have been concerns in Africa about the impacts of Chinese expansion in

Africa regarding governance, human rights, environment, product quality, local employment and labour conditions, and the sustainability of Africa's debt burden (ibid.). The interesting thing is that many African scholars and African governments of all stripes have soundly welcomed China's expanding influence on the continent, as they see the influence as a counter force to the colonial baggage and paternalism characterising their relationship with the West. They welcome "Chinese approach of cowboy capitalism." They appreciate the economic boost or impetus gained from Chinese investments and the pragmatic and speedy way in which the Chinese deliver aid projects, not bothering about corruption and environmental impacts. Of course, the Chinese could not worry about human rights violations because their record in this area is abysmal.

But this is not to say that all has been quite well and rosy. African governments have expressed their concerns when cheap Chinese investors wipe out local textile and other industries; when Chinese employers prefer Chinese over African workers, or when they violate local labour laws. There is no doubt that there will in the future be reasons for African countries and their leaders to be concerned about Chinese activities in the continent.

Taking the case of one country, a recent review of the China-Nigeria relations shows positive outcomes, however with potential problems in the future. First is the foreign direct investment (FDI) which has been on the increase, a ten-fold increase between 1999 and 2006. The review also observed that "while some of the Chinese investments and activities in the country are directed at addressing critical gap in the provision of basic infrastructure, these are not comparable to the level at which Chinese are seeking Nigeria's oil and gas and other raw materials" (Ogunkola, Sankole and Adewuyi 2008:11).

In trade relations, Nigeria's export to China is dominated by crude oil to the tune of around 95 percent. Considering the relative share of market, China constitutes a paltry 1.5 percent of Nigeria's exports in 2000 and 2005. On the other hand, Nigeria's import from China is quite diversified than exports. Nigeria's imports from China include electrical machinery, equipment, vehicles and nuclear reactors, boilers machinery and mechanical appliances jointly accounted for over 50 percent of Nigeria's imports from China. The authors of the review add that "the observed structure of trade pattern is inconsistent with Nigeria's quest to export manufactured or processed products. The need to diversify export products may be an uphill task given China's preference for raw materials and fuel and gas. More worrisome is the skewed balance of payments position which has consistently been in favour of China"(pp.11-12). In the final analysis, Nigeria and the rest of the continent will find out that not only the West, including the US, Japan and Canada have consigned Africa to the perpetual role in the international division of labour of producing and exporting cheap raw materials, that China also wants them to continue in that infamous role.

5

Debt, Capital Flight and Poverty

The massive external debt owed by African countries remains one of the most significant obstacles to the continent's development and significantly reducing the level of poverty. The more than $300bn that African countries owe to foreign creditors remains a crippling obstacle that undermines economic and social progress.

The continent has been tagged with the monstrous appellation of the poorest region in the world and the average African lives on less than $1 a day. Simultaneously, African countries are forced by the wealthy nations to repay billions of scarce dollars to them and their multinational corporations and institutions in the West such as the World Bank and IMF while millions of Africans continue to perish from poverty and associated problems. According to the World Bank, Africa spends about $15bn a year on debt repayments but receives only $12.7bn in aid during the same period. The World Bank states further that all developing countries, including those in Sub-Saharan Africa, pay $1bn every day in interest on debt. And, for every $1 African (and other developing) countries receive in grants, they pay $13 in interest on debt. Millions of Africans are HIV positive; millions are in urgent need of food aid; Africa's infant mortality rates are alarming; and African countries spend about three times more on health care, food, and education for their sick, illiterates, and millions of the hungry. African debts are also associated with capital flight.

Capital Flight and Poverty

There have been references to Nigeria's and other African countries' debts being "odious debts," for example Ndikuma and Boyce (2011), Ogunmefun (2005), and Offiong (2001). Odious debt is a legal theory that states that the national debt incurred by any regime for purposes that do not serve the best interest of the country concerned, should not be enforceable. By this doctrine, such debts are personal debts of the regime that incurred them and not debts of the state.

In 2011, Leonce Ndikumana and James Boyce published their book *Africa's Odious Debts: How Foreign Loans and Capital Flight Bled a Continent* (2011a) which has received numerous reviews. In the preview to that book titled "Funny Money and Stolen Lives" (2011b), Boyce and Ndikumana state that while Africa is widely perceived as being heavily indebted to international creditors including banks, western governments, and international financial institutions (World Bank and IMF), it is less known that Sub-Saharan Africa experienced an exodus of more than $700bn in capital flight between 1970 and 2008. In both absolute monetary values and relative to GDP, this magnitude of capital flight is quite staggering (p.1). The very sad thing has been that some of the very money loaned to African countries wound up in accounts at the very banks that made loans to African governments. According to Boyce and Ndikumana, "Africa is a net creditor to the rest of the world in the sense that its foreign assets exceed its foreign liabilities." But there is a catch. The unfortunate catch is that the assets are in the hands of private Africans, while the liabilities remain public, owed by the people of Africa at large through their governments (ibid.). Referring to the documentation in their book *Africa's Odious Debts,* Boyce and Ndikumana note that "for every dollar of foreign borrowing, on average more than 50 cents leaves the borrower country in the same year. This tight relationship suggests that a substantial portion of Africa's capital flight has been debt-fueled. Growing public external debts and private external assets are connected by a financial revolving door"(p.3).

How this works is explained by the authors. Common mechanisms include "inflated procurement contracts for goods and services, kickbacks to government officials, and diversion of public funds into the bank accounts of politically influential individuals" (ibid.). Other means of capital flight involve earnings from oil and mineral exports. "But foreign loans make an exceptionally easy mark in that there is no need to go through the messy business of extracting natural resources to convert them into cash" (ibid.).

These authors tell us that when foreign loans are acquired and a part of it is siphoned abroad, Africa still received an inflow of money, but this is less than the face value of the debt. The net drain on African economies is experienced in subsequent years when the creditors are repaid with interest. Using World Bank data on debt-service payments and public health expenditure by African governments, the authors show stark evidence of the human costs of debt-fuelled capital flight. The authors estimate that every additional dollar of debt service means 29 fewer cents spent on public health. "In economic parlance, the former 'crowds out' the latter" (ibid.). In their estimates, "debt-service payments on loans that fuelled capital flight translate into more than 75,000 extra infant deaths each year" (ibid.).

In his review of *Africa's Odious Debts*, John Weeks (2011) lambasts the public, the media and even economists in their perception of Sub-Saharan Africa as receiving large amounts of development assistance over the last three decades and yet continues to languish in abject penury. Weeks singles out Dambisa Moyo's *Dead Aid* and former World Bank economist

William Easterly's *The White Man's Burden* for castigation for their polemics that "trillions" in aid dollars have been "squandered" in Africa to no benefit, "with the lack of benefit typically attributed to corruption in African governments" (p.2). Weeks emphasises the importance of taking into consideration the fact that a significant part of the aid illicitly returns to the donors' countries. Capital flight significantly contributes to poverty. Having shown the extent of capital flight from Sub-Saharan Africa, and that while the assets remain private and hidden, its foreign debts become public, owed by the people of Africa through their governments, the authors of Africa's *Odious Debts* propose that African governments should repudiate such odious debts from which Africans derived no benefit. The authors ask the international community to assist in this endeavour. This reminds me of Nigeria's payment to Paris Club creditors which "exceeded public spending on health" (Addison 2006:211). We briefly examine this payment.

Nigeria's Foreign Debt Payment and Poverty

Nigeria in 2006 paid almost $20bn to two giant international syndicates: Paris Club and London Club of Creditors to settle her foreign debts. In the opinion of Chiakwelu (2009:1), "this transfer of wealth by a relatively poor nation contradicts the entire prudent financial judgment and rudimentary economic disposition preached to Nigeria by the rich donor nations that babbles about the ills of capital flight in developing nations."

President Obasanjo had secured the purported $18bn debt relief for Nigeria from the Paris Club of Creditors, which was the inducement for Nigeria to pay off $36bn foreign debt. The total foreign debt was $35.9bn as of June 2005, $31bn of which was owed to 15 of the 19 creditor-countries of the Paris

Club. Nigeria paid the final installment of $4.518bn on April 21, 2006 to get out of the Paris Club. Previously, Nigeria had to pay off $12.4bn in arrears and debts as was required to fulfill arrangement and concord reached with the Paris Club in June 2006 (ibid.). Additionally, Nigeria had to pay off the last batch of outstanding debts it owed to the London Club totaling $2.15bn. In settling its debts to Paris Club and London Club of Creditors, Nigeria paid a total of $20bn. This represents an enormously large transfer of wealth by a poor Third World nation to high income nation.

Interestingly, in 1985 Nigeria owed $8bn to Paris Club creditors, out of $19bn of its foreign debt. By the end of 2004, Nigeria owed Paris Club $31bn out of $36bn. As from 1992, Nigeria never had any loan from Paris Club and the question arises as to how the debt increased. The answer is found in what Chiakwelu terms "the malleable interest rate, interest arrears and interest charged on the arrears" (ibid.). Obviously, the creditors do not want their debtors to get off their grip. They want their creditors to be perpetually indebted to them and to continue to pay the interest *ad infinitum*. This is quite similar to what happens under bonded labour in which labourers take out a loan simply to survive. The debtor must work for the creditor to pay back the loan, but often the creditor makes it impossible for the debtor to complete the loan payment. Creditors determine to keep debtors in bondage indefinitely by charging the debtors illegal fines, or charge debtors for food, tools, transportation to the work site while keeping wages too low for the debt to be completely paid. Alternatively, creditors can simply say that all the labour the debtor performs constitutes collateral for the debt and cannot be used to reduce it (Miers 2003).

Interestingly enough, Britain, the erstwhile colonial master of Nigeria was the largest creditor of the debt, receiving

$3bn from Paris Club; and from the Paris Club to which Nigeria made a payment of $12.4bn Britain also received $3bn. Despite all the entreaties by eminent world leaders that Britain should return at least part of the money to Nigeria, all pleas fell on deaf ears. This suggests that all the platitudes of rich nations to assist poor nations in their war against underdevelopment and poverty remain mere hallow talks. Today, according to a recent study by the Nigerian National Bureau of Statistics published in February 2012, almost 100 million Nigerians live on less than $1 a day. What the amount of money paid to the rich countries in 2006 could have done to stem that poverty is anybody's guess.

One would have expected Nigeria to be cautious in its borrowing after the harrowing experience it had with external creditors. Some seven years after Nigeria's exit from the $31b Paris Club debt, this country in 2012 "is on the march again, dashing with reckless abandon on the slippery slope of another debt abyss." Nigeria is again on the march globe-trotting, "cap in hand, busy, tapping into the wallets of all manners of creditors" and the result is that as at April 2012, according to the finance minister and coordinating minister for the Economy and the person who negotiated the debt settlement with the Paris Club, Dr. (Mrs.) Ngozi Okonjo-Iweala, Nigeria's debt profile stands at N6.8tn or $44bn, in dollar terms. Nigeria's external debt stands at $5.9bn, while its domestic component is N5.96tn (Adigun 2012:1).

Debt and Poverty

Foreign debt has further compounded Africa's problem and poverty. The former UN Secretary-General Boutros Boutros-Ghali had said in December 1992 that "external debt is a millstone around the neck of Africa." The millstone is still very much around the neck of Africa; it is like a noose around the neck, tightening up every new day. Africa's debt rose dramatically during the 1970s, when prices of its commodities exports began a long steep nose-drive. By 1992, Africa's total debt had grown to $290bn, two and a half times greater than in 1980, while Sub-Saharan Africa's debt had more than tripled. Servicing this debt cost the continent $26bn, paid to its creditors in 1991 (UN 1993). Although Africa's debt is about one-fifth of the Third World's total debt, this is a burden much heavier than that faced by any other region primarily because of the relatively small size of African economies. Africa's debt is equivalent to 90 percent of its gross national product (GNP), and for Sub-Saharan Africa, it is 110 percent of its GNP. The continent of Africa can only meet about two-thirds (and Sub-Saharan Africa less than half) of its originally-scheduled debt servicing obligations, with the balance having built up arrears. These arrears totaled a massive $14bn in 1992, up from just $1bn in 1980 (ibid.).

The absence of significant debt relief has meant that the continent's debt servicing continued to increase throughout the 1980s, growing five-fold between 1983 and 1990 and accounting for 30 percent of Africa's export earnings, already hard-hit by commodity price drop. This is an extraordinarily onerous burden for the world's poorest region to carry. The continent spends four times more on debt servicing than it does for all health services it provides to its more than 1000 million people. Thus Mozambique alone loses more children to malnutrition and easily preventable or curable diseases than do all the struggling countries of the erstwhile Soviet Union (ibid.).

The debt burden also creates difficult problems for the economic recovery programmes that most African countries have embarked on in an effort to revive economic growth.

One of the basic goals is to generate additional resources through private investment. Unfortunately, the efforts of these debt-ridden countries to attract such investment have been a fiasco. More than 80 percent of the decline in private flows to the continent in recent times is attributable to the decline in private flows, since investors are not willing to take risks in countries which are "tagged as bad debtors." Foreign direct investment (FDI) has ceased in some African countries.

In the area of development assistance, which in fact for many countries remains the source of almost their entire financial inflows, the picture is not quite encouraging. The competition is keen because of the entry of Eastern Europe and the former Soviet Union, as well as other Third World countries whose deteriorating economies have made them quite dependent on aid.

Multilateral debt is a thorn in the flesh of African countries. In 1980, multilaterals accounted for 14 percent of the continent's debt, but by 1993 it was about 25 percent. Multilateral debts cannot be rescheduled and, because of preferred conditions, the World Bank and IMF tend to get paid first. The result has been that multilaterals loom rather large in Africa's debt servicing bill. In 1991 the multilaterals portion of the continent's debt servicing was 25 percent, but for Sub-Saharan Africa, more highly dependent on official flows, it was 36 percent (*Africa Recovery*, December 1992-February 1993:5).

Sixteen African countries owe 50 percent or more of their foreign debt to multilaterals, and another eight, 40 percent or more. Many of these countries, like Botswana and Lesotho, face little or no repayment problems. For others like Chad and Togo, multilateral debt service, while more than half of all payments, is still relatively light. But for many African countries, multilateral debt servicing is currently both large and burdensome part of their obligations. In 1991, payments to multilaterals were equivalent to over 36 percent of export earnings for Uganda and Zambia; for another eight countries, including Ivory Coast (14 percent), Ghana (17 percent), Kenya (13 percent), and Madagascar (17.6 percent) they constituted over 10 percent of export earnings. For others like Burundi, Malawi, Niger and Rwanda, multilateral payments were scheduled to take increasing share of debt obligations in 1993, even excluding the IMF, which is included in the above figures. This situation does not encourage the reduction of poverty in the continent. Debt burden has left most African countries in economic, social and political crisis of Himalayan dimensions (Offiong 2001).

Debt discourages investors. Foreign investors will not risk funds in Africa if domestic investors are not prepared to take the same risk. At the same time the stock of flight capital from the continent remains large at some 90 percent of regional gross national product. Efforts to attract foreign investors remain strained so long as the debt crisis continues. And, until the debt burden is taken care of, economic growth will remain limited since the meagre resources available will be devoted to debt repayments. Debt-service repayments are perhaps the greatest financial hemorrhage that the continent has experienced. This situation has prompted Mr. Luis Fernando Jaramillo, Columbia's representative to the UN and, at the time, Chairman of the Group of 77 to comment that, "the heavy and unbearable external debt burden of African countries has led to the paradoxical situation that such countries have become net exports of capital to developed countries and multilateral financial institutions." The fact remains that until significant debt relief is given to African countries, the continent will remain in its dark tunnel of economic difficulties for many years to come.

It was not surprising when the Central Bank of Nigeria in its 1994 mid-year report said that the Nigerian economy was declining and that the greatest problem for the economy since the beginning of that year was government's inability to secure debt relief from its foreign creditors. In January 1994 the military government had aborted the economic reforms of SAP and in its place introduced what it called "genuine regulation," an act that went against the thinking of the international lending community and thus Nigeria fell out of favour. World Bank officials quickly vetoed any request by Nigeria for debt relief until the country returned to its basic economic reforms (Ukim, November 14, 1994). The Paris Club of Lenders had tied all debt relief negotiations to the country's agreement with the IMF. The debt obligation put tremendous stress on the finances of the government. Government's debt at the end of June 1994 amounted to N946.3bn (about $43bn), representing an increase of 14.2 percent over the level for June 1993. Domestic debt increased by 45.8 percent from N199bn ($9.1bn) to N291.5bn ($13.3bn) by June 1993. External debt rose from $28.7bn to $29.8bn at the end of June 1994, representing an increase of 3.8 percent or $1.04bn (ibid.). The consequence of this is obvious: the road to economic recovery and hence a reduction in poverty is far beyond the end of the tunnel, even though Nigeria eventually paid off its external debt in 2006; Nigeria has already accumulated new external debts.

Most African countries have not yet restored their economic growth and they are currently even more deeply indebted than ever. This is a testimony to the almost insurmountable debt problem they face. Thus the goal of returning these countries to sustained growth and external credit worthiness is still far out of sight. As at 1990 there were 26 severely indebted low-income countries in the world, of which 24 were in Sub-Saharan Africa, and 19 severely indebted middle-income countries. The situation has not changed appreciably in the 21st century. In absolute terms the debt of 26 severely indebted low-income countries, amounting to $103bn in 1988, is not high compared with $516bn owed by the 19 middle-income group. The fact, however, is that some indicators of debt burden are really quite higher for the low-income group. The ratio of debt to GNP for this group, for example, was 111 percent in 1988, while for middle-income group of countries it was 54 percent (World Bank 1990:126).

There have been attempts to deal with the debt burdens of low-income countries, however. Since 1978 some bilateral donors have reportedly converted part of the official debt owed by these countries into grants. It has been claimed that about $3bn of official debt was cancelled this way; about $2bn of this amount represented claims on low-income Sub-Saharan African countries. It is, however, crucial to note that the cancelled debt amounts to a paltry 3 percent of the total outstanding debt of the low-income African countries at the end of 1998. Further, many of these countries will not benefit much from further conversions of loans to grants since most of their concessional loans have already been forgiven (World Bank 1990)

The arrangement agreed to at the Toronto Economic Summit in June 1988 provided debt relief on official bilateral nonconcessional debt under the auspices of the Paris Club for severely indebted low-income countries that were embarking on adjustment programmes. By March 1, 1990 the so-called "menu" of options agreed to at the Toronto (partial write-off, longer repayment periods, and more concessional interest rates) had been applied to some 16 Sub-Saharan African countries (World Bank 1990:126).

Despite the fanfare, just as with the conversions of concessional loans to grants, however, the amount of actual debt relief given accruing to twelve Sub-Saharan African countries participating in the special Programme Assistance in 1989 was around $50m (in relation to rescheduling under standard terms), or just 2 percent of their debt service. Projections suggested that Toronto-terms reschedulings were likely to have an almost negligible effect on the future stock debt. It was further projected that if there was no change in the debt-relief options offered by creditors and if Toronto Terms were applied regularly (that is, if rescheduled debts coming due were once again rescheduled on the same terms), the total reduction of debt to all bilateral creditors by the end of 2000 would be around $2bn, or just 11 percent of long-term nonconcessional debt in 1998 (World Bank 1990:126). However, there are no studies yet to confirm or repudiate those projections.

In 1988 interest payment on the external debt of the low-income countries of SSA (including Nigeria) amounted to about $2.9bn. This represented about 27 percent of net disbursements of official development assistance (ODA) to these countries in the same year. The ratio of interest payments to pure grants was more substantial; it was 47 percent in Kenya, 52 percent in Ghana, 50 percent in Madagascar, 73 percent in Togo, and 57 percent in Zaire (Congo). These high levels of interest payments critically limit the contributions that aid can make to increasing consumption and investment and reducing poverty (World Bank 1990:126-7). Many low-income countries in SSA find themselves with daunting debt and debt service burdens at a time they need to invest more, and at the same time to increase the consumption of large numbers of people languishing in poverty. Indeed, debt burden is a millstone around the neck of African countries and until this is relieved, there can never be a solution to the current economic quagmire.

Rather than decreasing, Africa's external debt was rising, reaching $227bn in 1996, representing $379 for every man, woman, and children in SSA (Collins, August 1998:15). The plight of poor countries resulting from the burden of external debt prompted the launching of Jubilee 2000, an international coalition of non-governmental organisations (GOs), churches and trade unions, other organisations and individuals. Its African chapter was launched in Accra, Ghana in April, 1998. This organisation argues that creditors and debtors have shared responsibility for building up unsustainable debt and for corruption. It calls for cancellation of unrepayable debt, a fair and transparent debt negotiation process, the redirection of savings from debt relief to benefit poor people in debtor countries, and civil society role in determining the conditions for debt relief and repayment (ibid.).

Influential international Catholic agencies have called for even deeper debt relief, and the World Council of Churches officially endorsed the position of Jubilee at its December 1998 World Assembly in Harare, Zimbabwe. There are other campaigns which focus on debt-reduction for specific countries (for example, the Democratic Republic of the Congo – given the "odious" nature of its debt; and Rwanda, given its recent emergence from genocide). In May 1998, South African NGOs met in Mainz with representatives of German and Swiss church groups and Jubilee 2000 to explore possible campaign for cancellation of South African debt caused by apartheid. It is interesting that Jubilee 2000 titled one of its studies "Chains Around Africa: Study of the Debt Burdens of 20 Sub-Saharan

African Countries." According to that study, "that region's debt service payments of $14.5bn in 1996 were the highest since 1990. The human impact...has been severe, with some African countries now spending at least twice as much on debt service as on health care...for every $1 Africa got in grants in 1996, it paid out $1.31 in debt service. And while Africa earns 5 percent of the developing world's income, it owes 11 percent of developing country debt" (ibid.).

Concerned with the debt chains around the neck of Africa, Jubilee 2000 met in Birmingham, England on May 16, 1998 to confront the Group of Eight (G-8) major industrialised countries at their meeting. About 70,000 people formed a human chain some ten kilometers around a conference centre, demanding that the world's richest nations provide deeper and faster debt relief to the world's poorest countries by the end of 2000. Their petitions carried 1.5 million signatures from some 65 countries which they submitted to UK Cooperation Minister Claire Short on behalf of the G-8, and summit president, UK Prime Minister Tony Blair. But before this activity, there was an attempt to assist the poorest countries with some relief.

In 1996 a special programme was set up for the Heavily Indebted Poor Countries (HIPCs) whereby the international creditors could have their debts reduced. Unfortunately, however, nothing really materialised except that in March and April 1998 Ivory Coast and Mozambique were cleared to have their debts reduced in 2000 and 1999, respectively. Uganda became the first country to benefit from the HIPC package in April 1998, since the programme was first launched in 1996. The G-8 summit in Birmingham did not accomplish anything to the benefit of African countries, in terms of debt relief. It is quite important to note that at the summit, the US, Germany and Japan "led opposition in the G-8 to UK proposals for deeper debt relief" (Collins, August 1998:15). Their final summit was laden with conditionalities and according to the summit president, Tony Blair, if HIPC demonstrate "a real will to pursue policies that will relieve poverty and build sound economy, we will do our part to contribute the funds necessary to reduce their debt burden to sustainable level" (p.14).

To qualify for the HIPC relief programme, a country must first endure a three-year torture by subjecting itself to the IMF's enhanced structural adjustment programme (ESAP) in order to reach the "decision point" – when HIPC relief is judged necessary or not. "If eligible, a country must undertake another three years of adjustment and donor supervision to reach the 'completion point' – when actual debt reduction occurs" (ibid.). The treatment of those poor countries reminds me of the treatment to which people on welfare in the US are subjected. Such people are often stereotyped as lazy, shiftless, dishonest, lacking in high IQ, and the like. Their private lives are greatly scrutinised and compromised, and the constant presence of social workers and welfare investigators in their homes clearly denies them the basic right to privacy. On the other hand, those who benefit from wealthfare (government programmes, subsidies, tax breaks, and more for the rich and wealthy) are free to spend their billions unsupervised. These are the rich and powerful that dominate the private economic sector. Poor African countries represent American welfare beneficiaries who must be subjected to conditionalities associated with indignities. African countries are banana republics, whose leaders have lost whatever respect and dignity they had and must kowtow to the whims of western creditors.

GNP as a Measure of Progress
Before ending this section, it is important to make a brief statement about GNP, because we earlier compared its ratio

between poor countries and middle-income countries. There is a tendency to heavily rely on GNP as a measure of progress and poverty reduction, but it is important to note that "high GNP does not equal well-being." Furthermore, according to UNICEF, "defining progress from the standpoint of ordinary people can sometimes reverse the prism of gloom through which most of the poor countries of the world are viewed" (*Africa Recovery*, December 1993-March 1994:11). UNICEF had monitored developments from the perspective of the one billion people in the world for whom "adequate food, clean water, safe sanitation, decent housing, reliable health care, and at least a basic education" remain a dream yet to be realised (ibid.). One of the interesting findings was that rich, as measured by GNP, does not necessarily correspond with achievement in child welfare or material well-being.

Despite Africa's precarious economic situation, there are four Sub-Saharan countries among the seven developing countries with per capita GNP of $500 or below that have maternal mortality rate under 200 per 100,000 live births, quite below the world average of 310. In contrast, Botswana is one of the countries with relatively high per capita GNP ($2,590) where maternal mortality remains high (250 per 100,000). However, only 11 African countries managed to maintain mortality rates below the world average, and the continent's overall average of 590 per 100,000 is the highest in the world. UNICEF then places such figures in a context where 20 percent of children in the US, with per capita GNP of $22,500, live below the poverty line, and one in eight does not get enough to eat. UNICEF adds that between 1979 and 1986 the percentage of families living in poverty doubled in the United Kingdom and also rose by 47 percent in the United States.

In the important area of female literacy, certain countries with relatively low GNP have also done better than others with high GNP. As examples, UNICEF presents the following cases: Madagascar's figures for GNP and female literacy in 1991 were $210 and 73 percent; Zambia's were $420 and 65 percent; and Zimbabwe's were $620 and 72 percent. This compared quite favourably with Morocco's $1,030 and 38 percent; Congo's $1,120 and 44 percent; and especially Gabon's $3,780 and 49 percent.

Concerning the number of years its children stay in school, Sub-Saharan Africa is at par with richer South American region, where 48 percent of those enrolled reach the fifth grade. This shows a significant achievement in view of the disparity in initial enrollment of 71 percent as compared to 99 percent. This regional average of 68 percent could also change substantially if data were available for such problem countries as South Africa, Liberia, Uganda and Sierra Leone. When African statistics are compared to those of other regions of the developing countries, one finds them disturbing, added to the fact that their regional average for under-five mortality of 183 per 1,000 births is the highest in the world and about twice the world average. The continent also harbours four (Nigeria, 1 million; Ethiopia, 0.54 million; Congo, 0.35 million; Tanzania, 0.23 million) of the 10 countries in the world that account for two-thirds of the 8.5 million annual under-five deaths (*Africa Recovery*, December 1993-March 1994:11). Finally, what the above analysis suggests is that countries with high GNP may not necessarily be quite healthy on the basis of the vital indicators. It shows that good management and perhaps political will can help in determining priorities and being able to spend resources diligently. However, the obvious fact is that Africa is still very poor, the poorest of the poor regions of the world.

To summarise, unequal trade patterns have plunged the poor countries of SSA deeper and deeper into debt to industrialised societies, mainly Western and Japan. As a group, the poor nations of the globe owe rich and powerful countries in excess of $1tn (World Bank 1993). This staggering debt has become a financial yoke few countries can bear. Excessive debt drains the resources of poor countries, destabilises their economies, making things worse for these countries already reeling from very high unemployment and rampant inflation. Thus apart from their narrow-export oriented economies, and lack of industrial capacity, they have external debt as a millstone around their neck. Their beggarly financial earnings from their mostly raw materials export are used in servicing debts. This means that the little money they could use for development is paid out to the rich countries. So instead of money coming to them from the rich nations, the poor ones are paying out money to the rich. An irony, that Robin Hood takes from the poor to the rich, instead of vice versa. And finally, GNP is not a good indicator of progress.

Debt Relief
To lessen the burden of debt payment, there is what has been dubbed a "menu of options" for keeping the real debt service payments within manageable limits. These fall within two broad categories which include debt reduction and flexible and concessional debt rescheduling, which postpones debt service payments or reduces long-term debt burden, and debt swaps.
Under debt reduction and debt rescheduling, for low-income countries several donors, such as Canada, Finland, Germany, Netherlands, Norway, Sweden, and the United Kingdom, have reconverted concessional bilateral loans to grants. Sub-Saharan Africa has benefited from about two-thirds of world-wide cancellations. In 1989 France wrote off concessional debt

owed it by 35 of the poorest African countries and the measure was to cancel some $2.4bn of debt. Belgium on its part cancelled about $200m. Beginning in 1990 the US began to forgive Development Assistance (DA) and Economic Support Fund (ESF) debt owed by Sub-Saharan African countries with reform programmes. However, this was conditional. Eligibility was contingent upon the debtor country having in effect an IMF stand-by, a structural facility or an enhanced facility, or a World Bank SAP. The total amount to be forgiven depended on the number of countries meeting the eligibility requirements. There were 23 Sub-Saharan African countries that carried DA or ESF debt amounting to about $1bn in 1989 (World Bank 1989:177). In addition to this was the agreement reached at the June 1988 Toronto economic summit, where the debts of IDA-eligible countries could be rescheduled.

In the case of swaps without local assets, proposals were made to relieve the pressure on foreign exchange resources by swapping local assets – physical or financial- for debts. In 1989 Nigeria converted about $1000m of its promissory notes. Most arrangements allowed the debtor to share part of the discount on debt, determine the sectors of the economy in which equity could be purchased, and placed restrictions on the dividends and principal that could be repatriated. The simplest form of swap remains debt for equity. However, this has limited application in Africa because of the lack of perceived investment opportunities and developed markets for financial instruments.

Many of these initiatives benefit only low-income countries whereas there are comparable special programmes for middle-income countries in Africa; they are subjected to long-term development problems not quite much different from the low-income countries. Besides, there are technical and legal problems to be settled. One such problem is that each country has its peculiar and special circumstances, and the solution to its debt problem has to be decided on a case-by-case basis. As a general principle, debt relief should go only to countries that are both debt distressed and also willing to adopt reforms to improve their capacity for growth and future debt service. In order to really benefit debtor countries, special finance for debt relief or concessional debt rescheduling should be purely "additional" and not taken out of the aid budgets already allowed to the beneficiary countries.

Africa's debts are devastating to the continent, but they are minor for creditors in relation to global debts. The kind of debt write-downs already arranged for large Latin American debtor countries are not expected to be offered to Africa. Africa's debt is not enough to disrupt global financial equilibrium. Significant debt relief from new money cannot be expected in the foreseeable future, and conventional debt restructuring is not likely to generate the debt relief required to restore growth. Thus we are back to square one.

UNICEF has put forward a series of proposals to ease Africa's debt burden. It has argued that the World Bank's scheme to buy back the commercial debt of low-income countries at prices prevailing on the secondary market clearly shows official approval for deeper debt relief, and this makes it essential for similar discounts to be offered to reduce the burden of official debt. Under the Bank's scheme, the private debts of Mozambique, Niger, and Uganda have been bought back at prices ranging from 10 to 18 percent of their nominal value (*Africa Recovery*, June 1993:29). In order to avoid differentials in the discount between countries, the entire stock of non-development debt of low-income nations should be written down so that its payment costs are equal to "fresh" lending from the Bank's International Development Association (IDA) – 10 years' grace period, 40 years to repay and 0.75 percent interest rate (ibid.).

Multilateral debt cannot be rescheduled and this represents an increasing burden to African countries. There is need for the Bank to extend current scheme to finance, through IDA, the interest on old loans from the Bank's main arm. The IMF continues to take "more money from Africa than it lends" and all lending, from whatever facility, should be concessional terms." This would have to include the repayment of interest arrears owed by countries like Zambia. This involves subsidisation of interest rates which could be paid for from special donor contributions or, preferably, from the sale of IMF gold (ibid.). It is obvious that simple debt relief, without considering how released resources are used, will have little medium-term impact on development. From the standpoint of UNICEF, the National Programmes of Action set up to realise the goals of the Children's Summit offer "a useful framework" to ensure that the financial resources freed by the greater debt relief are used on priority social areas. The proposal could be helpful to heavily indebted poor countries. This leads us to the case of heavily indebted poor countries initiative (HIPCI).

Set up in 1996, HIPCI provided that debts may be cancelled only after a six-year (or more) qualification period. Unfortunately, however, by 1998 the initiative was found not to have lived up to the expectations of African governments. By 1998 only seven countries qualified for debt relief initiative out of 41 candidates; five of the seven beneficiaries were African countries. The failure of the initiative to fulfill its expectations led to recommendations for changes by the African caucus of IMF and World Bank governors and Commonwealth finance ministers.

The recommendations include:

- Liberalisation of eligibility criteria.

- The time frame was considered too long. As it was, debtor countries had to adhere to IMF programmes for a minimum of six years (three years before the "decision point," and another three years to reach "completion point," after which actual debt relief could occur).
- Another problem was that eligibility was rather rigidly linked to an IMF track record. For example, after Ethiopia had been declared "off track" by the IMF in 1997, its debt relief was suspended and the same criteria threatened Tanzania's chances of debt relief because of its uneven performance under IMF and World Bank programmes.
- In order to be of benefit to the HIPCs, debt relief should be tied to poverty reduction. Poverty levels should be used in determining how much debt relief a country needs. The IMF and World Bank should promote schemes such as Uganda's "poverty action fund," which "channels the savings from debt relief into publicly monitored and audited social programmes."
- There should be more flexibility for post-war countries. As it was then, the World Bank and IMF allowed non-IMF reforms to be counted as part of a country's initial three-year track record; however, war-ravaged countries still confronted long waits for debt relief (*Africa Recovery*, November 1988:12).

In response to these recommendations, the IMF and World Bank in 1998 launched another initiative for Africa's most fragile economies. It is a trust fund similar to the HIPCI fund, designed to help finance reconstruction in post-conflict countries. However, since the World Bank and IMF cannot lend to countries in arrears, and most post-conflict countries are in arrears, the new initiative was already doomed to failure. So the HIPCI has not achieved anything and debtor countries have been asked to follow guidelines prescribed by the World Bank and IMF to produce Poverty Reduction Strategy Papers (PRSPs). The present focus is on poverty reduction from funds freed from debt relief. As has been obvious so far, the role of the World Bank and IMF in African economies has completely reduced African countries to neo-dependencies.

6
IMF and World Bank:
Enforcers of Neo-dependency

Of all Third World regions, Africa is the only one that qualifies for the status of "new neo-dependency" or "post neo-dependency." Callaghy (1993:209) has referred to Africa as "the lost frontier" experiencing "marginalisation and dependence without strategic importance." How did Africa come to acquire this monstrous appellation? To answer this question, even at the price of repetition, it is imperative to turn to the synopsis or scenario of Africa's economic crisis, beginning in the 1970s.

The Scenario
The decade 1973-1983 was quite harsh for Third World countries. An unfavourable global economic climate dominated by recession, protectionism, inflation, and high interest rates; in addition the oil shocks of 1973-74 and 1979-1980 took their toll on the Third World. Certain countries absorbed this impact much better than others, perhaps because of their economic structure and level of development, and their individual ability to adjust to such external impact. The result was that some fared better than others. Furthermore, the oil importing countries had to contend with paying higher prices for oil while simultaneously coping with depressed prices for their primary product exports and worsening terms of trade. At the same time high interest rates in world markets made debt service payments rather onerous and irksome for larger debtors with meaningful levels of private bank debt at floating interest rates. Efforts to manage

these developments resulted in large balance-of-payments deficits, enormous debt, runaway inflation, high levels of unemployment, and significant import cutbacks. Due to these developments, the average rate of growth in terms of real GNP of the less developed countries (LDCs) dropped by 2.5 percent in 1981, about half the rate prevailing in 1979-1980 and still further below the rates of 1977 and 1978. Their rate of growth dropped to 1.5 percent in 1988. Renewed growth in industrialised countries brought about some improvements in economic indicators of LDCs, and the gains were reversed in 1985. Sustained decline in international market prices for primary commodities, low levels of growth for LDCs exports brought about slower growth in the industrial countries, along with reduced net capital inflows (Leslie, 1987:3-4).

The countries of Sub-Saharan Africa have been hardest hit and their economic problem defies any short-term solution. Twenty-six of 36 least developed countries of the world are in Africa (*Transnationals,* July 1989:2). Having managed to absorb the 1973-74 and 1979-80 price increases in oil, imported foodstuffs, and manufactured goods, Africa had to contend with protectionist tendencies in the industrial countries and the impact of the recession between 1981 and 1983. Appalling trade performance, resulting from low commodity prices, declining demand in the West for primary products, and falling levels of domestic production resulted in depleted foreign exchange reserves and import strangulation, thus increasing debt service to extraordinary levels (Leslie, 1987:4).

The economic crisis in the region is multifaceted and a few macroeconomic statistics will convey its magnitude. Between 1980 and 1988, real per capita gross domestic product (GDP) dropped by about 25 percent. The deterioration in terms of trade suffered during the same period, resulting in per capita income falling by 30 percent, or by just a little less than one third. This is a staggering loss of income. Some countries such as Benin, Burkina Faso, Burundi, Malawi and Mali suffered declines in GNP per capita (1980-1987) of less than one percent per year (perhaps because of relatively high net resource flows) while countries like Liberia, Madagascar, Mozambique, Niger, Nigeria, Rwanda, Sudan, Togo, Zambia, witnessed drops of more than 3 percent. In particular, Nigeria's per capita income dropped from $1000 in 1980 to just $290 in 1991. The magnitude of the crisis in Sub-Saharan Africa is brought home by the fact that out of some 35 countries for which data were available, only 8 managed to escape a decline in GNP per capita. Of these 8, only Gabon, Botswana and Cameroon achieved substantial growth in per capita GNP (Ghai, 1991:14).

Let me try to answer the question I posed at the beginning of this chapter, namely, why is Africa the lost frontier, suffering from marginalisation and dependency without strategic importance? Callaghy (1993:210) says that Africa "is a continent on the edge" and that it is primarily economically marginalised. This marginalisation is also strategic because it has lost the importance it once commanded between the two ideological blocs, because the international situation is far from what it was between 1960 and 1989. In other words, with the collapse of communism in 1989, Africa lost its importance because it is no longer a battle field for communist and capitalist ideologies. Economically, Africa is not important to TNCs and international banks; it is not important to the economies of either of the major Western countries or of the industrialising countries like Korea, Taiwan, Brazil, and Mexico, except in recent years when China has become a force in the continent. Africa's share of world output has declined; its key export commodities are declining in importance or are being provided more effectively by other Third World countries, for example, Indonesia and Chile. Trade continues to decline, lenders are unwilling to lend, because they are not maintaining debt service; and few are interested to invest except "in narrowly defined mineral enclave sectors" (ibid.), something that China is currently doing.

I have already mentioned the decline in Africa's per capita income since 1973, the drop in real growth rate since about 1965, and that other developing countries did better despite the poor economic environment worldwide, especially in the 1980s. The continent's export levels have remained relatively flat, in some cases really declining after 1970, while those of other Third World countries have risen admirably. Africa's world market share for non-oil primary products dropped from 7 to 4 percent between 1970 and 1985. If the 1970 share of the world market had been maintained, 1986-87 export earnings would have been $9 to $10 billion per annum higher. Compared to other regions of the developing world, Africa's average annual growth rates for exports have fared rather poorly (ibid.).

The continent's marginalisation becomes quite obvious when its performance is compared with that of other Third World regions. This picture becomes quite clear when Africa is compared with South Asia, with which Africa has the most in common. Africa's per capita GDP growth declined dramatically while that of South Asia had risen but steadily until the recent economic crisis which made a mockery of their "economic miracle." Also while Africa's population growth rate continues unabated, that of South Asia has begun to drop. There are also startling differences in the level and quality of investment. While Africa's investment as a percentage of GDP dropped in the 1980s that of South Asia continued to increase, despite the difficult economic climate of the decade. In the area of comparative rates of return on investment, while those of Africa declined from 30.7 percent in the 1960s to 2.5 percent in the 1980s, those of South Asia rose slowly but steadily from 21.3 percent to 22.4 percent. The implications of these patterns are serious and clear. They set the stage for where Africa is today economically and the consequent pauperisation of the people in the continent.

Post Neo-dependency

Given the above bleak economic prospects of Africa, world captains of business have not shown much interest in Africa. Compounding Africa's predicament are the various changes that have taken place in the international scene over the last two or more decades. The Soviet empire disbanded, the Berlin Wall crumbled, and the tense situation in the Middle East has not yet escalated as it was in the 1970s or even 1980s. This is however not to say that the tinder box, known as the Middle East cannot explode any time, especially if Israel carries out its threat of attacking Iran's nuclear facilities. Russia has abandoned its communist ideology and has embraced capitalism. China and India have become emerging powers economically and politically. Thus there are many more scountries competing for scarce resources and there are many alternatives for investors. Meanwhile African countries need foreign exchange for their survival. Given this pathetic scenario, business executives have almost abandoned Africa. With the end of the cold war Africa has been forsaken by them because of lack of strategic value to them; there is no more need for satellite countries to fight their proxy wars. As observed by Callaghy (1993:211), "for the most dynamic actors in a rapidly changing world economy, even a neocolonial Africa is not of much interest anymore, especially after the amazing changes wrought in Eastern Europe and elsewhere beginning in 1989. According to this view, the African crisis really should be left to the international financial institutions as a salvage operation: if it works, fine, if not, so be it; the world economy will hardly notice." African economy is so insignificant that its collapse will not be noticed. In other words, it will have no adverse effect on world economy. This phenomenon in which Africa has been marginalised and left at the mercy of international financial institutions is what has been referred to as the new neocolonialism. It is another form of neocolonialism but it is far more pernicious than the former in that the dependence is much, much greater than in the case of neocolonialism. We call this phenomenon post-neocolonialism, neo-dependency or post neo-dependency. The insignificance of African economy to the world economy is evident in the way African economic crisis has been treated by the industrial countries *vis a vis* economic crisis in Latin America and Asia.

Against the background of heavy foreign debts and deteriorating economic performance, African countries were pressured by multilateral financial organisations, commercial banks and donor countries to accept intervention by international financial institutions. This pressure was quite effective because African countries were in dire need of foreign exchange to honour their debt obligations and also maintain a minimum level of imports. In return for debt rescheduling and new credits, the foreign creditors insisted on a wide-ranging but generally uniform package of economic reforms. In this process the initiative in formulating domestic economic policies shifted from the national authorities to international sources (Ghai, 1991:5). Thus Africa has been handed over to a variety of external actors who have exploited their leverage to "encourage" economic liberalisation. As a new neocolonialist region, Africa is experiencing an acute dependence on international financial institutions like the World Bank and IMF, and major Western countries for design of national economic reform packages and the resources required to implement them. This leverage has been transformed into intense economic policy conditionality, that is, specific economic policy changes in exchange for borrowed resources. The basic drive of these reforms is to enable the West to fully integrate African economies into the world economy by reviving the primary product export economies that existed at the eve of independence and supposedly improving upon them through a more "liberal political economy" and this is a strategy that has been referred to as "back to the future." These economic policy changes or reforms are what have been dubbed "structural adjustment programmes" (SAPs). Let us examine this programme more closely.

Structural Adjustment Programme (SAP)
Structural adjustment, again, is a term that describes the policy changes implemented by the IMF and the World Bank in developing countries. The policy changes are conditions for getting new loans from the IMF or World Bank, or for obtaining lower interest rates on existing loans. The conditions are implemented to make sure that the money lent is spent in accordance with the overall goals of the loan. The SAPs are created with the goal of reducing the borrowing country's fiscal imbalances. The SAPs are supposed to prompt the economies of the developing countries to become more market-oriented, which in turn forces them to concentrate much more on trade and production so it can boost their economy (Wikipedia 2010:1). Through the conditions, SAPs

force poor countries to implement "free market" programmes and policy. These programmes include internal changes involving privatisation and deregulation and external ones which center around the reduction of trade barriers (ibid.).

It is important to note that while both the IMF and World Bank loan to depressed and developing countries, their loans are meant to address different problems. The IMF lends mainly to countries that are confronted by balance of payment problems (inability to pay their international debt), while the World Bank gives loans to fund particular development projects. IMF SAPs are concerned with temporarily fixing problems that countries face as a whole. On the other hand, World Bank SAPs center on providing loans and grants to countries that provide funding on a project basis, for example, granting a loan to improve infrastructure in a region of a developing country.

Historically, as just stated, SAPs came about as a result of global economic disasters during the late 1970s; these included the oil crisis, debt crisis, multiple economic depressions and stagnation. It is important to state that the debt crisis was primarily triggered by an abrupt increase in interest payable on international loans. The debt crisis gave the World Bank and IMF extraordinary power to dominate and control the South. Debtor countries were forced to accept austerity measures as demanded by the IMF before their debts could be rescheduled. In addition, borrower countries demanded the "seal of approval" from the IMF if they were to become eligible to borrow money from any other source.

By 1985, it was clear that in spite of the austerity measures in place, the debt crisis could not be contained and SAPs were introduced to mostly Sub-Saharan African countries. As stated before, adjustment programmes brought with them anti-inflationary monetary policy, the privatisation of public enterprises, dismantling of foreign exchange controls and more flexible labour markets (Fact Sheet on Debt Africa, Feb. 8, 2008). It further reduced the public sector by eliminating subsidies, and government was forced to withdraw its involvement in price setting and increase its role in creating an enabling environment for foreign investment (ibid.), conditions which favour the North.

In 1977, the World Bank and IMF launched the Heavily Indebted Poor Countries (HIPCs) scheme, an initiative that promoted debt relief for 41 low income countries so long as they continued to live by SAPs. HIPC initiative simply proposed to write off debt that was deemed uncollectable. When HIPCI and HIPC11 failed to realise the expected results, poverty reduction was grafted on the SAPs. The debtor countries are being asked to follow guidelines prescribed by the World Bank and IMF to produce Poverty Reduction Strategy Papers (PRSPs). Stating it somewhat differently, in 2002 SAPs underwent some transition, the introduction of Poverty Reduction Strategy Papers. These came about because of the belief by the Bank that "successful economic policy programmes must be founded on strong country ownership" (Wikipedia 2010:1). The World Bank favours "poverty reduction" and because of this "SAPs have attempted to further align themselves with the Millennium Development Goals (MDG) (ibid.) The present focus is on poverty reduction from funds freed from debt relief.

Much has been said about the impact of SAPs in the Third World in general and Africa in particular. Mohameden Ould-Mey (1996: xvi) has noted that SAPs have been "unleashing a profound process of denationalisation of the state where it is restructured from a national to multinational state, virtually deprived of its sovereignty over development policies." The national economies of African countries are presently "controlled by a complex multitude of international economic investors" and are "experiencing a systematic process of devaluation, a phenomenon that is contributing to the bizarre acceleration of net resource transfer from the South to the North" (ibid.). The process of democratisation, which is a central target of SAPs, is preparing the path for a fundamental "socio-political fragmentation" that has the great potential to diffuse and contain "the explosive social impacts of economic reforms." Unfortunately, this process of democratisation is going to remain superficial amid undemocratic relationship at the global or international levels where SAPs are actually conceived and designed.

The UN Economic Commission for Africa (UNECA) (1989) after analysing the efforts to implement the adjustment policies in Africa concluded that in spite of the efforts, the "crisis remained unabated." It went on to say that many African economies had moved from stagnation to declining growth; food deficits had reached alarming proportions; unemployment had mounted; under-utilisation of industrial capacity had become widespread; and that environmental degradation had threatened the very survival of the African people.

Other analysts of SAPs have come up with similar conclusions. Susan George (1992) has contended that the pressure exerted by SAPs has been responsible for the collapse and chaos in Liberia, Somalia, and Sierra Leone; it has equally been responsible for the destruction of tropical forests, urban pollution, hunger, desertification, and sickness. Paul Mosley and John Weeks (1993) in their study found no evidence that SAPs are helping the African continent along the path to economic recovery. Richard Sandbrook (1993) observed that aid is offset by debt servicing and that the export-led growth model in the continent of Africa is inadequate in the long run because the industrialised countries practice protectionism; they can develop synthetic substitutes; and that their technological advances require less or different material inputs. Adebayo Adede (1985) argues that the exported growth model has enhanced Africa's dependence on the global market while destroying intra-African cooperation, which is not only desirable but also an imperative for reducing the impact of the economic crisis on the continent. In all this the continent remains the most heavily indebted region in the world in terms of the ratio of debt to GNP, as will become apparent subsequently.

Furthermore, a Staff Study Mission from the US Congress visited Britain, France, Senegal, Ghana, and Cote d'Ivoire in 1988 to assess the impact of SAPs in Africa. In their report they stated that structural adjustment had produced little enduring poverty-alleviation, and that certain policies had worked against the poor. The report stated further that the price of groundnut in Senegal had plummeted from $1,000 to $500 per ton between 1985 and 1987 and that poverty among urban Senegalese had been made much worse by structural adjustment. P. Adams (1992) in his assessment of SAPs in Sub-Saharan Africa estimated that the collective GNP of the region had lessened by 20 percent, even though the region had benefited from cash infusions to the tune of $100 billion. In Mauritania, the World Bank "Structural Adjustment Report" (January 12, 1990) noted that after six years of adjustment programmes, the Mauritanian economy was "far from achieving sustainable economic growth"; a rare admission by the Bank.

According to Ould-Mey (1996:20), SAPs are not designed to either solve or aggravate the economic crisis in Africa. Adjustment programme is the manifestation of the industrialised countries to "expand their markets, increase their exports, and secure debt payments through a carrot-and-stick policy of providing loans to fiscally bankrupt Third World governments in exchange for fundamental reforms in their political economy." SAPs are not designed to necessarily overcome the budget and balance of payment deficits of Third World countries; their main purpose is to maintain an open global trade and payment system and prevent national governments from trying to place further restrictions on capital movement and import of goods and services from the rich industrialised countries. Viewed from this perspective, Ould-Mey (p.21) states further that adjustment is then a success because nationalistic policies are for the most part reversed, resource transfer from the South to the North has accelerated, and liberalisation policies are now sweeping the entire Third World, opening new markets and strengthening the umbilical cord between developed and developing countries through what many describe as the debt trap, where a nation seeks new loans to pay old ones. In short, SAPs succeed in preventing any disruption in the world trade and payment system, which continues to transfer resources from developing to developed countries.

The result of all these orchestrations is further impoverishment of a very poor region like Sub-Saharan Africa. Having made the above assertions, Ould-Mey proceeds to provide documentation to support his contentions.

It is misleading to blame only the IMF and the World Bank for the economic woes resulting from SAPs, because these two institutions serve merely as instruments of a development policy that carries out strategies developed by the industrialised countries, particularly the G-8 (originally G-7 before Russia was invited into it) and "their spearhead, the United States." This was relatively well-planned policy by the then G-8, whose regular summit meetings since 1975 "reflect a heightened recognition of the need for close cooperation as a result of the growing integration of the world economy and the globalisation of financial markets" (US Department of State *Dispatch*, 16 September, 1991). The G-8 had started planning on a global strategy of coordination and cooperation on international economic and financial policies, with particular reference to debt credit issues worldwide, ever since their first summit meeting in France in 1975. Thus by 1982 they had succeeded in attaching stringent conditions to any additional provision of credits or rescheduling of debts through vigilantly planned SAPs. The developing nations were "seduced by foreign loans," frightened by their acute fiscal problems and balance of payment deficit and tormented by the possibility of being declared insolvent by the World Bank and IMF. The recipe of the strategy is that national economies must be reformed or adjusted to make them automatically adjust to the incentives and "adapt to the imperatives of the global market" in an effort to "homogenise the law of value worldwide, despite the fact that this very attempt at homogenisation persistently produces differentiation because of basic advantage of capital mobility beyond national boundaries compared to labour fixity" (Ould-Mey, 1996:15-16).

The G-8 summit of 1975 was followed by the Economic Declaration of Rambouillet, (US Department of State *Bulletin,* 8 December 1975), which warned against "a return to protectionism" and then went on to urge trading nations of the world triad "to pursue policies which will permit the expansion of world trade to their mutual advantage" and to use "the IMF and other international fora in making urgent improvements in international arrangements for the stabilisation" of developing economies. They went on to emphasise the need to intensify cooperation on all the relevant international organisations."

The declaration concluded with a threat to the Organisation of Petroleum Exporting Countries (OPEC) that the G-8 would do everything "to secure the energy resources" they needed for their growth. Of course, Secretary of State Henry Kissinger did not disguise the threat to use force when during the presidency of Gerald Ford he said on numerous occasions that America would go to war if oil stopped flowing from the Gulf to the US and other Western countries. The Gulf war of 1990 was a fulfillment of that promise. At the 1976 summit in Puerto Rico, President Gerald Ford was in attendance and the main concern of the summit was stabilisation rather than adjustment. At the 1977 summit the G-8 vowed "to seek additional resources for the IMF and support the linkage of its lending practices to the adoption of appropriate stabilisation policies" (US Department of State *Bulletin*, 6 January, 1977).

These institutions were directed by the G-8 to consult with other industrialised countries on how the strategy could be well articulated. The World Bank responded with publication of *World Development* series beginning in 1978. Not surprisingly, the 1978 issue concentrated on interdependence among nations and why this should be paramount when designing development policies. The 1979 issue laid out what they saw as a systematic series of development scenarios and gross domestic product (GDP) growth projections. The 1980 issue laid out the strategic agenda of development studies in the 1990s. The first chapter of the 1980 issue reads, "Adjustment and Growth in the 1980s." The 1980 summit of the G-7 at Venice endorsed the new strategy of adjustment. In the Venice Declaration, the G-7 welcomed the Bank's innovative lending scheme for structural adjustment" (Ould-Mey, 1996).

The need to tighten lending standards might have become urgent following Mexico's default on its debts. The G-

8, according to Harvey (1989), designated the IMF and the World Bank "as the central authority for exercising the collective power of capitalist nations and states over international financial negotiations." Subsequently, the strategy of adjustment was detailed by US Secretary of Treasury Donald Reagan in a hearing before a congressional subcommittee on 15 September, 1983 (cited in Ould-Mey, 1996:33). Reagan told the subcommittee that "a broad international strategy has been adopted." He said that the strategy has five elements. First, adjustment in borrowing countries must be quite effective. Second, the IMF has the responsibility to ensure that the use of its resources is tied to implementation of essential policy measures by borrowers. Third, governments and banks of lending countries should give "a bridge financing in exceptional cases of system-wide danger." Fourth, commercial bank lending should be continued for those countries that pursue sound adjustment programmes. And finally, protectionism must be avoided. Reagan further told the subcommittee that "the IMF is a bank" and it "is the linchpin of our strategy and much of the success that has been achieved is due to the IMF's effort to promote and support adjustment" (ibid.). As noted by J. Boughton (1994), since 1982, the IMF has assumed the role of alleviating the liquidity pressure that otherwise would have necessitated the indebted developing countries to default, "defaults that would have threatened a collapse of international banking system."

It is important to note that the increased contact between the developed and underdeveloped countries and the present globalisation of the world economy has been a frontal attack on the dependency theory which has all along contended that such relationships have always worked to the detriment of the developing countries. By emphasising interdependency the developed countries have been pursuing the recommendations of Walt Rostow in his book *Stages of Economic Growth: A Non-Communist Manifesto.*   African countries have been implementing SAPs.   Africa is the region worst affected by SAPs.   In the 1980s, as reported by Oxfam (1993) 36 Sub-Saharan African countries initiated some 241 adjustment programmes.   Most of these countries have had multiple programmes, with eleven of them implementing 10 or more.   Yet, the region's foreign debts increased from $84 billion (amounting to 91 percent of the value of exports) in 1980 to $199 billion (237 percent of the value of exports) in 1993.   In the final analysis, this trend resulted in both the dependency and marginalisation of the region.   This has spelled worsened poverty.   The IMF and the World Bank, agents of the Summit of 8, have been wringing substantial concessions from weak Third World governments while exacting very few or none at all from First World governments. Consequently, at a time of increasing protectionism in the industrialised West and Japan, Third World countries are being forced to open their economies to a competition that is grossly unfair to them (Rapley, 1996:154).   This is likely to severely damage their economies and further increase their dependence on the industrialised countries.

Ghana was one of the early customers of adjustment and also one of the most faithful to the IMF and World Bank formula, thus attracting the most generous aid and credit. Ghana is often mentioned as the success story of SAPs in Africa. As the test case in the region, Ghana's experiment *had to succeed.* Thus its foreign backers pumped aid and credit into the economy in order to sustain its recovery.   It was a self-fulfilling prophecy (ibid.). As observed by Kusi (1991), without the official foreign investment, it would have been quite unlikely for the Ghanaian economy to have fared that well.   But most other African countries cannot expect to be as lucky because the rich nations' governments have been slashing aid to Africa.

Nigeria, Ghana's neighbour did not fare as well as the latter. Under the programme, cocoa production increased but cocoa processing by local plants did not. The reason for this was because inputs used for those plants, for example, spare parts and technical expertise, are imported and their prices were hiked by currency devaluation. Whatever increase may have occurred in Nigeria's GDP emanated from expansion in the primary sector. Growth in manufacturing has stagnated if not retrogressed. A layer of new export manufacturers that appeared to be developing at the initial stage of the programme soon ran out of steam. In the mean time, many large firms have shut down while small ones, despite improved access to credit, have not been doing well. They have been negatively affected by rising input costs, "the contracting domestic market, and the lack of linkages to large firms that might otherwise have shifted from imported inputs to local sources to reduce their input bills" (Rapley, 1996:82).

What has happened to Nigeria, namely, increase in primary production and not the value added to that production in local economy, is no increase in industrial processing of that output and the products are exported raw. Governments have been forced to cut spending and this inevitably has affected "human-capital formation, the development of the pool of skilled labour, managerial talent, and engineering capacity. This obviously jeopardises future industrial development" (ibid.).

SAPs and Tightening Dependency

From the perspective of the World Bank, IMF and bilateral and multilateral foreign aid donors, Sub-Saharan Africa's economic problem must be solved by SAPs. Thus by 1989, 35 Sub-Saharan countries had adopted SAPs aimed at relieving external and internal imbalances and facilitating the resumption of growth. SAP "generally involves a set of policy reforms to minimise reliance upon markets in domestic and external trade and capital flows, minimise the government's interventionist role by reducing public ownership, subsidies and regulation, and improve the state's efficiency in allocating and using resources" (Sandbrook, 1991:L95). To elaborate a little, governments no longer promote industrialisation by deliberate policy measures and greater incentives are focused on production of primary commodities. Nations are forced to give up the push for more export promotion. National ownership and control of the economy give way to emphasis on incentives to foreign investment and privatisation of state business and their sale to foreign interests. Intentionally or otherwise, social services have been very seriously and negatively affected.

In sum, the main policy objectives of SAPs include the following: reduction in the size of the public sector and improvements in its management; elimination of price distortions in different sectors of the economy; more trade liberalisation; and promotion of domestic savings in the public and private sectors. To accomplish these policy objectives, the international financial institutions employ the following policy instruments: exchange rate adjustment which centers around currency devaluation; interest rate policies to enhance domestic savings and achieve appropriate allocation of resources; control of money supply and credit; fiscal policies to reduce government expenditures and deficit financing; trade and payment liberalisation; and regulation of the prices of goods, services, and factor inputs (DeLancey, 1993:114). Once again, these requirements have been dubbed "conditionalities."

The above conditionalities are not all, as more continue to be added and these have tended to erode the sovereignty of African countries.

Interestingly enough, the so-called Tokyo International Conference on Development's (TICAD) declaration held on 5-6 October, 1993 simply affirmed the ongoing SAPs by specifically asking Africa to continue "structural adjustment programmes to improve access of the poor to income earning opportunities and social services; give increased priority alleviation to investment in human capital through nutrition, health and education programmes" (*Africa Recovery*, December 1992-March 1993:33). What TICAD does is to simply ratify the conditionalities imposed on Africa and other Third World countries. It further endorses the myth that SAPs and all that they conjure are the panacea for African economic problem.

Apart from the initial conditionalities which formed the basis of the policy instruments, more have been added and African countries have almost lost the "flag" or "sham" independence they won in the 1960s because they can hardly make any political or economic decisions which are not popular among (or even approved by) the Western powers that dominate (in fact, control) the international financial institutions. African leaders have been so frustrated with conditionalities that at a September 1993 meeting with World Bank President, Mr. Lewis Preston, Guinean finance minister, Mr. Soriba Kaba, charged that the constant imposition of new conditionalities is used "as a pretext" to reduce resource flows to the continent.

Some recent "fundamental amendments" to aid conditionality include "a definite seal of approval" to adjustment policies, good governance and democratisation, and suspending any form of aid for governments accused of human rights violations. European Union (EU) even insists on intensive "dialogue" with African, Caribbean and Pacific (ACP) "governments on their economic priorities, with EU development experts getting a larger say in how ACP countries manage their economies" (Islam, December 1993-March 1994:L21). To ensure ACP "fidelity to economic commitments," the practice of allocating funds to each ACP country at the start of the Lome cycle was "replaced by a more rigorous system of step-by-step aid disbursement." This installment plan is aimed to "encourage countries to spread up the implementation of projects and programmes" and "the size of subsequent allocations and the speed with which they are released" will be contingent on ACP countries' "ability to put its first installment to good use." The "special allocations for human resources development and environmental protection" are released only on "approval of specific country projects." ACP countries must also "encourage the growth of their private sector and make sure that local entrepreneurs can get access to EU funds" (ibid.). The US-Africa trade bill of 1998 contains conditionalities which clearly state that the bill will apply only to those African states judged by the US to be pursuing market-oriented economic policies, such as privatisation of state industries, the elimination of tariff and non-tariff barriers to trade, and the reduction of business and commercial taxes and regulations, among others (Madarshahi, August 1998:12).

One problem with these conditionalities is that they hold up quick-disbursing adjustment loans whenever "strict policy implementation and macroeconomic performance conditions are not attained" (Smith, December 1993-March 1994:15). Conditionality is "essentially coercive" in nature and often arouses resentment by those who have to implement them and also "live with their consequences." In a sense, it may be good for African leaders to be treated this way hoping that they will learn some lessons by properly managing their resources and also stop embezzling and stockpiling billions of dollars in Western and Lebanese banks. Early in 1994 African franc-zone countries succumbed to France's pressures and accepted its conditionality of devaluating their currencies before France would support their bid for some aid. The result of that devaluation was disastrous and those countries are today much more dependent on France, their erstwhile colonial power, than they have ever been.

The control that the international financial institutions have on African leaders and their countries is so strong that they have been treated like a village headmaster treats his pupils.   If they do not "behave" they are suspended immediately.   Cameroon was suspended in March 1994 because it was 60 days overdue on a $46.6 million loan payment. Sierra Leone was suspended by the IMF on April 25, 1988 following the accumulation of overdue financial obligations to the lending agency totaling $55 million.   On March 28, 1994 the IMF approved loans totaling $163 million for Sierra Leone after lifting a six-month band on lending to that country.   This new loan was made because Sierra Leone had paid outstanding obligations to the lending agency facilitated by bridge financing by France, Norway and the US. The IMF approved SDR47.56 (about US$66.7 million) for Senegal in April 1994, contingent on good economic behaviour for twelve months.

In 1991 bilateral donors suspended aid to Kenya and in 1993 agreed to resume disbursements in 1994, on condition of "progress in implementing the economic reform agenda" as "strong positive steps on human rights, governance and corruption." They also directed Kenya to go after its first ever Paris Club deal in January 1994 over its $500 million debt arrears.   But on March 23, 1994 while speaking to Kenyan Parliament, President Daniel Arab Moi announced a reversal of economic restructuring measures demanded by the IMF in favour of domestic measures, and instead of "waiting to be guided by prescriptions from international agencies." Moi referred to the IMF measures as "unrealistic" and then said he was moving away from a programme of government austerity and economic change because of the IMF's "hard-line and uncompromising attitude." Reforms sought by the IMF and World Bank would cause severe problems for the measures already hit by rising and plummeting real wages. This reaction came because the IMF and World Bank had asked for free exchange of the Kenyan shilling, domestic interest rate links, reductions in government reserves of strategic crops, mass retrenchment of civil servants and privatisation of state-run industries. Moi contended that these measures would "wreck the already weakened economy." Of course, Moi knew that Kenya depended very much on aid, approaching one billion American dollars a year. As a new neo-dependent, Moi knew that he could only bark because he could not bite. It was not long before Moi caved in. In 1993 Zambia was told that disbursement of $800 million in pledges depended on economic policy performance and "good governance." Thus, it is no exaggeration that the IMF and World Bank officials treat African leaders like a village headmaster treats his pupils and these African leaders and their countries are so dependent that they have swallowed their pride.

At a conference on "Economic and Social Policy Options for the Third Republic [of Nigeria]" organised by the Frederick Ebert Foundation and African Centre for Development and Strategic Studies, Professor Bade Onimode noted that apart from the well known objectives of SAP, there were "unstated objectives of the programme which its originators (the West) want to reap." These hidden objectives include: to recolonise Nigeria and other Third World countries; to ensure the payment of often "bogus" foreign loans; to keep Nigeria and other countries of the South down and deny them opportunity to rise and challenge the hegemony of the West; imposition of massive currency devaluation; and to ensure that industrialisation eludes Nigeria and other countries implementing the SAPs conditionalities. Onimode further contends that the visible achievement of SAP has been the polarisation of the Nigerian society where about 10 percent of the population has catapulted into a new position of affluence, leaving 90 percent to recline in abject penury. In his view, "stabilisation before growth, which the programme preaches, is wrong." Rather, both should progress simultaneously (Nwosu, March 1993:11). The position of Onimode is at the heart of the suspicion of not only Nigerians, but also Africans all over the continent about the objectives of SAP. What Onimode must appreciate, however, is that the West use coercion to accomplish their goal. The coercive instrument is conditionality.

By using the case of Nigeria, I want to demonstrate how the IMF and World Bank coerce poor countries of Africa (and other Third World countries) to open their national economies up for the control of Western companies and corporations. When General Adulsalami Abubakar came into power in June 1998 following the death of his predecessor, General Sani Abacha (perhaps the most notorious dictator Nigeria has ever known), one of the demands the West made of Abubakar in exchange for their support was economic liberalisation, something that Generals Babangida and Abacha had either done half-heartedly or resisted. The road to liberalisation meant setting in motion a privatisation programme. When General Abubakar sought to negotiate an interim programme to be monitored by IMF staff that would make it possible for talks on a medium-term economic strategy agreement for

Nigeria, the General was given the condition that he must begin seriously to privatise. Furthermore, in order for Nigeria to establish accord with the IMF and the World Bank to try to get debt relief talks with the Paris Club, Nigeria had to show its effort at privatisation and liberalisation. Paris Club members then accounted for 70 percent of Nigeria's total foreign debt of about $31 billion as at 1996. Because of this arm-twisting or conditionality, in 1998 General Abubakar conceded and announced the programme of privatisation which he initiated before restoring civilian democratic rule on May 29, 1999 (Obadina, December 1998:4).

Following this coercive demand by the international institutions and foreign creditors, Nigeria sold about 40 percent of its equity in government corporations and companies to "strategic investors," a veiled reference to foreign companies (generally Western), which then ultimately took over management control of the enterprises. The shares were sold through international open tenders to investors said to possess proven technical and financial capabilities. Some 20 percent of the shares were sold allegedly to Nigerian investors through public share offers, while the government kept about 40 percent of the shares. When Nigeria undertook privatisation in the 1970s, many of the enterprises allegedly bought by Nigerians were actually owned by foreigners for whom Nigerians fronted (Offiong, 1980a). Some of the enterprises auctioned away in 1998 included the National Electric Power Authority (NEPA), Nigerian Telecommunications (NITEL), the National Fertiliser Company, hotels, rolling mills, paper companies, vehicle assembly firms, a cement company, and a sugar plant. The goals of this privatisation programme include enhancing efficiency and increasing foreign investment, and this in turn drags Nigeria even more inextricably into the global economy and further compounds her post neocolonial status.

It is certain that hundreds of jobs have been lost and the poor people have been forced to pay more for the services rendered by those enterprises auctioned away. We must bear in mind that the essence of private enterprise is profit maximisation. No wonder, then privatisation remains one of the most controversial and odious aspects of economic liberalisation, not only in Nigeria, but also everywhere in Africa. There is no doubt that the Nigerian government was urged by "local private sector groups and foreign creditor institutions to off-load inefficient, under-funded and corruption-ridden state enterprises." For example, in 1996 the federal government of Nigeria invested $4.6 billion and received an average rate return of only about 2 percent (Obadina, December 1998:4). But it was the coercive conditionalities of the financial institutions that had the job done – forced the government to initiate the privatisation programme.

Not surprisingly, trade unionists and nationalists have been opposed to the sale of government equity holdings in the enterprises, because of the potentially negative social consequences of privatisation. Jobs are lost in addition to increased cost of essential services and loss of national pride. Some "sections of the ruling elite that rely on state enterprises for patronage oppose the sell-offs" (ibid.) People are worried that privatisation has led to concentrated ownership of former state enterprises in the hands of members of certain wealthy ethnic groups in a country that has had its own share of fratricidal conflicts. Already there were complaints about the privatisation exercise of the 1970s that the Yoruba and Hausa/Fulani were the beneficiaries because the Igbo had not yet recovered from the civil war. The sales of sensitive state enterprises to foreign corporations did not go well with Nigerians. An influential Nigerian commentator Ken Ogbuagu, whose view has been echoed by many in and outside Nigeria, has said that the federal government has "headed on a [path] of unprecedented national calamity with the foreign ownership of any part of NEPA, NITEL, the refineries or the railways... There is an international conspiracy whose aim is to grab the central nervous system of Nigeria, hence Africa. The sale of strategic national assets [to foreigners] is absolutely wrong" (cited in ibid.)

Certainly, there are concerns not only among Nigerians but also all over Africa that such acts of privatisation will prevent the spread of development to poor sectors of society, especially the rural areas where the bulk of the population lives. This situation is likely to be so because private companies want to be where the infrastructures already exist. In Africa the few infrastructures already in place are largely in urban areas. Because conditionalities work, the IMF and World Bank continue to tighten them.

The tightening of conditionalities has been vehemently protested by African countries. For example, Zambia's Finance Minister, Ronald Penza, complained of "undue interference by donors" and generally, there have been protests against multilateral institutions and bilateral agencies that they are applying criteria on such key issues as governance and performance "without agreed parameters and precise definitions" (Smith, December 1993-March 1994:15). The situation is so bad that one economist, David Finch in a research paper for UNCTAD said, the "association by the Paris Club of IMF conditionality with renegotiation of debt terms ... has forced many countries in Africa with debt problems to submit to perpetual negotiation with the IMF over their economic policy. This exercise in external control ... promotes a relationship with the IMF akin to that of colonial power and colony" (ibid.).

The proliferation of conditionalities has resulted in "impossibly large numbers of commitment." From the World Bank data, Uganda is said to have made 79 specific policy commitments to donors for the fiscal year 1991-92. Between 1980 and 1992, African countries conducted about 8,000 separate negotiations with debtors. African countries have many more negotiations ahead and conditionality is intensifying and "swamping" African policy advisers. The tendency is to significantly reduce African input and increase the danger of economic programmes "inappropriate to local circumstances because they are donor-designed." The result of all this is that every proliferation of conditionality by international financial institutions and every additional demand on overburdened debtor governments "will reduce the probability that each conditionality will be observed, leading again to a misapplication of human and financial resources" and avoidable human hardship (ibid.). What is evident here is that even the "political kingdom" which Africans fought for and won has been lost to new neocolonialism or neodependency. The "economic kingdom" which they had hoped to achieve through the instrumentality of the political kingdom now seems an impossible dream. The present situation of neodependency or new neocolonialism, has more than integrated African economies into the world economic system in an entrenched and irreversible position of economic subserviency.

There seems to be a lot of hypocrisy in what the international financial institutions claim they seek to accomplish in Africa through SAPs. Why do they pursue liberalisation in Africa when industrial nations themselves are becoming more and more protectionist? Africa's share of world trade, according to GATT, declined significantly to only 2.6 percent of world merchandise trade in 1992. World prices for agricultural exports have been spiraling down-ward and by 1992, real export prices of coffee and cocoa had dropped 69 percent from the start of the 1980s, while the price for palm oil had dropped 49 percent and for sisal and cotton by 47 percent. This situation represents sluggish demand for some tropical commodities. Why then encourage them to produce more primary products to flood the world market and continue to depress prices further down? Perhaps more than sluggish demand for tropical commodities, it is protectionism in industrial countries that diminishes international market opportunities for Africa.

SAPs have created many problems for African policy implementers, at least in the short-run. Costs of imports have increased astronomically, including essential imports of resources, supplies and capital to enhance economic growth. Prices of domestic goods have risen because so-called subsidies have been removed and prices regulated. The poorest have been hardest hit, particularly with respect to food prices. This point was underscored by the former UN Secretary General, Mr. Boutros Boutros-Ghali, when he said in his speech to the Panel of High-Level Personalities that "structural adjustment is not popular on the streets of Africa" and warned that "political will alone cannot guarantee results." He went further to say that the fruits of SAPs were yet to ripen "but the hardships they have brought are already very apparent. Dislocation, unemployment and declining living standards are only a few of the immediate difficulties that many countries are now experiencing. Governments must be encouraged to stay the course; greater care must also be taken to help governments address the dire human consequences of such reforms" (*Africa Recovery*, December 1993-March 1994:37).

Despite the protestations and the negative results of SAPs, Mr. Edward Jaycox, then Vice President of the World Bank for Africa, arrogantly stated that "adjustment is a *sine qua non* for alleviating poverty, because without adjustment we can't get growth, and without growth we cannot expect to have any positive impact on poverty, given that [Africa's] population is growing over 3 percent a year" (*Africa Recovery*, April-September, 1994:9). The implication of Mr. Jaycox's statement is that in order to get out of poverty, the condition must first be made intolerable through SAPs and all the attending hardships they unleash, and then after the terrible shock, they will suddenly find themselves affluent. The unfortunate thing about the hardships unleashed by SAPs is that those feeling the effects of the hardship are the very poor who had no hand in bringing about the terrible economic condition.

7

Impacts of World Bank and IMF SAPs

We have in the last chapter demonstrated how the World Bank and IMF have exploited SAPs to tighten the noose on Africa's dependency. We also pointed out the disastrous impacts of SAPs promoted by the World Bank and IMF on African people and their societies. No matter how well intentioned, the impacts of SAPs have been quite devastating to those they were purportedly intended to save; "purported" because the basic concern of the two international financial institutions has been to open up poor countries' markets to Western countries and their multinational corporations and, to serve as international tax collectors for Western creditors. In this chapter we further describe the impacts of SAPs on selected topics, reactions of research and advocacy organisations to the work of the two banks including the US Senate, and finally we discuss the reaction of the World Bank to the criticisms leveled against it.

Impact of Currency Devaluation in CFA Countries
Devaluation is a major policy instrument of the World Bank and IMF and its impact on the people, particularly *the wretched of the earth*, has been devastating. We proceed to examine the impact of the January 1994 currency devaluation in franc African countries.

For many years France had defended the CFA franc against devaluation. But a few months after Prime Minister Edouard Ballander assumed office in Paris and barely a month after the death of the Ivorean strong man, President Houphouet-Boigny, a self-styled apologist for Western nations' imperialism, the situation changed one hundred and eighty degrees. France quickly joined forces with the World Bank and IMF to emphasise to the African leaders of the franc zone the dire need to devalue their currencies to "restore competitiveness" to the zone's economies which had been in recession since 1986; and failure to agree to devaluation would mean another decade of recession in the zone. Determined to force the countries involved to devalue their currencies, France notified the franc countries in September 1993 that it would stop plugging budget deficits with effect from January 1, 1994 unless they agreed to implement SAPs under the auspices of the IMF. This threat amounted to arm twisting.

Meanwhile, poverty in Ivory Coast had doubled between 1985-92 to 60 percent of the population and across the franc zone, "average per capita and household incomes had fallen some 40 percent in the same period. The drop in living standards ... was akin to the 1930s' Great Depression of Europe and the U.S. and the ... crash in Russia and Eastern Europe" (Bentsi-Enchill, December 1993-March 1994:42). These countries' economies were experiencing decreasing agricultural output, declining export revenue and a 40 percent decline in trade since 1985. The argument was that since the CFA franc zone was pegged to a French franc that had appreciated by 40 percent against the US dollar in 1985-92, local industry had suffered from high product costs, declining investment, and low levels of maintenance and productivity. There was a tendency for people to evade tax, leading to eroded government revenue with the consequent cuts in services in order to protect civil service incomes purely "for political reasons." This was the argument advanced by the World Bank.

This chain of events led to an increasing diversion of predominantly French aid to service ballooning arrears to the financial institutions; which in fact had suspended most SAPs in the CFA zone. By 1993, the CFA countries required external financing of $8.6 billion to bring down arrears on foreign and domestic payments. According to Bentsi-Enchill (ibid.), "economic circuits were seizing up with a banking system crippled by the growing burden of bad loans to the public and private sectors, and a general liquidity shortage worsened by accelerating capital flight. The outflow of bank notes from the West African zone alone rose from $289mn in 1986 to $1.26bn in 1993, over a third of money supply. To stem the rapid outflow, the two CFA central banks suspended the convertibility of bank notes outside the West and Central African zones" in August 1993.

With devaluation, the IMF was willing to come to terms with the franc zone countries. Cameroon, Niger and Senegal had IMF standbys. Ivory Coast and Mali got ESAFs, Comoros, a structural adjustment facility (SAF). Benin, Burkina Faso and Equatorial Guinea were "in line" for ESAFs, and Chad, Central African Republic and Gabon for standbys, all expected by the end of March 1994. These countries were promised an increase in loans for their budget deficits ($896 million in 1994, up from $586 million in 1993). France in addition cancelled development debts ($1.1 billion) of the ten low-income countries; half the development debt ($3.2 billion) of Cameroon, Congo, Ivory Coast and Gabon; and wrote off $569 million arrears to its central aid agency, the Caisse francaise de de`velopment (p.3).

In the social sector, France and the World Bank agreed to launch a $52 million fund to promote education, health and public works for the youth. The financing of these projects depended on donor contributions. Since devaluation doubled foreign debt in CFA terms, France, the IMF and World Bank agreed to seek 50-60 percent cancellations by the Paris Club.

Initial efforts at discharging this commitment did not appear to be encouraging.

The reaction to the devaluation was quite predictable. There were strikes and protests in several countries and riot police were called in resulting in several deaths. The parity of the CFA franc set in 1948 was changed from a rather staggering ratio of 50 to 100 equal 1 French franc; the Comoro franc rose from 50 to 75 equal IFF. The range was very high and the impact was equally debilitating. The impact brought about volatility in several CFA countries and the governments, France and the World Bank frantically sought emergency solutions. UNICEF screamed that devaluation would further damage the already poor health system; France agreed to subsidise for three months, half the post-devaluation price increase of the 20 French medicines most widely used in the 14 franc countries. It is interesting to note that in the wake of riots, strikes and protests following the devaluation, governments were forced to do what in some cases were essentially the very things that SAPs sought to stop.

Specifically, the following measures were taken, and even though they were said to be temporary, some flew in the face of SAPs. Benin imposed price freeze on foods, pharmaceuticals and construction; salary rise was promised; and project for unemployed youth was also launched. Burkina Faso raised education grants by 8 percent; increased public sector salaries by an average of 6 percent; imposed controls on prices and profit margins; and cut industrial tax rates. Central African Republic announced price freeze on goods and services while Congo lifted import taxes on stable foods; price freeze on basic foods; announced the postponement of public sector wage cut of 20-35 percent. Ivory Coast increased pay for civil servants by 5-15 percent; voluntary retirement with 18 months' salary to replace retrenchment plans; minimum wage of up to 10 percent; value-added tax and customs tariff cut; export bonus stopped; three-month price freeze on 34 goods; high-cotane petrol and rice up to 15 percent; pharmaceuticals up 46 percent; cocoa, coffee, cotton producer prices up 20, 30 and 50 percent and 30-50 percent for bananas, rubber, and palm oil (ibid.).

The impact of the currency devaluation did not end there. Gabon announced price freeze on basic goods, petroleum products, and utilities. Niger on its own made plans for import subsidies, civil service pay raise and price controls. Senegal cancelled an earlier announced 15 percent public sector pay cut and instead promised a 10 percent raise in March 1994. President Dious frantically prepared decrees on salaries, custom duties, food prices and taxes; 20-30 percent increase in rice, flour, cooking oil, milk; 22-30 percent for petroleum products, electricity, gas, transport, cotton, rice, groundnut producer prices up 43, 30 and 6 percent. Finally, Togo announced price freeze on petroleum products, pharmaceuticals, foodstuffs; export controls imposed (ibid.). I have detailed the various actions taken by different governments in reaction to their currency devaluation in order to emphasise how debilitating the impact of the currency devaluation was. The impact has been the same in practically all the countries where this measure has been applied. It is always a disaster.

While the people are suffering under the grinding teeth of SAPs, what is the prospect of these reforms in overcoming the economic crisis? The Ivorean Prime Minister, Kablan Duncan optimistically said that the devaluation "will considerably improve the competitiveness of our export commodities, considerably increase the level of productive investment, free our economic potential and generate new jobs" (ibid.). This statement should not be surprising because

Ivory Coast leaders have often appointed themselves defenders of France's practices in Africa. They have always chosen to be apologists of French imperialism, neocolonialism or neodependency. The fact of the matter is that even if devaluation stimulates export production, it will not increase external demand for raw materials on which revenue prospects are still dim. Furthermore, local producers are subject to higher input costs; tighter, more expensive credit and lower effective demand for a long time to come. Even though France gave $52 million to help ease the cash-flow problems of French Businesses in the region, indigenous businesses in the area had to face a far more difficult and uncertain future. This is the real needy group that deserves adequate attention; it is impossible for them to compete with French businessmen. They are disfranchised even in their own countries.

According to the World Bank (1989), formal sector wages were "way out of line" with franc zone productive capacity and "must fall initially" during SAPs. To make this "politically feasible", "temporary" general subsidies on basic foodstuffs and transport had to be introduced. The idea was to delay the comprehensive impact of lost purchasing power on the "most vocal and most important short-term losers," the urban students, unionised workers and civil servants. The second stage was to work on "narrowly targeted" subsidies and safety nets for the "truly poor and vulnerable" of the urban informal sector, which France, the World Bank and IMF had promised to help. But the World Bank and IMF are aware that such programmes are often in-efficient and do little to reduce poverty (p.42). The franc zone governments have been pushing SAPs policies such as liberalisation of markets, privatisation of public enterprises, elimination of monopolies, quantitative restrictions and 'other rent-creating mechanisms.'

Previous efforts were slowed or reversed by "politically powerful interest groups" whose economic power was trampled by such policy changes. Similar interest groups retain their power in most franc zone countries but they currently face the challenge of spreading the burden of more stringent austerity programmes outside many "short-term losers" from devaluation and SAPs. Certainly, the road to promoting a controversial route to economic recovery in the already turbulent democratic transition in many countries is tortuous, indeed. Currency devaluation simply makes the local currency buy much less than it was and the result is that to buy a cup of garri, a basic food in West Africa, you have to carry a bucketful or basketful of the local currency.

UNCTAD Reacts to SAPs

At this juncture, a visit to UNCTAD's reaction to the policy objectives and policy instruments of the World Bank is rather germane. Obviously such programmes as imposed on the franc zone countries (and this has been the same all over SSA) require massive sums of money but what these countries receive are trickles. The amounts used in reviving German economy after World War 11 was massive and the impact was felt. However, one must admit that the infrastructure was already there as opposed to the case of Africa. Africa must not bear this blame alone; the West must accept a large chunk of the blame for their actions under colonialism and neocolonialism. In his review of *Trade and Development* (1993), Mr. Kenneth Dadzie, Secretary-General of UNCTAD comments on "insignificantly funded" SAPs, with often misplaced objectives. According to him, aid was increasingly used "to induce policy change" instead of to finance growth and investment. The result is that many countries are dependent on aid "simply to sustain a low level of activity.... Despite more intensive application of SAPs in Sub-Saharan Africa than in any other region ... its per capita income fell 15 percent in 1980-92, with average economic growth one-half to one-third that of all developing countries" (*Africa Recovery*, October 1993:30).

Although SAPs have emphasised macroeconomic stability and agriculture, "little, if any, genuine diversification has occurred" and "no effort" had been made to prevent overproduction of primary commodities. Sub-Saharan commodity prices fell by almost 15 percent in 1990-92, and terms of trade dropped by 40 percent, compared to 25 percent for all developing countries. Mr. Dadzie notes further that inadequate levels of official development aid (ODA) never compensated for these loses, let alone provide new investment. In 1980-90, for 25 African countries "there was an additional ODA flow of $2.4 billion against GDP loss of $16.45 bn." Dadzie argues that SAPs policies of trade liberalisation, often involving the sudden withdrawal of import protection, also while industrial countries maintain protectionism against export markets result in acute shortages of foreign exchange and that SAPs relied too much "on devaluations and other purely market-based mechanisms ... The main aim appears to be to privatise or close down public enterprises," on the pretext that "Sub-Saharan governments cannot be counted upon to correct market failures." There are a few private firms able and willing to undertake long-terms risks and UNCTAD called for "an active government role", particularly in countries with widespread market failures. It then recommends "pragmatic rather than doctrinaire approach" to country-specific needs and realities. African governments' commitment to SAPs has been weak because of their limited participation in the conception and design of the programmes. Education and health are the two social institutions often overly affected by

SAPs (ibid.). When SAP programmes are imposed upon African countries by IMF and World Bank, the people do not have a high sense of commitment whereas if they were involved from the beginning to the point of implementation, the outcome might be different.

In sum, devaluation does not stimulate exports from Africa primarily because the continent relies heavily on the export of primary goods the demand for which is largely inelastic. Africa's market for its primary products is fundamentally in the First World. Devaluation leads to increases in output which in turn lowers world prices. Unfortunately, however, these lower prices do not result in increased demand the way they are likely to do for other goods. On the other, devaluation brings about inflation due to the rise in import costs; removal of subsidies on inputs brings about the same result. This problem becomes quite pronounced when farmers rely very much on imported inputs, such as fertiliser. Inflation wipes away the gains in producer prices. A clear example of what happened to Ivory Coast currency devaluation was when coffee and cocoa prices rose by 50 percent, but the price of insecticides rose by as much as 60 percent. There is no doubt that regardless of where devaluation of currency takes place in Sub-Saharan Africa, rising input prices will more than offset producer-price increases, making nonsense of market liberalisation.

Impact of SAPs on Education

The impact of SAPs is not limited to currency devaluation and the disaster it brings upon the poor, the rising input prices, among others. The 1993 *World Education Report* published by the UNESCO, describes conditions in African education for school-age children as "catastrophic" and that economic and other pressures (the derivatives of SAPs) have further pushed away the continent's education goals. Funds have been cut due to SAPs. It is interesting to note that in the 1960s and 1970s Western experts were making huge sums of money as education consultants, purportedly helping African governments to plan and expand education to more and more people because it was the *sine qua non* for modernisation. In the 1980s education was no longer seen as the panacea to rapid modernisation and as part of the conditionalities, African governments were (and still are) required to cut down on education expenditure.

Apart from outright cuts in education expenditure, other factors involved in the dwindling education sector include shortages of foreign aid funds, declining personal income due to SAPs and high population growth. These factors have combined to bring about a disastrous decline in the overall quality and quantity of African education, leaving the African region far behind literacy rates in other Third World regions. However, in countries like Tunisia and Botswana children can expect to have quality and quantity of education comparable to those in industrial nations. On the other hand, drop-out rates are more pronounced than enrollment levels. In the poorest societies, the average number of years a child spends in school is quite below the four years UNESCO considers the minimum needed to achieve literacy and basic skills. Examples include Niger where a five year-old boy may spend only 2.1 years in school; Burkina Faso 2.4 years; Guinea 2.7 years; and Djibouti 3.4 years. This situation is much worse for girls, because traditionally, girls' education is not generally well appreciated. Boys have preference over girls, the situation becoming worse when parents are forced to make the choice.

In the area of adult education, not much has been achieved. Only nine out of 39 Sub-Saharan countries had a decline in adult literacy in the 1980s, and in most countries very few pupils complete their formal education to reduce the growth of illiterate population. Informal education is not widespread enough. In some countries women constitute 65 percent of adult illiterates and this emphasises the importance of "family literacy." Evidence abounds that "the higher the education level of women, the lower their fertility rates and the better their children's health and education" (Noonan, December 1993-March 1994:23).

The economic crisis of the 1980s and the consequent SAPs have so adversely affected Sub-Saharan African countries that they have been forced to devote more of their current spending each year barely to keep the same percentage of children in school. But economic decline has been more than compounded by SAPs which slice education budgets at the same time bilateral aid to education is declining. This has led to a drop in recurrent spending per pupil in Sub-Saharan Africa from $83 in 1980 to $76 in 1990, thus intensifying existing shortages of textbooks and worsening teacher-pupil ratios that were 1:40 to 1:60 (ibid.). In Senegal, for example, SAPs forced a decline in education spending from 33 percent of the national budget to 26-27 percent. Drop-out rates in Senegal record 45 percent; building of new schools was rendered impossible, and there was a freeze on hiring new teachers.

In Nigeria, the disastrous impact of SAPs had the tendency to intensify the pre-existing crisis in the Nigerian education sector, as evidenced by:

- chronic under-funding, relative to the sectors such as defense;

- increasing inadequacy as well as physical disrepair of existing infrastructure and educational facilities;
- insufficiency of trained staff and basic teaching aids and equipment (e.g., university teacher-student ratio over 1:20, far in excess of UNESCO's recommended 1:10, and NUC's [National University Commission] target of 1:12);
- deteriorating conditions of service of teachers relative to supporting staff; and
- demoralisation and oppressive conditions in the educational institutions, etc. (Jega, 1993:104).

In 1988 and 1989 the Nigerian government barely increased the absolute level of funding of education; the raise was "inconsequential because of the inflationary trend unleashed by SAP" (Tella, 1989:7). Government allocated N800 million to primary school education with some additional grants of N40 million for the purchase of books. Assuming that all was disbursed, each state of the federation could expect to get $39 million out of $800 million. In five of the 30 states (as at that year because more states were subsequently created) their shares would hardly pay salaries of teachers for four months. Each of the 30 states would expect to get N2 million from the special book grant which was N500 per school in each state. This amount in the 1989 value of the *naira* (Nigerian currency) could just purchase a few books since SAP had hiked book prices by as much as 600 percent relative to their pre-SAP costs (ibid.).

UNESCO's figures show that even at its peak, educational expenditure per pupil, the key "indicator of the educational priorities of each state," has never gone beyond US$24.10 in Nigeria. This placed Nigeria above barely 20 countries in the world, according to G. T. Kurain (cited in Jega, 1993:105). In 1984 Nigeria's total expenditure on education as a percentage of its GNP was below 4.9 percent. Jega (1993:105) charges that "today, education is fast becoming a huge private enterprise with even the World Bank coming up with loan packages (and conditionalities) for Nigerian universities given the gross underfunding of the university sector occasioned by SAP; the attack on university autonomy; the threat of retrenchment of staff and increasing arbitrariness of university authorities in violation of statutes, ASUU [Academic Staff Union of Universities] declared an industrial dispute with the government in 1987 and, failing to reach an amicable settlement, called out its members on a general strike on 1 June 1988." Since then, the impact of SAPs and the authoritarian military regimes have been the constant causes of strikes by ASUU.

The contentions of Jega have been independently confirmed by the findings of a study on the impact of SAP on Nigerian universities. In his findings, Ubani (1992) concluded as follows:

- economic austerity and SAP have had a negative impact on the Nigerian government's financial support for the university system;
- quality of instruction in Nigerian universities have fallen as funding for the university programmes were decreasing under economic austerity and SAP; and
- facilities/utilities, faculty stability, government financial commitment, research, students' accommodation and adequacy of funding have had severe negative impacts on the quality of instruction due to economic austerity and SAP.

As one who had the opportunity to serve in a Nigerian university for sixteen years, during which period I served as Head of Sociology, Dean of Social Science, Dean of Graduate School, and Chairman of Committee of Deans, I can only concur with the above findings. For, things changed for the worse beginning in the 1980s and the deterioration continues to date. Commenting on the inadequacy of higher education in Sub-Saharan Africa, UNESCO notes that "a country cannot generate the skills it needs for independent management of its own development without a viable system of higher education. And this is precisely where the chasm is largest between Sub-Saharan Africa and the rest of the world" (cited in Noonan, December 1993-March 1994:23). UNESCO went on to say that while a country like Canada has an enrollment ratio of 5,102 students in higher education per 100,000 inhabitants, Tanzania, for example, has only 21, and Mozambique 16. In addition, the number of African students abroad has been in relative decline (ibid.).

The result is that Sub-Saharan Africa has few scientists and engineers involved in research and development, despite the vital importance of this activity for adapting and developing technologies essential to socio-economic progress. SAPs have also forced the shrinking further of previously nominal levels of Africa's research and development spending. UNESCO argues that education is not a priority for multilateral financial institutions, and the World Bank, for example, continues to emphasise budget cuts, as we earlier stated. This is saddening because over the last 30 years or so, multilateral institutions have taken over from bilateral donors as principal external sources of education funding.

Because of its concern in enforcing public spending cuts, the World Bank's proposals emphasise "cost sharing" which include either instituting or increasing tuition fees, requiring upkeep of facilities or clerical work of students, reducing teachers' salaries and lowering the qualifications required for teachers. Many of these recommendations violate major international conventions on education because they would contribute to a further decline in the quality and coverage of education.

In Third World countries as a whole, the World Bank (1991:68) itself admits that in the 1980s the share of education and health in bilateral aid to developing countries dropped from 18 percent to 16.3 percent, and in multilateral aid, from 14 percent in 1985 to 12 percent in 1988. Almost 10 percent of bilateral aid and 5 percent of multilateral aid were allocated to education, which represented an average annual funding of $4.3 billion. Between 5 and 6 percent of bilateral aid and 8 to 9 percent of multilateral aid was spent on health and population programmes, with an average yearly flow of $2.7 billion.

Some evidence suggests that aid has not been allocated to priority areas. Well over 95 percent of education assistance was targeted at secondary and higher levels of education, instead of the primary level. Furthermore, the bulk of aid earmarked for primary education was allocated to increasing supply of essential resources for learning, such as teaching materials and teacher training, which have been found to be most cost-effective. In low-income countries, quantitative expansion remains the focus; buildings, furniture, equipment represent 57.8 percent of all aid. Only 1.5 percent of total aid is given for primary health care, and only 1.3 percent for population assistance. In the specific case of the impact of SAPs on education, Babalola, Lungwangwa and Adeyinka (1999: 96) in their study of education under structural adjustment programme in Nigeria and Zambia concluded that "it is crucial for countries with developed economies to know that SAP, being a donor-driven programme, has negative effect on education in receiving countries."

In the final analysis, although several other factors have coalesced to force a decline in African education, SAPs have made their mark felt in this area. As earlier stated, it is difficult to see the rationale behind the demand by the World Bank and IMF that expenditure on education be cut as a condition for loans. The situation in the universities is that many professors in medical, engineering and other areas have left the universities for other professions or moved to other countries where they have the facilities to practice their profession. The hardship imposed by SAP reforms has seen university professors and their students go on strikes to demand better pay and facilities. It has turned the universities into centers of political activism and this has often elicited vendetta from military juntas.

Nigerian and other African universities used to compare well to other international universities but they have been deteriorating over the years, with SAPs compounding the problem and making the situation much worse. The January 2012 report of Webometrics, a tertiary education ranking institutions organisation, has shown that African universities are not doing well. For example, only three institutions in Nigeria made the list of first 100 best universities in Africa and absolutely none in the first 1,600 in the world. (For more on the deterioration of education in Nigeria, see Offiong 2008).

Africa is fast urbanising and by 2030, it is projected that half of its population will be living and working in cities and towns. Africa faces some serious challenges because it must prepare its population to participate in a globalising economy. The International Development Research Centre (IDRC), UNESCO and World Bank have provided some data about Africa that speak to the challenges ahead.

- Despite the improvement in literacy rates, approximately 40 percent of Africans over the age of 15, and 50 percent of women above the age of 25 remain illiterate.

- Illiteracy among persons over the age of 15 is about 41 percent; gender disparity in education exists in 75 percent of countries. Between 2000 and 2006, Seychelles had the highest adult literacy rate of 92 percent, while Mali and Burkina Faso had the lowest – 24 percent.
- Early childhood development in most countries is left to private sector actors primarily working in urban areas in aid of more advantaged groups.
- Over 50 percent of countries are unlikely to attain the goal of universal primary education by 2015; and nearly 40m children are not going to school.
- Liberia is said to have the lowest primary student-teacher ratio of 19. In Mozambique the ratio is 67. Cape Verde is credited for having the highest gross enrollment rate, that is, 80 percent, in secondary education; Niger on the other hand has the lowest – 11 percent.
- Enrollment in lower secondary schools rose to 46 percent in 2003 from 28 percent in 1991. The gross secondary school enrollment rate exceeds 20 percent in half of the countries, and yet remains below 8 percent in some 10 countries.
- It is further noted that higher education and other levels and forms of education do experience problems with respect to access, quality and relevance.
- HIV/AIDS pose the danger of claiming 10 percent of the lives of teachers within five years, and 20 percent of school-age children will be orphaned. Further, a minimum of three million more teachers are required in SSA to achieve the goal of universal primary education by 2015.

- The continent loses an estimated 20,000 skilled personnel a year to developed countries, what we have referred to here as brain drain.
- More people in New York are connected to the Internet than on the entire continent of Africa. In Liberia only 0.03 per 100 have access to the Internet; Seychelles does much better with 34 in every 100 people (Africa Grantmakers Affinity Group 2011a and 2011b).

The impact of SAPs has also been felt in the area of health care and we proceed to discuss it.

Impacts of SAPs on Health Care

Available evidence suggests that SAPs have severely aggravated the poverty and health problems of Africans, as indicative of the figures in the preceding paragraph. The World Bank had asked African countries to increase health spending once the adjustment reforms "start paying dividends," according to Zimbabwe-based World Bank representative, Christian Portman. Portman adds further that increasing the income of those in poverty is the most efficacious means for improving their lot, since people are most certain to spend it on health care, better food, safe water, sanitation and housing, all of which reduce disease (*Africa Recovery,* October 1993:15).

On the other hand, in direct response to the World Bank representative, Zimbabwe's Minister for Health and Child Welfare, Dr. Timothy Stamps, said that SAPs had been "playing havoc with the nation's health and threatening to swallow major health achievements." Since independence in 1980 Zimbabwe had been making significant progress in life expectancy, infant mortality and in repairing and expanding health care facilities throughout the nation (ibid.) but SAP had caused the deterioration of health care in that country.

The impact of SAPs on healthcare has been so devastating that the Canadian Council of Churches (CCC) and Inter-Church Coalition of Africa (ICCA) protested in a letter to the former World Bank President, Mr. Lewis Preston. According to the two bodies, orthodox SAPs have had "devastating impact" on health and livelihood in Sub-Saharan Africa. They stated that World Bank policies constitute an "assault on both the physical welfare and the basic human dignity of the poor." The churches argued that "access to health care is a basic human right" and that the World Bank's strategy of privatising health care "only increases inequities in access to health services" in a period of severe unemployment, skyrocketing prices and growing poverty. What the World Bank has done has been imposing the US marketplace approach which views health care as a commodity that is ultimately subject to demands and spending power of consumers. The churches argued further that multilateral debts of debt-distressed low and middle-income countries should be cancelled. They also charged the World Bank with worsening both health and development crises in the 1980s by shifting resources from development aid to debt repayments.

These have been happening at a period when foreign aid is shrinking. Foreign aid accounts for one-fifth of Africa's health spending and over 50 percent in Burundi, Chad, Guinea-Bissau, Mozambique and Tanzania. In several countries like Mozambique, it in addition finances over 90 percent of capital spending for health. Allocations for health have been declining at a time when Africa needs to wage war against a monstrous virus disease called AIDS. This killer disease is estimated to have caused 8.5 million premature deaths by the year 2000. The ten most affected African countries lose an estimated 0.6

percent in annual per capita income growth due to loss of productivity and expensive treatments, and while about one in three in some cities, is now HIV-Positive, total spending on AIDS prevention in the continent was only $90 million in 1992 (*Africa Recovery*, October 1993:14). In addition to AIDS, Africa must combat malaria which in a decade may cause double the number of deaths, that is, from one to two million. Africa has also been alerted that tobacco-related diseases cause more premature deaths in developing countries by the year 2025 than AIDS, TB and childbirth complications combined. AIDS statistics on Africa are staggering. Before giving current statistics, the following are the statistics in the height of the epidemics in the 1990s.

- With only 10 per cent of the world's population, Africa has 63 per cent of global HIV/AIDS cases. There are 21 million Africans infected with HIV/AIDS, and an average of more than 3,800 adults is infected with the virus every day in Africa.
- Some 95 per cent of Africans infected with HIV/AIDS live in abject poverty, with no hope of obtaining the new miracle drugs (for which Africans were the guinea pigs) that patients in developed countries use to combat the virus and lead comparatively normal lives.
- About 90 per cent of all HIV transmission in Africa occurs via heterosexual sex. This is 100 per cent preventable.
- An estimated 87 per cent of the world's children infected with the HIV virus live in Africa. More than eight million children in Sub-Saharan Africa have been orphaned by AIDS.
- AIDS has lowered average life expectancy levels by as such as 10-17 years in some African countries. In

hardest-hit Zimbabwe, AIDS has reduced life expectancy by more than 20 years.

- In the early 1980s HIV was found mainly in the swathe of territory from West Africa to Eastern Africa; countries north of the Sahara and in Southern Africa apparently were untouched. Today [1998] no part of the African continent is unaffected.
- AIDS has overtaken malaria and other diseases as the leading cause of death for adults between the ages of 15 and 49 in Botswana, Burundi, Malawi, Rwanda, Tanzania, Uganda, Zambia, and in capital cities such as Abidjan, Addis Ababa, Nairobi and Ouagadougou.
- HIV infection has spread far beyond the original sub-populations with high-risk behaviour into the general population of as many as 19 African countries.
- Up to 50 per cent of hospital beds are occupied by HIV/AIDS patients in many parts of Sub-Saharan Africa *(Africa Recovery,* November 1998: 11).

The situation is not better more than a decade later and I proceed to present some data drawn from various sources, including UCSF (University of California at San Francisco) (June 2011), USAID (2011),UNAIDS (2011), and Kates and Carbaugh (2006). The world has a population of 7bn and 34m are estimated to live with HIV/AIDS. As at 2009, Africa was estimated to have a population of about 1bn, while SSA was estimated to have a population of 836,000,000m. Out of the total of 34m living with HIV in the world, Africa has 22.5m (23m); North Africa and Middle East 470,000, South and South-East Asia 790,000, and Oceania 54,000. UNAIDS (2011) gives us estimated percentage as 68 percent of all people living with HIV/AIDS are in SSA. The top seven countries in Africa in which people are living with HIV/AIDS are South Africa (5,600,000), Nigeria (3,300,000), Kenya (1,500,000), Mozambique (1,400,000), Tanzania (1,400,000), Uganda (1,200,000), Zimbabwe (1,200,000). African women (aged 15+) living with HIV/AIDS number 12,100,000; children with HIV/AIDS number 2,300,000, and 1,300,000 die of AIDS each year.

It is clear that SSA continues to bear an inordinate burden of the global HIV/AIDS. The epidemics in SSA vary significantly, with the southern region being most severely affected. An estimated 11.3 million {10.6 million) people were living with HIV/AIDS in that part of the continent in 2009, accounting for nearly one third (31 percent) more than the 8.6 million {8.2 million – 9.1 million} people living with HIV/AIDS in the area a decade earlier. Globally, 34 percent of people living with HIV/AIDS in 2009 resided in the 10 countries in southern Africa; 31 percent of new HIV/AIDS infections in 2009 took place in these 10 countries, as did 34 percent of all AIDS-related deaths. And, about 40 percent of all adult women with HIV live in southern Africa (UCSF 2011). UNAIDS published some new statistics in November 2011, reflecting the end of 2010. Those statistics are not different from those of 2009 in that Africa still comes out worst.

As noted by Kates and Carbaugh (2006), the epidemic in SSA is increasingly female. Women account for the majority of those estimated to be living with HIV/AIDS. For example, in Kenya, approximately two thirds (65 percent) of all people living with HIV/AIDS are women; in Uganda, it is 60 percent.

The future seems dim. Africans were used as guinea pigs in the studies leading to the development of drugs, the so-called cocktail, now used in the US and in other Western countries. After the efficacy of the drugs had been ascertained, Africans could not benefit from their exploitation, because they cannot afford to pay the cost. This is exactly what happened in the development of the vaccine for hepatitis B. Africans are once again being used as guinea pigs in the study to develop vaccine for AIDS. They are likely to come out losers in the end. African countries should emphasise prevention of this deadly disease rather trying to acquire the miracle drugs that prolong life, because most have no money for them.

African countries are deeply immersed in SAPs and they are committed to public cuts, as demanded by the World Bank. The argument is that very few countries can boost health spending by 50 percent over the next five years, as urged by the World Bank. Zimbabwe is a relatively economically strong country and yet its per capita health spending has declined by 30 percent since its SAP began in 1991. Besides the drop, qualified nursing staff levels and drug supply, new medical fees have supplanted subsidies on health care, and some old fees have risen by between 40 and 105 percent. As evidence that few people could afford hospital treatment, bed occupancy in Harare's central hospital has fallen by 34 percent since 1991. A trade union study in Zimbabwe found that failing to afford medical fees, many workers in the clothing and textile sector resort to traditional healers and prophets. This, in fact, is exactly what has been happening in Nigeria (Offiong, 1989). According to *Africa Recovery* (October 1993:15), a UNICEF survey in 1992 found that after one year of SAP, the number of women dying in childbirth recorded in Harare had risen by 100 percent. This is a reflection of the current harsh socio-economic conditions now translating into mortality trends" (ibid.). UNICEF accused the World Bank of running with the hare and hunting with the hound, when it demands adjustment and simultaneously recommends investment in health. According to Paul Nwabuikwu *et al* (*The African Guardian,* June 19, 1989:11), the World Bank defines SAP as "the reform policies and institutions to improve resource allocations, increase economic efficiency, expand growth potential and increase resilience to future shock." What SAPs seek to accomplish in the short-run constitute a millstone around the neck of Africans.

Even the World Bank itself in its report on adjustment lending (RAL-111) concedes that total sector spending was often maintained at the cost of "excessive cuts" in related operations and maintenance spending, resulting in "schools without teaching materials, health clinics without drugs and supplies. Adjustment lending rarely pushes for improved delivery of basic social services, rather important imbalances within sectors have persisted or worsened, with few cases of successful reallocation of social spending in favour of primary education and health. For the World Bank, health care, and primary and secondary education are cost-effective ways of increasing the productivity and welfare of the poor *(Africa Recovery,* December 1992-February 1993:13).

Higher spending can conceal declining social returns, according to the World Bank. Fast increases in current education spending in both Ivory Coast and Kenya have reflected increase in increasing staff costs while enrollment stagnated. The impact of declining spending for operations and maintenance include decaying and often unsanitary infrastructure and lack of drugs and teaching materials, "leading to serious deterioration in the efficiency of personnel and the quality of basic social life." The World Bank even admits that poverty reduction and general social sector concerns were "largely absent" from SAPs until 1987. From that time on the World Bank has supported special social funds and action programmes "should not be a substitute for more fundamental restructuring of social sector spending to increase efficiency and reduce poverty," as they hope to soften the blows of adjustment on vulnerable categories only in the short-term.   The RAL-11 report further stated that the 1980s witnessed an average decline of 25 percent in spending on economic infrastructure – in addition to transport and communications – in an example of 11 intensive adjustment countries.   "This decline reflects the falling budget share of materials, supplies and maintenance, 'most notably roads' which have been rehabilitated at substantial foreign currency cost,   only   to   become   impassable   for   lack   of maintenance"(ibid.).

Africa's problem goes much deeper than lack of priority and lack of funds, the debt servicing and payments to foreign creditors, adjustment policies and declining commodity prices have disproportionate pressure on health and education budgets (Ogan, December-1993-March 1994) and have serious repercussions on poverty. In her study of SAP and the delivery of health care in the Third World, Bianca Brunelli (2007: 25-26) conclude that the World Bank and IMF have adopted neoliberal inspired policies to try to "alleviate the economic difficulties" faced by poor countries. However, despite their intentions, the World Bank and IMF's "involvement has exacerbated poverty... key factors in structural adjustment programmes have impeded health delivery and have contributed to increased rates of morbidity and mortality." In short, their programmes have worsened matters for poor countries.

SAPs Intensify Poverty

I have repeatedly made references to the impact of SAPs on poverty in the continent of Africa and it is time to expatiate on it. The IMF and World Bank provide financial assistance to those countries that seek it, but impose conditionalities. Among such conditionalities are cutbacks, trade liberalisation, privatisation of public companies, minimising the role of government, currency devaluation, eliminating subsidies, among others. All these have adverse repercussions. Because the poor countries have to export more to stay afloat, there is a large-scale price war, which makes the resources of these countries cheaper.   Since they have to compete for new businesses from abroad, they have to try to give the most favourable conditions to would-be investors. The culmination of all these is that governments become authoritarian by being overprotective of foreign investors by promoting starvation wages as part of the spiraling race to the bottom.   People become dissatisfied and what usually follows is social unrest and the government aligns with foreign companies to oppress the very people they are supposed to serve and protect.

The policies of the two international financial institutions have encouraged dependency and poverty in Africa. As observed by Global Exchange (2001: 1), "by insisting that national leaders place the interests of international financial investors above the needs of their citizens, the IMF and the World Bank have short circuited the accountability at the heart of self-governance, thereby corrupting the democratic process." The subordination of social needs to concerns of foreign financial markets has, in turn, made it quite difficult for national governments to ensure that their people receive food, health care, and education – basic human rights as defined by the Universal Declaration of Human Rights. Both banks have eroded basic human rights; they have perverted the democratic process, and have made themselves "a clear and present threat to the well being of hundreds of millions of people worldwide" (ibid). This negative effect of the policies of these financial institutions has been further succinctly stated by Colgan (2002): "Over the past two decades, the World Bank and International Monetary Fund ... have undermined Africa's health through the policies they have imposed." The dependence of poor and highly indebted African countries on World Bank and IMF have indeed forced the poor African governments to orient their economies toward greater integration in international markets at the expense of social services and real long-term development priorities. They have reduced the role of the state and cut back government expenditure to the detriment of the people (ibid.).

Continuing its criticism of the World Bank and the IMF, Global Exchange (2001) states that for well over 50 years, the IMF and the World Bank "have advanced a form of economic 'development' that prioritises the concern of wealthy leaders and multinational corporations in the industrialised north while neglecting the needs of the world's poor majority"(ibid.). These institutions "work as a kind of international loan shark, exerting enormous influence over the economies of more than 60 countries" (ibid.). As stated before, in order to get loans, international assistance, and debt relief, affected countries must first agree to conditions set by the two financial institutions. Operating under the guise of promoting "free trade," market liberalisation, and financial stability. These two institutions have imposed cuts in health care, education and other social services for millions of people across the planet, thereby deepening poverty and increasing inequality. By elevating concerns about all other competing values, the institutions have created a human rights catastrophe" (ibid.). In the same vein, Cogan (2001) states that because of the imposed conditions of the two banks 48 Sub-Saharan countries spend about $13.5bn every year repaying debts to rich foreign creditors for "past loans of questionable legitimacy." These huge debt repayments divert money directly from basic human needs such as health care and education, and further fundamentally undermine African government's ability to fight against AIDS pandemic. There are numerous ways in which the international financial institutions have negatively affected Africa. Such huge transfer of capital to already rich countries makes it difficult to engage in any meaningful development. And, as we can see, Robin Hood has been taking from the poor and giving to the rich, the very opposite of what should be happening.

Kicking the Habit

In its report titled "Kicking the Habit: How the World Bank and the IMF are still addicted to attaching economic policy conditions to aid," Oxfam International (2006) laments that despite numerous commitments to reform, the two banks continue to use aid to force developing countries to implement "inappropriate economic policies, with the tacit approval of rich countries, this undermine national policy-making, delay aid flows, and often fail to deliver for poor people" (ibid.). If the world really intends to eliminate poverty, this practice has to end. The only appropriate condition should be for aid to be spent transparently and on reducing poverty.

Rich countries have the right to demand that their aid be spent appropriately. But what they should not be doing is use their aid to push economic policy reforms such as privatisation and liberalisation on poor countries, which in the end benefit the rich countries. This is exactly what the two financial institutions have been doing, with the tacit approval and support of their rich-country shareholders. Oxfam argues that economic policy conditionality "stops aid working." It interferes or undermines "national decision-making, vital for successful development."

For a long time, there has been a growing international consensus that economic policy conditionality does not work. "Policy conditionality ... is both an infringement on sovereignty and ineffective as observed by Africa Commission in 2005 (ibid.). In 2006, the Norwegian government studied IMF conditionalities and came to the conclusion that 26 out of 40 poor countries still have privatisation and liberalisation conditions attached to their IMF loans. Even the World Bank which favours economic policy conditionalities seems to have realised the inimical nature of this requirement and then "agreed to use it far more sparingly and only when two important safeguards were met" (ibid).

Using Mali as a case study, Oxfam shows how conditionality hurts that country. It reveals that far from leading to economic growth and poverty reduction, conditions have instead "hike electricity prices and are likely to hurt cotton farmers as well as delaying aid flows and undermining country ownership policies" (ibid.)

With reference to the particular case of privatisation, as required by SAPs, the ostensible outcome it seeks is increasing the efficiency and investment and decreasing state spending. But the fact is that state-owned resources are required to be sold regardless of whether they generate a fiscal profit or not. When resources are transferred to foreign corporations and/or national elites, as they always are, the goal of public prosperity gives way for private accumulation. State-owned firms may show fiscal losses because they play a wider social role, such as providing low-cost utility jobs. But privatisation has negatively affected many developing countries. For example, the privatisation of water in Bolivia and the privatisation of the health system in SSA have had negative repercussions (Wikipedia 2010:4).

Development Injustice

In its 2006 research report titled "World Bank and IMF Conditionality: A Development Injustice," Eurodad examines the conditions that the World Bank and IMF attach to their development lending in some of the world's poorest countries. The report discovered that "impoverished countries still face an unacceptably high and rising number of conditions in order to gain access to World Bank and IMF development finance" (p.3). The report notes further that on average poor countries face as many as 67 conditions per World Bank loan; but some face a far higher number of conditions. It cites Uganda as having "a staggering 197 conditions attached to its World Bank development finance in 2005," and this is a country where 23 percent of all the children under five are malnourished (ibid.).

In addition to exacting massive administrative burden on already over-stretched developing governments, the proliferation of World Bank and IMF conditions often force highly controversial economic reforms on very poor countries, like trade liberalisation and privatisation of essential services. These reforms regularly go against developing countries' wishes, a known and accepted prerequisite for any successful development. The tendency is for them to have a harmful impact on poor people, by increasing their poverty, rather than reducing it, and denying them access to vital services.

Bail-out or Blow-out

According to Molina-Gallart (2009:3), author of the Eurodad research report, titled "Bail-out or blow-out: IMF policy advice and condition for low-income countries at a time of crises," the leaders of the world's two richest countries did at the London summit in April 2009 decide that the IMF will become "a major instrument to respond to the financial and economic crisis." They agreed to quadruple the IMF's resources from $250bn to $1tn. But Eurodad questioned the fitness of the IMF for the purpose, because the IMF has been in the habit of imposing harmful conditions on countries in the wake of the 1990s crisis which helped to sink their countries further. They wondered what would be the outcome of the G20 decision for the tens of millions of people who are already suffering from the combination of the food, financial, economic and climate crises. In its report, Eurodad states that IMF "is still advising stringent fiscal and monetary policies to low income countries as well as controversial structural reforms" (p.3). Eurodad continues that if the IMF is to provide funding to poor countries to meet the financial gap created by the crisis, it must change real soon.

The World Bank and IMF policy on SAPs has drawn a number of criticisms but the banks have always insisted that their programmes work well. We now visit the reaction of the World Bank (and indirectly the IMF) to the vituperative criticisms following their activities all over the developing world.

The World Bank and IMF Reactions to Criticisms

The World Bank has had some colossal failures that have generated biting criticisms, as presented above. For so many years, the World Bank has been accused of promoting a brand of market fundamentalism that has so far served rich corporate interests at the expense of impoverished hundreds of millions in the developing world. We have reported in this work bank-imposed privatisation and downsizing of the public sector that has left poor countries quite unable to educate their citizens, promote health care or build up their weak economies. The

World Bank has a penchant for mega development projects that have devastated ecosystems of countries all over the developing world, destroyed the livelihoods of millions of indigenous populations and small-scale farmers and "set developing countries on a dirty and unsustainable energy pathways" (Weissman 2012:5).

What has been the World Bank's reaction to all the vituperative complaints about SAPs' performance? This answer can be found in the World Bank reports. I will first present the reports and then take issue with them. According to the World Bank (September 1992), about a decade of structural adjustment has left low-income Sub-Saharan countries still "barely growing" in per capita terms, and at rates quite inadequate for reasonable reduction in poverty. In yet another report, the World Bank (October 1992) said that structural adjustment had left much to be desired in terms of restoring growth and social welfare to Sub-Saharan Africa. The World Bank (October 1992) noted that adjustment lending helped Sub-Saharan export performance but also led to a "significant drop in investment ratio," and had minimal effect on inflation and domestic savings. The World Bank's third report on adjustment lending (RAL-111) claimed that both exports and savings reacted weakly in African and other low-income countries; that total investment dropped, on average, and with few exceptions, private investment "remains generally at inadequate levels." Even in countries like Ghana and Kenya where yearly growth averaged about 5 percent in the late 1980s, relative successes were "fragile, with ... risks of reversal" (Bentsi-Enchill, December 1992—February 1993:13).

Sub-Saharan African countries were not among the World Bank's "star performers" of adjustment such as South Korea, Indonesia (before the collapse of the Asian economic miracle), Mexico and Morocco. These poor results for African and other low-income countries are explained in terms of often stringent adjustment measures than middle-income countries. The RAL-111 report lays blame on the lower levels of development in the sub-region which is characterised by inadequate human resources, institutions and infrastructure, as well as poor governance. SAPs had disappointing results in Sub-Saharan Africa partly because they were "too ambitious and included too many conditions" to ensure sustainability. Compared to other regions, Africa's success in implementing SAP conditions was "below average," thereby damaging the credibility of the reforms and investor uncertainty. But the World Bank noted that the poor performance of adjustment in Sub-Saharan Africa "lends credence" to the demands for economic reform programmes of which the conception and time-frame are clearly adapted to Africa's economic structures.

SAPs did not reduce poverty in Africa, instead poverty "almost certainly increased" in low-income countries, before getting better in the late 1980s. Despite this condition, the World Bank contended that the poor were "clearly better off" under most SAPs than they would have been without systematic adjustment, and suffered greatly in countries that abandoned adjustment. According to the World Bank, Zambia, Ivory Coast and Tanzania have been failures because they abandoned SAPs and consequently fared worse than those that stock to intensive adjustment. Thus, despite its admission of the woeful failure of SAPs in the continent, the World Bank is still willing to argue that SAPs are succeeding and that they are still essential for development.

To prove its point, the World Bank undertook a study of 26 African countries implementing SAPs. The World Bank then came out with a 1994 report, titled *Adjustment in Africa: Reforms, Results and the Road Ahead.* For the analysis of this report, I draw from Laishley (December 1993-March 1994a) and Lone (December 1993-March 1994). According to the World Bank, adjustment is working in Africa and countries that underwent the most comprehensive and terribly demanding reform programmes reaped the fastest turnaround in growth rates, while those that undertook modest reforms and those that did not reform at all realised little improvement or deterioration. These findings remain valid "even after allowing for the impact of external factors such as aid flows and trade losses" (Laishley, December 1993-March 1994:1). The World Bank states that a lot more still remains to be done, for a continent that many observers say is already suffering from "adjustment fatigue." At the launch of the report in 1994, Mr. Edward Cox, then World Bank's Vice President for Africa said that "the good news is that some African countries have improved their policies and reaped the gains in higher rates of growth." However, there is still some bad news, and that is, African countries "still have a long way to go in implementing the policies needed for growth sufficient to reduce poverty at a reasonable rate" (ibid.).

After closely monitoring 26 Sub-Saharan African countries, the World Bank concluded that six – Burkina Faso, The Gambia, Ghana, Nigeria, Tanzania and Zimbabwe – have improved policies the most and realised the returns. However, "current growth rates among the best African performers are still too low to reduce poverty much in the next two or three decades." As if the World Bank was reacting to constant criticisms, the report stated that adjustment in general had not engendered a high social cost and was helping to reduce poverty, even though evidence remains inconclusive due to inadequate data. The World Bank's Vice President sought some refuge by stating that adjustment simply represents "the tip of the iceberg of development efforts in Africa ... it is not a substitute for strong public investment programmes, capacity-building and better public sector management" (ibid.).

The World Bank contended that the foundation for growth involves reduction in "budget deficits, flexible exchange rates, controlling inflation, freeing agriculture from price controls and taxes, reducing trade barriers and reforming the public and financial sectors" (Laishley, December1993-March 1994b: 16). In ranking countries by their policy performance, however, the World Bank chose just three areas - fiscal, monetary and change rate policy. The six countries which did the best in putting appropriate measures into practice during "adjustment period" from 1987-1991, had a median improvement of 1.8 percent. The nine moderate adjusters experienced a median improvement of 1.5 percentage points in average per capita growth rates between the two periods, though their average per capita remained negative. As for those countries where policies degenerated, there was a median decline in growth rates 2.6 percentage points.

The World Bank said that the differences in performance between countries with improving and degenerating policies, was the same for most indicators. Countries which made the most sweeping changes in policies realised the largest upturns in growth of exports and industrial production and, where agricultural reforms were undertaken in addition, for farm output as well. But the World Bank admits that less satisfactory progress has been achieved in the vital areas of public sector and financial reform. The World Bank further admits that reforms are accompanied only by very modest growth of 0.4 percent per capita during 1987-91 for all 15 countries where policies showed improvement. It also admits that countries have experienced difficulty in sticking with "the reform process in all its necessary rigour," with 11 out of 26 countries demonstrating a degeneration in policies and Nigeria, one of its best performers, abandoned the measures the World Bank contends are most crucial for growth.

Despite available data to the contrary, the World Bank in its reports states that adjustment is helping the poor in Africa. It notes that "the poor are probably better off and almost certainly no worse off ... There is every reason to think that (adjustment) has helped the ... Often the poor would have benefited from more adjustment ... It is a sorry state of affairs when we know least about poverty in the region where poverty is most a problem" (cited in Laishley, December 1993-March 1994:19). These statements seem to suggest that the World Bank is trying to cover up something. From what we know about adjustment in Africa, the poor have been getting poorer. The World Bank's claims that social costs have largely been confined to the relatively well-off urban areas, with the "silent majority"- Africa's poor, small farming households – benefiting from reforms are ridiculous. These claims are quickly qualified. Madagascar and some other countries have been hurt by reforms by way of reductions in subsidies; that early adjustment programmes "did not pay enough attention" to ensuring adequate provision of services to the poor; and it admits that the primary objective of adjustment is not conquering poverty and that the direct fight against poverty must come from wider development and investment programmes. The World Bank concedes that early advocates of adjustment had anticipated immediate returns from reforms but it adds that "opponents have wrongly cast and criticised adjustment as an alternative to measures supporting long-term development."

Responses to this report from various quarters were swift and critical. Africa is concerned with two aspects of the programme namely, "how to make more socially and politically sustainable, and how to ensure it reduces poverty in what is already the world's most impoverished continent" (ibid.). These concerns are strengthened by the World Bank's statement that in Ghana, the country it considers as having the most effective adjustment policies, the poor "will not cross the poverty line for another fifty years," and that after a decade of implementing structural adjustment programmes, not even one African country has achieved a sound macroeconomic policy (Lone, December 1993-March 1994:18).

Not surprisingly, Oxfam, an English non-governmental organisation referred to the report as "a blend of half-truths, over-simplifications and institutional propaganda." And, Douglas Hellinger of the Development Group for Alternative Policies, testifying before the US Senate, blasted the report as "deceptive" and as an "insensitive attempt to dismiss the realities and suffering of the poor with self-serving assumptions." The optimistic tone of the Bank's report prompted Tim Carrington of the *Wall Street Journal* to write that "the report's message belies the huge size of Africa's development task. The amount of growth that African states can generate by sound macro-economic policies alone is too paltry to relieve significantly the wretched poverty of the continent" (cited in ibid.).

The World Bank report dodged the central issue that commands the attention of various groups in the continent of Africa, namely, the trade unions and non-governmental organisations (NGOs), that the World Bank's version of adjustment reform is deepening misery in the continent. The UN General Assembly was so concerned that in its December 1993 session it demanded that proper attention be given "to eradicating poverty and addressing the social impact" of adjustment. In the same vein the former UN Secretary-General, Boutros Boutros-Ghali remarked that "structural adjustment is not popular on the streets of Africa. The fruits of these efforts have yet to ripen, but the hardships they have brought are already very apparent" (ibid.).

As we noted earlier, the World Bank President, Lewis Preston had stressed that reduction of poverty and economic growth were the two benchmarks by which the Bank would measure its success in Africa in the 1980s. Despite this report being its "most comprehensive" attempt on what the Bank considers "one of the most controversial aspects of its involvement in Africa," the Bank failed to investigate the impact of adjustment on poverty. Instead, the Bank simply asserted that "the poor are probably better off and almost certainly no worse off" as the result of adjustment, but the same Bank admits that it does not have concrete and systematic evidence to support the claim. It could not, because such evidence does not exist. What exists is the preponderance of evidence to the effect that poverty is ubiquitous and that it is growing much worse as the result of the Bank's version of adjustment. Having asserted that not even one Sub-Saharan African country has succeeded in achieving a sound macro-economic policy, the Bank should have attempted to evaluate how long it can keep proposing policies which as they now are, remain largely inoperable. There is need to tackle the central issue of how to make "the advocated reforms more sustainable politically and socially" (Lone, December 1993-March 1994:47). By exhibiting an aloof attitude, the World Bank consigns itself to the accusation that it is a "foreign" institution that is far removed from Africa's reality. It lends support to the charge that it is an imperialist institution bent on re-conquering and strengthening or consummating the new neo-dependency status of the continent.

There are also some "questionable interpretations" of the Bank's data. Although the Bank says that countries which were the best reformers registered the best turnaround in GDP, some of the Bank's own data do not allow one to draw such a categorical linkage. Lone (December 1993-March 1994:47) has listed some of the contradictions arising from their data:

- Two of the Bank's best four performers, The Gambia and Burkina Faso, appear in the bottom half of the ranking for economic performance. Further, six countries whose economic performance places them in the top half – Mozambique, Uganda, Sierra Leone, Niger, Zambia and Gabon – were considered by the Bank to be poor performers. Mozambique and Uganda really placed first and third in economic performance.

- In agriculture countries in the top categories of macro-economic policy reformers recorded a decline in average yearly growth rates, and were outperformed even by those countries in the "deterioration" category.

- Although the Bank tends to take issue with "aggregative analysis" that seems to obscure variations in performance by individual African countries, the Bank's report is not averse to smaller "aggregations" which may suit its own purpose. It is difficult to justify the inclusion of Zimbabwe among the top performers between 1987-1991' when that country never began implementing a Bank adjustment programme until 1991.

- The Bank's contention that the "adding up" problem, that is, where higher agricultural commodity production lowers international prices, is restricted to only a few exports raises concerns because these account for more than half of the continent's export revenues. Further the Bank's conclusions on the impact of increased production on revenues will produce happy hunting grounds for skeptics.

- It is surprising that the Bank concludes that declining terms of trade did not have any significant impact on the continent's economic performance. This is contradicted by a study subsequently released by the IMF. We briefly review that report.

The publication of the IMF report in September 1993 never clearly brought out the value of SAPs to Africa. The report entitled *Economic Adjustment in Low-Income Countries – Experience Under the Enhanced Structural Adjustment Facility*, was a study of 19 countries, fifteen of which are in Africa, using the IMF's enhanced structural facility (ESAF). For the Managing Director of IMF, Michael Camdessus, the study was a forthright proof that ESAF was responsible for the progress of the 19 countries studied, and that "on average" the 19 countries experienced improvements in most economic indicators. However, he also said that debt relief and favourable terms of trade had been at least as important as adjustment policies in bringing about positive economic performance. The claim is that performance was strongest in those countries with "sustained and comprehensive" SAPs. The best macroeconomic improvements took place in countries that carried out "the most forceful reforms and suffered the least from weakening terms of trade," and "clear-cut conclusions on the reasons for differences in countries' performance have proved difficult to draw." The ESAF is a 1987 follow-up to the structural adjustment facility (SAF) set up by the IMF in 1986 to provide highly concessional loans to debt-distressed, low-income countries. By mid-1993, some 36 countries had SAF agreements and 29 countries had moved on to the more stringent conditionality of the ESAF (Wall, December 1993-arch 1994:20).

As its main criterion for measuring the impact of the ESDAF, the IMF uses progress toward external viability, that is, reduced debt-to-export ratios and debt-service burdens. However, the IMF associates progress in 11 countries not only to the advantageous impact of the ESAF, but also to "increased concessions on debt (cancellation and easier terms)" as well as to "strong export growth." In other countries, "debt and debt service remain so high that even the strongest domestic policy efforts would be insufficient to restore external viability in the foreseeable future." A successful reform in these countries will require "substantial" concessional financing and debt cancellation. The study noted that in all 11 countries with improved viability, average yearly growth in the previous three years was 2 percent higher than in the three pre-SAF/ESAF years. Over comparable period, yearly growth dropped slightly in the eight countries with little or no progress towards external viability (ibid.).

For countries experiencing degenerating terms of trade, the IMF recommended "highly concessional" financing and debt relief "particularly when there is no strong reason to believe that deterioration will be reversed soon." It added further that "the strength of adjustment" should immediately be re-evaluated, indicating a need for more flexible conditionality. The report contains something slightly encouraging. In general, ESAF countries as at 1993 had "on the average" witnessed overall progress of GDP, trade volumes, inflation and debt ratios. On the other hand, there was "relatively small response of investment ratios and the persistence of low savings ratios," thus confirming the critique that SAPs emphasise deficit reduction at the expense of increasing productive capacity. The study noted that capital expenditure tended to decline during adjustment. Other than in Mozambique and Uganda, capital expenditure dropped by almost 1 percent of GDP. According to the study, in Ghana, Guinea, Niger, Tanzania, Togo and Uganda, where higher producer prices and marketing board reforms made for improved conditions and incentives for agricultural production, the result was improved living standards for the rural poor. Simultaneously, "weak information bases made it difficult to evaluate the social impact of adjustment." According to Wall (ibid.), "ambiguous data ... hampers the evaluation of SAP fiscal policies." The study states that on average, "most countries" managed modest cuts in budget deficits of some 2 percent relative to GDP, but that the two-thirds of them were already making some progress in deficit reduction before entering SAF/ESAF agreements. The IMF then recommended continued efforts to rein in fiscal deficits, credit expansion and inflation. It further called for more technical assistance from multilateral institutions to reinforce the administrative capacity of African governments.

From the data presented thus far, it is clear that SAPs do not work in Africa; they have not been helping in reducing poverty. Few, if any, reform programmes have achieved the targeted growth rate or increase in per capita agricultural production, or improved the present account balance and external debt position (Sandbrook, 1991:95). All that we have seen are attempts by the financial institutions trying to whitewash very gloomy reports of their performances in the continent. The causes of the feebleness of Africa's recovery efforts are several and I agree with Sandbrook (ibid.) who has contended that "international factors form a major set of impediments."

The IMF/World Bank's policy of export promotion is often misconceived in a world where commodity markets remain soft and many developing countries continue to specialise in the same primary commodities. The continent's payments on its enormous external debt also hobble recovery. The major trading partners, key aid donors and creditors in the West have not been supportive of the painful economic reforms with the requisite level of financing and improved traditional conditions.   In addition to appropriate prices, agricultural production requires credit availability, reliable infrastructure and research; but these non-price factors have often suffered as a result of austerity induced declines in development expenditures.

On the domestic front, "political and administrative" factors which structural adjustment programmes have unintentionally exacerbated have constituted impediments. State incapacity and economic crisis are closely related and "the technocratic orientation of structural adjustment" has perhaps unintentionally aggravated the ungovernability of countries already reeling from sagging living standards. SAPs have failed to produce favourable results in Africa. It is this failure that prompted the May 1994 conference of the UN Economic Commission for Africa (ECA) in Addis Ababa, Ethiopia and I proceed to discuss the conclusions of that conference.

ECA's Reaction to Failure of SAPs

According to Harsch (April-September 1994:1), "increasing Africa's capacity to implement its own development plans was the prime concern" of the Addis Ababa conference. If Africa is to double average per capita income and reduce poverty by 50 percent within two decades, Africa will need both much higher rates of gross domestic savings (GDS), and massive increase in external financing. Africa, according to ECA, needs to raise and maintain GDI at 35 percent and GDS at 25-35 percent GDP to attain 6 percent a year economic growth for the 1993-2005 period. The "enormity of the task" is testified to by the fact that since 1980 Africa's GDI has averaged a paltry 20 percent of GDP and only about 15 percent in Sub-Saharan countries.

Furthermore, the ECA noted that for the period 1993-2005, Africa would also need external financing of $950 billion (in 1990 dollars) of which $490 billion "would cover external debt service payments, leaving $460 billion for capital investments in Africa." The ECA emphasised the domestic imperative for the continent maintaining commitment to structural reforms that increase economic efficiency and competitiveness; it however, noted two external factors that "will continue to exercise veto power over the pace of Africa's development" in the 21st century. These are the "structural trade balance," particularly for low-income countries, and the external debt burden.

On trends as they were at that time, the ECA forecast a cumulative trade deficit of some $654 billion for low-income Africa by the year 2015. It contended that Africa would need substantial credits and grants, otherwise "capacity building will be slow, especially in the areas of physical infrastructures and production plants; competitiveness will continue to be lost, diversification of the production and export base will be slow and hesitant; and economic stagnation and social decline will continue" (*Africa Recovery*, April-September 1994:31). Africa's export losses from the Uruguay Round, which we discussed earlier, are "simply not sustainable" when it is already "the most structurally disadvantaged region in the world trading system," according to the ECA Executive Secretary, Layashi Yaker (ibid.).

The ECA also estimated that almost half of low-income Africa's external financing gap in the 1995-2015 period will be due to debt-service obligations which will total over $499 billion. Creditors have taken "only weak measures" to address Africa's 'old' debt although they generally know that it is "largely unpayable and an impediment to recovery." The ECA stated that debt reduction is essential in order to revive confidence, attracting foreign investment and flight capital, and restoring growth in the short-to-medium term, and "depends entirely on the goodwill of the creditors." The ECA then called on creditors to show their commitment to Africa's recovery by reducing the debt burden "to a point where it ceases to inhibit investing in Africa's future."   The ECA conference then concluded that the immediate task for African governments was to significantly improve their debt payment capacities, to better handle the 'old' debt and negotiate reductions, as well as to prudently manage 'new' debt from the beginning. African countries must not depend on official development finance flows to cover financing gaps. Rather, "they must do their utmost" to attract investment; long-term bank lending; and short-term lines of credit to cover imports (*Africa Recovery,* April-September 1994:31).

Conclusion
It is evident from the analysis that SAPs are not doing Africa much good. The international financial institutions that direct and manage SAPs have assumed the role of colonial administrators and administrations. In designing SAPs, African leaders' views are never sought.   The leaders of the international financial institutions assume the role of authoritarian rulers who act on behalf of their people because they "know" exactly what is good for them. The World Bank

and IMF have assumed a role that smacks of colonial authoritarianism. Like colossuses they bestride the narrow economic world of Africa and African leaders must inevitably walk under their huge legs and make themselves dishonourable graves. Financial administration is part of the "unique" Western experience. Some call it "civilisation." Under colonialism the colonial imperialists ruled the people without their consent, churning out authoritative proclamations, because it was they, and they only, who knew what was good for the people; and whatever was good for the people must first benefit the colonialists. Whatever benefits the colonised may have received were mere by-products of their exploitation. Under neocolonialism, the neocolonial powers ruled through remote control, so that despite all their involvements in the daily running of African countries, their hands never really showed. Even when their hands showed, the doctrine of plausible deniability allowed them to quickly deny it and blame every upheaval they helped to instigate on the war lords or evolutionary atavism.

Under the new neo-dependency, however, the foreign actors control the show. Cheered on by the Western countries that dominate the World Bank and IMF and the Paris Club – the key aid donors – the two international financial institutions impose incessant conditionalities which are not only related to economic and financial management, but also to the overall running of government. In other words, these conditionalities even directly affect governance. The basic interest of the financial institutions is to make sure that these poor countries continue to pay their debt, even when their people are starving to death. They also want to make sure that the poor countries remain perpetually attached to the imposed international division of labour, that of producing raw materials for the industrialised countries.

As the poor countries compete for limited customers in the raw materials market, it is certain that the prices of these primary commodities will remain cheap. Economically powerless because of the irksome debt burden, African leaders can only kick and scream, but they must comply if they are to get the foreign exchange on which they depend to service their debts and purchase whatever they can afford from the industrial countries. This is where power theory manifests itself. The West controls what the poor countries of Africa need in this asymmetrical relationship, the interests of Africa must be subordinated to those of the West, represented by the World Bank and IMF. Having been abandoned by the captains of industries and having lost its importance due to certain changes in the international political and economic order, Africa has been greatly marginalised and almost totally dependent on international financial institutions and aid donors. Thus whoever pays the piper must dictate the tune. Even though there may be some resistance here and there by special interest groups and even governments, lacking in any better alternatives, they must comply with the ever multiplying conditionalities or they are immediately cut off from their main source of funds. Indeed, Africa is a new neodependency.

It does seem that the World Bank has a penchant for trying to mislead the world. It used its near total monopoly of control of global poverty figures to support its policies of deregulation, privatisation, market liberalisation, and increased economic growth through free trade as the panacea for and the *sine qua non* to fighting poverty. As we noted in a previous chapter Adam W. Parsons of Share the World Resources (STWR) has accused the World Bank for misleading figures. In August 2008 the World Bank published its revised figures on poverty by saying that there were extra 430 million more people living in absolute poverty. This contradicted the

Bank's celebrated decline in extreme poverty it reported previously. The number of poor rose from 986 million in 2004 to 1.4bn in 2005. Despite this accelerated increase, the Bank still stated that poverty eradication was progressing well. Again, we have to state that in Africa the number of the poor doubled under globalisation, from 200m in 1981 to 380m in 2005, with half the population of SSA still living below the poverty line. It is impossible for this continent to meet the Millennium Development Goals set at 2015. This goes a long way to confirm the failure of SAPs and the very poor work of the World Bank and IMF.

Let me end this analysis of the negative impacts of SAPs by summarising Naiman and Watkins (1999:2) who in their survey of the impacts of IMF structural adjustment in Africa, in which they examined growth, social spending, and debt relief, came to the following conclusions:

- All developing countries in the world implementing IMF's Enhanced Structural Adjustment Facility (ESAF) "have experienced lower economic growth" than those who have not participated in the programmes; that African countries "have fared even worse than other countries pursuing" the same programmes; that African countries "have actually seen their per capita income decline;" and that it will take "years before these populations recover the per capita incomes that they had prior to structural adjustment".

- At a time when African countries should be increasing spending on health care, education and sanitation, IMF SAPs have compelled them to reduce spending. For those countries pursuing SAPs, the average amount of per capita government spending on education actually declined between 1986 and 1996.

- As we already noted, these two authors conclude that neither IMF-mandated macroeconomic policies nor debt relief under the IMF-sponsored HIPC Initiative have in any significant way reduced these countries' debt burdens. Total external debt as a share of GNP for ESAF countries increased from 71.1 percent to 87.8 percent between 1985 and 1995. For SSA debt rose as a share of GDP from 58 percent in 1988 to 70 percent in 1996. Clearly, IMF debt relief has not in any sufficient way reduced the debt service burden of Uganda or Mozambique, the two African HIPC countries that qualified to move further under the HIPC initiative. The result has been that poor countries continue to divert resources from expenditures on health care and education in order to service their external debt ibid.).
- They finally conclude that "efforts to increase economic growth, increase access to health care and education, and reduce the burden of debt repayment are likely to fail so long as the IMF remains in control of the economic policies of countries in Sub-Saharan Africa" (ibid.). They call for continued efforts to reduce Africa's debt burden and this must be coupled with efforts to reduce the role of IMF, and that "debt cancellation or relief should not be conditioned upon compliance with the IMF's structural adjustment programmes or policies" (ibid.).

In sum, SAPs have not been able to solve the problems of developing countries. Despite the professed intensions, they have turned out to be quite detrimental to the societies they have been designed to assist; they have compounded and made the solution impossible. They have further tightened the dependency of the countries involved. The benefits of SAPs go to the creditors on whose behalves the IMF and World Bank work.

8

Illicit Financial Flows
from Developing Countries

From the failures of SAPs engineered or orchestrated by the World Bank and IMF, we discuss the enormous amounts of money that leave poor, developing countries to rich, powerful countries. Africa, for example has been described as a beggar continent. A lot has been said about foreign aid squandered by leaders of the continent. Little, however, do people realise that much of the funds that come to Africa by way of aid and other sources find their way back to the very countries that provided the aid in the first place. The facts we present here will show that illicit financial flows compound the problem of development and poverty in the continent.

Introduction

In 2005 Raymond W. Baker, then Senior Fellow at Center for International Policy, published his world celebrated book *Capitalism's Achilles Heel: Dirty Money and How to Renew the Free-Market System.* For more than 40 years in more than 60 countries, including Nigeria, Baker witnessed the free-market system operating illicitly and corruptly, with terrible consequences. He provides a fascinating analysis of the way criminals, terrorists, and business people move dirty money around the globe, impoverishing billions and making capitalism look terribly bad. Drawing on his experiences in Africa, Asia, Latin America and Europe, Baker demonstrates how Western banks and businesses employ secret transactions and completely ignore laws while handling some $1tn in illicit proceeds every year. Baker further illustrates how business people, criminals as well as kleptocrats employ the same techniques to move funds by using transfer pricing, false documentation, fake or fictitious corporations, tax heavens, secrecy jurisdictions, and other tricks and vices of the trade. He shows how these tactics negatively impact on individuals, institutions and countries.

In September 2006 and following the publication of his *Capitalism's Achilles Heel* in 2005, Baker launched Global Financial Integrity (GFI), a non-profit, research and advocacy organisation located in Washington, DC, with him as the Director. GFI focuses its research on illicit financial flows, an illegal form of capital flight. They define illegal financial flows as pertaining to "the cross-border movement of money that is illegally earned, transferred, or utilised" (GFI 2011). Illicit financial flows generally concerns the transfer of money earned through illegal activities "such as corruption, transactions involving contraband goods, criminal activities, and efforts to shelter wealth from a country's tax authorities" (ibid.). As the title of this chapter suggests, these are the things to be discussed because they contribute immensely to the underdevelopment of the poor countries. As will become evident, we will draw heavily from GFI research findings, which have shown that illicit outflows are approximately 10 times the amount of official development assistance (ODA) going into the developing world. The ratio of illicit financial flows leaving developing countries compared to ODA is 10:1, that is, for every $1 in economic development assistance which goes into a developing country, $10 is lost through illegal outflows. As will become evident, most of the illegal outflows go to developed countries (Kar and Freitas 2011) confirming our contention that Robin Hood has not been fair to developing countries, particularly Africa.

Illicit Financial Flows from Africa: Hidden Resources for Development

In December 2008 GFI released a report authored by Dev Kar and Devon Cartwright-Smith titled *Illicit Financial Flows From Africa: Hidden Resources for Development.* This report covers the 39-year period from 1970 through 2008. The study used the World Bank Residual Method and IMF Direction of Trade Statistics and came to the conclusion that illicit financial flows "totaled $854bn across the period examined". The authors consider the figure "conservative" since it "addresses only one form of trade mispricing, does not include the mispricing of services, and does not encompass the proceeds of smuggling." Adjusting the $854bn estimate to take into account some of the illicit flows not accounted for the total illicit outflows from Africa, across the 39 years would be around $1.8tn.

The report states that this massive flow of illicit money out of the continent of Africa is "facilitated by a global shadow financial system comprising tax heavens, secrecy jurisdictions, disguised corporations, anonymous trust accounts, fake foundations, trade mispricing, and money laundering techniques" (ibid.). The impact of this structure and the funds it smuggles out of Africa is dumbfounding. This drains hard currency reserves, heightens inflation, reduces tax collection, cancels investment, and undermines free trade. It takes away the resources that could otherwise be used to fight poverty and enhance economic growth (ibid.).

In the 39-year period the $854bn lost in cumulative capital flight was enough to wipe out Africa's total external debt outstanding of about $250billion and potentially leave

$600bn for poverty alleviation and economic growth. Sadly, cumulative illicit flows from Africa increased from about $57bn in the decade of the 1970s to $437bn over the nine years 2000-2008.

The overwhelming bulk of the above loss in capital through illicit channels was from Sub-Saharan African countries. However, there were significant disparities in the regional pattern of illicit flows. Most of the illicit flows are from the West and Central Africa region, with Nigeria as a principal contributor. Nigeria's influence is also a factor in the illicit flows from the group of "fuel exporters." Illicit flows from the continent are great at an average rate of 11.9 percent annually in real terms over the 39-year period except in the 1990s when real rates declined across every region. This report places Nigeria at the top of the list of countries with the highest cumulative flows for the period 1970 – 2004. SSA as a whole lost $282bn in real 2004 dollars for the period 1970 – 2004; extending the period to 2008 significantly increased the cumulative total to $533bn (p.13). Then in December 2008, GFI released another report showing illicit financial flows from developing countries between 2002 and 2006. We proceed to present the findings of the report.

Illicit Financial Flows from Developing Countries: 2002 – 2006

This (main) report begins by describing legal and illegal flight capital. Legal flight capital is calculated in what Kar and Cartwright-Smith (2008: iii) refer to as "Hot Money Method analysis" as "portfolio investment and other short-term investments, but not including longer-term foreign direct investment. Legal flight capital is recorded on the books of the entity or individual making the transfer, and earnings from interest, dividends, and realised capital gains normally return to the country of origin.

On the other hand, illegal flight capital is designed "to disappear from any record in the country of origin, and earnings on the stock of illegal flight capital outside of a country do not normally return to the country of origin" (ibid.). This kind of capital can be generated through numerous means that are never revealed in national accounts or balance of payments figures, including trade mispricing, bulk cash movements, *hawala*, transactions, smuggling and other means. (Hawala transactions refer to a process in which large amounts of black or dirty money is converted into white).

The study resulting in the 2008 report used World Bank and IMF data to estimate the quantity and patterns of illicit financial flows coming out of developing countries. In the executive summary, Kar and Cartwright-Smith (20078: v) state that in the report, illegal flows include "the proceeds from both illicit activities such as corruption (bribery and embezzlement of national wealth), criminal activity, and the proceeds of illicit business that become illicit when transported across borders in contravention of applicable laws and regulatory frameworks (most commonly in order to evade payment of taxes)." There are no official statistics on illicit financial flows since these outflows escape the detection of regulatory agencies. In the absence of official statistics on illegal outflows of capital, researchers have relied on "proxy measures" to study the phenomena. The proxy measures are based on economic models and therefore have limited capacity to reflect the real volume of illicit financial flows. But the authors of the report are convinced that if anything, the estimates of illicit financial flows for the developing countries presented in the report "are likely to be understated," which means that the estimates presented in the report are conservative.

This ground breaking report has some very perplexing findings.   In 2006, according to the executive report (p. v), illegal flows out of developing countries were approximately US$1.06tn. Furthermore, the volume of illicit financial flows leaving developing countries increased at a compound rate of 18.2 percent over the five-year period of the study.   On average, Asia accounted for approximately 50 percent of all the illicit flows from all developing countries.   Asia became the dominant region in overall illicit financial flows from developing countries due to a large volume of illicit flows from mainland China. Europe became second in the share of overall illicit financial flows from developing countries, accounting for about 17 percent of the total. The Middle East and North Africa (MENA) region and the Western Hemisphere region shared approximately 15 percent of total illicit financial flows from developing countries.

The report further noted that the smallest share of illicit financial flows comes from Africa region at about 3 percent of the total. The share would have been higher if more complete and reliable data were in place. Over the five-year period of the study which resulted in the report, illicit financial flows grew at the fastest pace (49.4 percent) in the MENA region followed by Europe (25.4 percent), Asia (15.7 percent) and the Western Hemisphere (2.8 percent) in that order. The report notes that illicit financial flows from Africa declined (-2.9 percent) but this decline is more the result of lack or incomplete data "than supportive economic or political factors." Finally, the report submits that the nearly 50 percent compound rate of growth in illicit financial flows from the MENA region is an index of the humongous growth of the present account surplus and external debt of many oil producing countries in the region, instead of the flight of capital through trade misinvoicing. Finally, although the total illicit flow out of Africa is pegged at 3 percent, this is quite significant considering the size of African economies.

Having concluded in their 2002-2006 report that between $850m to $106bn a year was disappearing from poor countries as proceeds from vices such as bribery, theft, criminal activity, and commercial tax evasion, the GFI then asked the question: where are these huge financial outflows absorbed? GFI answered this question in their publication authored by Kar, Cartwright-Smith and Hollingshead (2010). We now turn to this publication.

The Absorption of Illicit Financial Flows from Developing Countries: 2002-2006

The GFI study of 2008 had shown that "even at its most conservative estimate, illicit financial flows ... from developing countries increased from US$372 billion to at least US$859 billion over the period 2002 to 2006 or at a compound annual rate of 18.2 percent" (Kar, Cartwright-Smith and Hollingshead 2010:1). The objective of this report then becomes that of shading light on the absorption of illicit funds by banks in developed countries and offshore financial centres. It is essential to know where illicit flows are absorbed because they have deprived developing countries of really scarce financial resources for development and poverty reduction and have also undermined the effectiveness of foreign aid. Attempts by developing countries to stem the tide of illegal outflows have been thwarted because there are many institutions quite willing and actively seeking to absorb these illicit outflows. The study revealed that "both offshore centres and banks have been complicit in the absorption of illegal funds" and this calls for "regulatory measures and oversight to bring about greater transparency and accountability" which "must be applied evenhandedly in order to penalise and discourage such transactions" (pp. 1-2).

The report stated that cash absorption exceeded illicit outflows by a significant margin. It observed that "on average, banks account for about 76 percent of total cash absorption while offshore centers absorb the rest (24 percent)" (p. viii). The report further noted that offshore centres increased their share of holdings of illicit deposits from 21.8 percent in 2003 to 34.2 percent in 2006, reflecting a corresponding decline of the share held by the banks for the same period from 78.2 percent to 65.8 percent (ibid.).

According to the report, offshore centres absorbed more illicit flows from Asia (43.9 percent) than any other region for the period 2002-2006. Their role in the absorption of illicit flows from MENA (36.0 percent), Africa (26.8 percent), Europe (15.8 percent) and Western Hemisphere (10.4 percent) is significant. The suggestion here is that developing countries in the Western Hemisphere and Europe deposit the bulk of their illicit funds in developed country banks rather than offshore centres (pp. viii-ix).

Finally, the authors state that their "most interesting finding ... was that developed country banks hold a significant portion of the total of illicit funds, ranging possibly from 46 to 67 percent. On average ... the proportion of total illicit funds that find their way into developed country banks was anywhere from 20 percent to 72 percent between 2003 and 2006" (p.30). In his press report released on the report in May 2010, Baker, Director of GFI remarked that "we are crossing a threshold in global finance regulation and poverty alleviation with these illicit flows studies." He goes on to state that "For every $1 in aid that the Western world is sending into developing countries, $10 is lost." While the first report looked at how much these countries were losing, the current report has given an idea of where that money is ending up. It follows that halting this annual loss of capital is crucial to successful poverty alleviation and economic development. Knowing where the illegal funds are absorbed is an excellent beginning but the problem is the political will to stop or at least minimise the problem. The fact that there are vested interests in the phenomenon makes it quite a Herculean task to overcome. Already Canada, Germany and Japan are yet to ratify the UN Convention Against Corruption; half of OECD countries have ratified; only 13 of the 54 jurisdictions classified by the IMF as offshore financial centres have ratified it. So it is a long way from illicit out flows being stopped. One very important handicap of the decisions of the UN is that each nation jealously protects its self-interest and guards against any decision that might affect it. The leaders must always play to the interest of their populations at home, how any decision might affect them politically in the next election. So that after decisions are taken, it is uncertain they will be ever be implemented.

Discussion Paper - Illicit Financial Flows from the Least Developed Countries: 1990-2008

The concerns for the staggering illicit flows from poor countries prompted UNDP to commission "discussion paper" on the illicit financial flows as a contribution to the United Nations 1V Conference on the Least Developed Countries (LDCs), Istanbul, Turkey in May 2011. This discussion paper was authored by Dev Kar (2011). Of the 48 countries classified by the UN as LDCs, 33 of them are in SSA and all of them together lost a cumulative total of $246bn in illicit financial flows for the period 1990 to 2008. Six of the top ten countries in cumulative outflows were in Africa, including Angola (No.2),

Lesotho (No.3), Chad (No.4), Uganda (No.7), Ethiopia (No.9) and Zambia (No.10) (see Chart 4, p.13 of the discussion paper).

The discussion paper explores the composition of illicit flows of the 48 least developed countries. The UN recognises the importance of illicit financial flows from poor countries in development as well as its importance in the Millennium Development Goals (MDGs). The UN also recognises that wherever illicit capital takes place, it constitutes a major hindrance to mobilisation of domestic resources for development. Further, it significantly reduces the amount of resources available for investment in the MDGs and productive capacities, which makes it very difficult for them to wage adequate war against their nemesis, poverty.

According to Kar (2011:3), illicit financial flows from poorest countries have increased from US$9.7bn in 1990 to US$21.3bn in 2008, implying an inflation adjusted rate of increase of 6.2 percent annually. Conservatively, illicit flows have jumped from US$7.9bn in 1990 to US$20.2bn in 2008. The top ten exporters of illicit capital are responsible for 63 percent of total outflows from LDCs while the top 20 account for almost 83 percent. The paper further states that trade mispricing is responsible for the bulk (65-70 percent) of illicit outflows from the LDCs, and this tendency for mispricing has increased along with increasing external trade.

Table 1: Top 20: Excerpted from Chart 4 of Discussion Paper: Cumulative IFFS from LDCs by Country, 1990 to 2008 (in US$ million)

Bangladesh	34,790
Angola	34,046
Lesotho	16,823
Chad	15,436
Yemen	11,979
Nepal	9,128
Uganda	8,757
Myanmar	8,535
Ethiopia	8,354
Zambia	6,800
Sudan	6,732
Equatorial Guinea	6,503
Laos	6,062
Liberia	5,863
Guinea	4,928
Malawi	4,171
Djibouti	3,885
Mozambique	3,773
Madagascar	3,746
Congo (DRC)	3,499

By way of summary, the discussion paper succinctly states that illicit flows:

- do divert resources needed for poverty alleviation and economic development;

- that approximately US$197bn flowed out of the 48 poorest countries and straight into largely developed countries, on a net basis over the period 1990-2008;
- that the top 20 account for almost 83 percent;
- that on the basis of the data available, African poorest countries accounted for 69 percent of total illicit flows, followed by Asia (29 percent) and Latin America (2 percent);
- that trade mispricing accounts for the bulk (65-70 percent) of all illicit outflows from the poorest countries, and
- the tendency for mispricing has increased along with increasing global external trade. Illicit financial flows remain a cancer in the system of developing countries and until there is a cure for it or at least a remedy that significantly reduces its spreading or growth, it will be quite difficult for these countries to get out of poverty and the MDGs are doomed to failure.

We proceed to examine yet another report by GFI on the topic of illegal flows, authored by Ann Hollingshead (2010).

Privately held, Non-resident Deposits in Secrecy Jurisdictions

This report seeks to quantify deposits held offshore by private entities on a country-by-country basis. It also examines the changes in these deposits in their historic and economic context. In the absence of sources providing comprehensive data on private, non-resident deposits, the author relied on "a variety of proxy measures to estimate figures by jurisdiction" (Hollingshead 2010a:3). The author then came up with some interesting findings: The private, non-resident deposits in secrecy jurisdictions have been growing markedly since the 1990s with "totals currently standing just under US$10tn. Over the same period, these deposits grew at a compound annual rate of 11.4 percent in nominal terms and 9 percent in real terms" (ibid.). Table 5 of the report (p.15) shows that the US, Germany, Jersey, Netherlands, Ireland, Switzerland, and Hong Kong top the list of jurisdictions, with the US topping the list with a total of more than US$2tn. These jurisdictions dominate the offshore market. Cayman Islands and United Kingdom hold over US$1.5tn in private foreign deposits.

Hollingshead further notes that "Contrary to expectations of perceived favourability for deposits, Asia only accounts for approximately 6 percent of worldwide offshore deposits, although Hong Kong is the tenth largest secrecy jurisdiction by deposits ..." (p.1). An analysis of case studies of selected jurisdictions reveal measurable fluctuations in financial deposits correlated to events in which financial secrecy or overall solvency became threatened. The report goes on to state that the rate of growth of offshore deposit holdings in secrecy jurisdictions had expanded at an average of 9 percent annually, thus outgrowing the rise of global wealth in the previous decade. This suggests an increase in illicit financial flows from developing countries as well as tax evasion by residents of developed countries. The report then recommends greater transparency to be introduced into the offshore financial market in order to curtail tax evasion and illicit financial flows.

In another study titled "The Implied Tax Revenue Loss from Trade Mispricing," Hollingshead (2010b) sought to estimate the loss of tax revenue to developing country governments resulting from a form of trade mispricing called 'reinvoicing.' According to Gascoigne (2011), 'trade mispricing' is a phenomenon where individuals and corporations use fraudulent commercial invoices to smuggle money out of the country, usually in order to facilitate tax evasion." On the other hand, reinvoicing occurs when goods are exported from one country under one invoice, then the same invoice is redirected to another jurisdiction, which means a low-tax or no-tax jurisdiction or tax heaven – where the invoice is sent to importing country for clearing and payment purposes (Hollingshead 2010b:1). This study was a follow-up to its 2008 report titled "Illicit Financial Flows from Developing Countries: 2002-2006" which estimated illicit outflows from the developing countries to be $1tn annually. On the basis of this report, GFI conducted an analysis of the tax revenue loss developing countries suffer due to trade mispricing. The conclusion of this study or analysis was that the average tax revenue loss to all developing countries amounted to between $98bn and $106bn per annum during the years 2002 through 2006. This figure represents an average of around 4.4 percent of the entire developing world's government revenue (p. 2). GFI followed up with another crucial report and we now turn to that report.

Illicit Financial Flows from Developing Countries over the Decade ending 2009

In analysing this report, we rely on the original report, authored by Dev Kar and Sarah Freitas (Decembber 2011), GFI press releases, Clark Gascoigne (12-15-11), AfricaFocus, and AfricaFocus Bulletin. The general conclusion is that despite a drop in 2009 due to the global recession, the developing world lost between US$723bn and US$844bn annually on average through illicit flows over the decade ending 2009. The illicit financial flows rose in current dollar terms by 15.19 percent annually from US$386bn at start of the decade to US$903bn in 2009 (AfricaFocus, 17 December 2011). The findings of this report are not only heartbreaking but also monumental.

The developing world lost US$903bn in illicit financial outflows in 2009, despite the massive financial crisis which affected the global economy in late 2008. The capital outflows stem from crime, corruption, tax evasion, and such like illegal activity. The report further states that the vast majority of the drop from US$1.55tn to US$903bn was due to a decrease in volumes of global trade, foreign direct investment, and new external loans, rather than any government action. From 2000 to 2009, the developing world lost US$8.44tn to illicit financial outflows (Kar and Freitas, December 2011:p. vii). A conservative estimate places illicit financial flows in current dollar terms at 14.9 percent per annum from the beginning until the end of the decade. Real growth of illicit financial flows by regions over the nine years is as follows: Africa 22.3 percent, MENA 19.6 percent, Developing Europe 17.4 percent, Asia 6.2 percent, Western Hemisphere 4.4 percent (ibid.). Asia accounted for 44.9 percent of total illicit flows from the developing world followed by MENA (18.6 percent), developing Europe (16.7 percent), Western Hemisphere (15.3 percent) and Africa (4.5 percent).

The study tracked the amount of illegal capital flowing out of 157 developing countries over the 10-year period from 2000 - 2009 and in the report ranks the countries by magnitude of illicit outflows. The following 20 biggest victims of illicit financial flows over the decade are abstracted from Table 5, page 42 of the report.

Table 2:   The 20 Biggest Victims of Illicit Financial Flows
              2000-2009.

China	$2.74tn
Mexico	$504bn
Russia	$501bn
Saudi Arabia	$380bn
Malaysia	$350bn
United Arab Emirates	$296bn
Kuwait	$271bn
Nigeria	$182bn
Venezuela	$179bn
Qatar	$175bn
Poland	$162bn
Indonesia	$145bn
Philippines	$142bn
Kazakhstan	$131bn
India	$128bn
Chile	$97.5bn
Ukraine	$95.8bn
Argentina	$95.8bn
South Africa	$85.5bn
Turkey	$79.1bn

Although only Nigeria and South Africa rank among the top twenty countries worldwide in illicit financial outflows (8th and 19th respectively), and SSA accounts for only 4.5 percent of all illicit financial outflows worldwide, such outflows from the continent are quite significant in comparison to the size of African economies. There are countries ranked

In the middle as Botswana that lost about $760m a year each and countries with relatively modest losses of about $90m a year each (e.g., Ghana and Mozambique).

The report also reveals the top victims of illegal capital flight. The following were the top 20 countries suffering the highest illicit outflows in 2009:

Table 3:   Top 20 Victims of Illicit Outflows in 2009

China	$291bn
Saudi Arabia	$82.3bn
Poland	$66.3bn
Malaysia	$46.8bn
Mexico	$34.6bn
Nigeria	$33.4bn
Russia	$23.4bn
Indonesia	$20.5bn
United Arab Emirates	$19.5bn
Venezuela	$18.8bn
Iran	$18.1bn
Azerbaijan	$14.3bn
Chile	$13.1bn
South Africa	$12.9bn
Vietnam	$12.5bn
Philippines	$12.1bn
Argentina	$11.7bn
Thailand	$10.8bn
Romania	$10.0bn
Ukraine	$9.8bn

Trade mispricing accounted for the average of 50.6 percent of cumulative illicit outflows from developing countries over the period 2000 to 2009, down from its high in 2004 when it was responsible for 57.2 percent. It still remains the major channel for the transfer of illicit capital from China. Illicit transfers of the proceeds of corruption, bribery, theft, kickbacks, and tax evasion, accounting on average for 49.4 percent of illicit outflows over the decade, are on the increase as a percentage of total illicit financial outflows (AfricaFocus, 17 December 2011:4). China continued to lead the world in illicit outflows, losing a staggering US$291.8 billion in 2009. Asia accounted for the largest portion of illicit financial flows from the developing countries. Over the period (2000 – 2009) examined by the report, 90 percent, on average, of total illicit flows from Asia were transferred abroad through trade mispricing (Kart and Freitas, December 2011: vii).

Further, over the decade, illicit outflows from Africa far outspaced the rest of the world, with a dumbfounding rate of 32.5 percent between 2000 and 2009, compared with 9.7 percent for Europe and 7.7 percent for Asia, possibly due to weaker customs monitoring and enforcement regimes (p.10). Corruption, kickbacks, theft and bribery are the basic conduit for the unrecorded transfer of capital from oil exports such as in Kuwait, Nigeria, Qatar, Russia, Saudi Arabia, the United Arab Emirates, and Venezuela. Mexico is reported as the only oil exporter where trade mispricing is the preferred method of transferring illicit capital abroad (AfricaFocus, 17 December, 2011:4-5). Bribery, kickbacks, and proceeds from corruption continue to be the dominant channel for the transfer of illicit funds from MENA, developing Europe, while trade mispricing remains the basic channel out of Asia and the Western Hemisphere (Kar and Freitas, December 2011:vii). The report calls for "combined global effort to curtail illicit financial flows" (p. i).

Because corruption has been repeatedly cited as a common means of siphoning illegal money out of poor countries, the author is tempted to briefly present a report emanating from the investigation by the permanent committee of the Senate of the US. This report treats four cases, showing how the practitioners are adepts in the art of crookery.

Keeping Foreign Corruption out of the United States: Four Case Studies

As observed by AfricaFocus (February 8, 2010:1), "corruption is not a solitary activity, and the networks that promote corruption are rarely confined to one country or one continent. For corruption in Africa, countries outside the continent enter the picture not only when foreign companies pay bribes for access. They are also a preferred location for stolen wealth." This statement is supported by the contents of the last chapter as well as the findings of the US Senate of February 4,, 2010. The Senate investigation concerns how politically powerful foreign officials, their relatives, and close associates – referred to in international agreements as Politically Exposed Persons (PEPs) – have used the services of US professionals and financial institutions to transfer large sums of suspect funds into the US to advance their interests. By using four case histories, the report shows how some PEPs have used lawyers, real estate and escrow agents, lobbyists, bankers, and even university officials, to circumvent US anti-money laundering and anti-corruption safeguards (US Senate 2010:1). By this investigation the Senate was able to develop four case histories that enabled them to decipher some of the tactics being employed by PEPs and their facilitators to bring suspect funds into the US, and "identify some of the legal gaps, poor due diligence practices, and inadequate PEP controls that, at times have made these tactics possible" (p.1).

Obiang case history: In November 2009, the *New York Times* complained bitterly regarding the blatant violation of US laws by Obiang who regularly flew into the US with a one-million dollar cash on hand, undeclared, in addition to the millions already stashed in US banks. The paper went on to list his assets in the US, which included: Oceanfront home in Malibu, California listed at $35 million; Gulfstream V jet at $38 million; four Ferraris, valued at $250,000 each amounting to $1 million; two Rolls-Royce Phantoms, at $350,000 each, amounting to $700,000; 2 Maybachs, at $350,000 each for a total of $700,000; 1 Bentley Arnage valued at $240,000; and 1 Rolls-Rolls-Royce Park and two speedboats not valued. The *New York Times* cited United States Immigration and Customs Enforcement as its source for the information. *The New York Times* report may have been the last straw that prompted the Senate to take up the investigation of the activities of Obiang.

The Senate report observes that beginning from 2004 to 2008, Teodoro Nguema Obiang Mangue, son of the President of Equatorial Guinea, used US lawyers, bankers, real estate agents, and escrow agents to move over $110 million in suspect funds into the US. He used attorney-client, law office, and Shell company accounts as conduits for his funds and without alerting the bank to his use of those accounts. If a bank subsequently uncovered Obiang's use of an account and closed it, the lawyers would quickly help him to open another one. The US shell companies they formed for Obiang were Beautiful Vision, Inc., Unlimited Horizon, Inc., Sweetwater Malibu, LLC, Sweetwater Management, Inc., and Sweet Pink, Inc.

Two real estate agents helped Obiang to buy and sell high-end real estate in California including his purchase of a $30 million Malibu residence with funds wire transferred from Equatorial Guinea. Once, an escrow agent refused, for fear of anti-money laundering precaution, to assist him purchase a $38.5 million US-built Gulfstream jet, another escrow agent, International Airline Title Services Inc., quickly filled the void and completed the transaction with no qualms, no questions asked. Obiang also brought large sums of suspect money into the US. He is under criminal investigation (ibid.).

Bongo case history: Omar Bongo, President of Gabon for 41 years until his death in June 2009 and between 2003 and 2007, had employed a US lobbyist to purchase six US-built armoured vehicles and obtained US Government permission to buy six US-built C-130 military cargo aircraft from Saudi Arabia to support his regime. He used offshore shell companies to move over $100 million in suspect funds through accounts at Citibank Private Bank.

In connection with the armoured car and C-130 transactions, Bongo wire transferred over $18 million from Gabon into US bank account held in the name of The Grace Group LLC. A United States corporation formed by Mr. Jeffrey Birrell received the funds primarily from President Bongo and an entity known as Ayira. He subsequently transferred $9.2 million of the funds provided by Ayira to a foreign account held by Bongo in Malta. He then wired over $4.2 million to foreign bank accounts opened in the name of a senior Bongo adviser, and over $1 million in payments to foreign bank accounts held in the name of various "consultants." Mr. Birrell's corporate accounts provided the conduit for those Bongo funds.

There were other illegal transactions by Bongo. For example, by providing large amounts of cash to his daughter who was unemployed, and was also a student, cash totaling in excess of millions of dollars. Inge Lynn Collins Bongo, wife of current president of Gabon formed a US trust, the Collins Revocable Trust, and opened accounts in the name of that Trust at banks in California. She received multiple large offshore wire transfers into the Trust accounts and then used the illegal funds "to support a lavish lifestyle and move money among a network of bank and securities accounts benefiting her and her husband" (p.3).

Abubakar case history: Jennifer Douglas, a US citizen and the fourth wife of Atiku Abubakar, former Vice-President and former candidate for president of Nigeria, had between 2000 and 2008 helped her husband transfer over $40 million in suspect funds into the US through series of wire transfers sent by offshore corporations to US bank accounts. Ms. Douglas was slapped with a civil complaint by the US Securities and Exchange Commission for receiving over $2 million in bribe payments in 2001 and 2002 from Siemens AG, a major German corporation. She then denied the charges while Siemens pleaded guilty to US criminal charges and settled civil charges related to the bribery (ibid.).

According to the Senate report, $25 million of the $40 million, was wire transferred by offshore corporations into more than 30 US bank accounts opened by Ms. Douglas, primarily by Guernsey Trust Company Nigeria Ltd., LetsGo Ltd, Inc., not aware of her PEP status, and they therefore allowed the multiple, large offshore wire transfers into her accounts. When questioned about the offshore wire transfers, Ms. Douglas said the funds came from her husband and feigned ignorance of the offshore corporations actually sending her money. One bank closed her account due to the offshore wire transfers, but her lawyer was quick to convince other banks to provide a new account (ibid.).

Furthermore, two of the offshore corporations wire transferred about $14 million over five years to American University in Washington, DC to pay for consulting services in connection with the development of a Nigerian university founded by Mr. Abubakar. American University accepted the wire transfers without enquiring about the identity of the offshore corporations or the source of their funds, apparently because there is no law requiring them to do so.

In some countries in the case Abubakar would have been irreparably damaged to the point that he would have been politically consigned to the dustbin for disposal; the kind of information contained here would have been a political tsunami which would have shred Abubakar into pieces. Not in Nigeria. He again ran for nomination of his People's Democratic Party (PDP) to contest for the presidency of Nigeria in 2007 but failed to get it. He is poised to run again in 2015. Abubakar was once described as the most corrupt politician in Nigeria by his former boss, President Obasanjo (see Offiong 2008a for Abubakar's and other corrupt politicians in Nigeria).

Angola case history: This case history involves three Angolan PEP accounts. Pierre Falcons, a notorious arms dealer supplied weapons during the Angolan civil war and he is a close associate of Angolan President Jose Eduardo Dos Santos. "He used personal, family, and U. S. shell company accounts at a bank in Arizona to bring millions of dollars in suspect funds into the United States and move those funds among a worldwide network of accounts" (p.4). This man has been in and out of prison and because banks did not know about his

PEP status, he was able to maintain 30 accounts for the Falcon family.

Another Angolan, Dr. Aguinaldo Jaime was head of Banco Nacional de Angola (BNA), the Angolan central bank. He tried on two occasions in 2002 to transfer $50 million in government funds to a private account in the US but his transfers were reversed. Because of those transfers (which were reversed) and the corruption concerns raised, Citibank closed BNA accounts as well as accounts for Angolan government entities, and then closed its office in Angola. But there are still banks in the US and elsewhere that continue to provide banking facilities or services to BNA, thus encouraging the illegal outflows of funds from Africa.

Finally, Banco Africano de Investimentos (BAI) is a $7bn private Angolan bank whose largest shareholder is Sonagol, the Angolan state-owned oil company. BAI offers banking services to Sonagol, Angolans in the oil and diamond industries, and Angolan government officials. Around the year 2000, BAI gained entry to the US financial system via accounts at Honkong and Shanghai Banking Corporation in New York (HSBC), using HSBC wire transfer services, foreign currency exchange, and US dollar credit cards for BAI clients. HSBC refused until 2009 to designate BAI as a "special category of client," requiring additional oversight, despite the presence of PEPs in BAI's management and clientele (ibid.).

These four case histories show how ingenuous and clever those who want to engage in illicit capital transfers are. This really underscores what the United Nations Commission of Experts on Reforms of the International Monetary and Financial System said on March 19 2009, namely that, the welfare of both developed and developing countries are intricately or mutually interdependent in an increasingly integrated global economy; all must work together otherwise the goal of eliminating poverty will remain elusive. The global society must seek to stem the tide of corruption, a cancerous tumor that must be removed before the body can have a wholesome living. It is only after the cancerous tumor is annihilated that the world can have a meaningful hope of successfully tackling poverty. This leads me to the effort to recover stolen assets.

Stolen Asset Recovery (StAR) Initiative

In 2011, the World Bank Group issued what they called "Fact Sheet on Stolen Asset Recovery." According to this fact sheet,

1. The cross-border flow of the global proceeds from criminal activities, corruption, and tax evasion is estimated at between $1tn and $1.6tn per year.

2. 25 percent of GDP of African states lost to corruption every year, amounting to $148bn, but the problem is seen in all continents.

3. Corrupt money associated with bribes received by public officials from developing and transition countries is conservatively estimated at $20bn to $40bn per year - a figure equivalent to 20 to 40 percent of flows of official development assistance (ODA).

The fact sheet continues by stating that every $100m of stolen money could fund:

1. First-line treatment for over 600,000 people with HIV/AIDS for a full year, or
2. 50 – 100 million in drugs for the treatment of malaria; or
3. Some 250,000 water connections for households

Having given the above facts, the World Bank Group fact sheet then proceeds to announce how much money has been recovered through the Stolen Asset Recovery Initiative. One billion dollars was recovered from Ferdinand Marcos of Philippines; $1800m was recovered from Vladimiro Montesino of Peru; $700m was recovered from Sani Abacha of Nigeria; $17.7m was recovered from Diepreye Alamieyeseigha of Nigeria; and Kazakhstan recovered $84m from US and Swiss banks. This is a very small fraction of the billions, perhaps trillions, of dollars stolen and stashed mostly in Western banks and offshore accounts. But it is a good beginning.

Some of the successes came as the result of what happened on September 17, 2007 when the World Bank in partnership with the United Nations Office of Drugs and Crime (UNODC) launched an initiative to help developing countries recover assets stolen by corrupt leaders. These efforts will go a long way to making it a little difficult for corrupt leaders to try to ship their loots to foreign banks. Unfortunately, however, Canada, Germany, Italy and Japan are yet to ratify the UN Convention Against Corruption as we stated earlier; there are still numerous organisations yet to ratify the convention. There does not seem to be the political will to do what is right because of political expediency: Western banks are glad to receive the illicit funds and their governments must give them protection.

The information presented so far has clearly shown that much of African poverty can be attributed to illegal outflows of funds from the continent and the sooner something is done about it the better. Finally, before coming to the end of this chapter I want to briefly examine what have come to be known as "vulture capitalism" and "vulture funds," in so far as they involve exporting funds from poor countries and the harm they inflict upon them.

Vulture Capitalism and Vulture Funds

Before confronting the term "vulture funds", we first attempt to explain the term "vulture capitalism". The term or phrase "vulture capitalism" gained wide currency in early 2012 during the Republican presidential primaries. This term has been used with regard to the past business transactions of Mitt Romney with Bain Capital, a company he headed. He was accused by his fellow Republican opponents of buying distressed companies and then restructuring them for his personal benefits. We all appreciate that vultures are unsightly scavengers that play some important role in the eco-system; in the same sense "vulture capitalists" are claimed to play a significant and beneficial role in the free market economic system. One common factor between the two is that both "consume the dead or dying for personal gain" (Mayer 2012:1).

Most carnivores do not show any interest in eating smelly, rotten carcasses because of the risks to their lives they pose. But vultures and certain other scavengers have adapted themselves to taking the risk of devouring and feasting upon carcasses and this has been to the benefit of the eco-system.

In the same way "vulture capitalists" provide overwhelming cleansing role in the free market economy. What vulture capitalists do is that when they know of a business that is dead or is dying they evaluate the risk involved and then proceed to do what scavengers are noted for, take the risk and the resultant profit is completely their reward for the risk taking. This is what vulture capitalism is all about. What liberals or progressives refer to as vulture capitalism while conservatives or rightwingers call "liquidation capitalism" (Bohan 2012:10).

Vulture capitalism is closely related to vulture funds. In fact vulture funds are vulture capitalism personified – vulture capitalism in operation. Vulture funds are private equities or hedge funds that invest in distressed debts of commercial companies or sovereign nations at cheap price and then turn round to sue for the entire value of the debts. The name is a metaphor comparing these investors to vultures for profiting from the debts of failing companies or poor nations. Thus Fukuda (2008:1) defines vulture funds as "exploitative financial funds in which private fund buys up cheap foreign debt, and sells it at a much higher cost." And, Haperskij (2010:1) sees vulture funds as "the more smarmy and marginal investment houses which buy the defaulted debt of poor countries for pennies on the dollar, and then proceed to give them for immediate repayment." As an example, a developing country sells bonds on which this country eventually defaults. A vulture fund then purchases the debt from the lender at "bargain basement prices" and then proceeds to sue the issuing country, or then employs whatever available tactics to summarily exact the bonds' full worth as compensation. The vulture funds have won more than half of the resulting court cases, and in many instances making unconscionable profits of more than 400 percent (ibid.).

As from the middle of the 1990s vulture funds have been suing poor, developing countries demanding payment of their debts which they had purchased for pennies on the dollar. By this practice, they have exacerbated the economic problems of poor countries in Africa and Latin America. About 20 African and Latin American countries have been involved in this situation and most of them are among the HIPCs. In Latin America Paul Singer, a staunch Republican in the US and the owners of the firm Elliot Associates Ltd sued Peru for $58m in 1996, after the firm had purchased $11m (one-tenth of its original value before the country had defaulted) worth of debt. The US Federal Court ruled in favour of the firm. Peru paid Paul Singer $58m and he made a $47m dollar profit on the debt (ibid.).

In Africa American vulture funds have pursued Zambia, Liberia, the Congo, Cameroon, Sudan, Uganda and other HIPCs. The case that sparked most outrage was that of vulture fund Donegal International against Zambia in 2007. Donegal International is owned by a Republican Michael Francis Sheehan. Sheehan bought $15m Zambian debt of the 1970s worth a paltry $3m and proceeded to sue Zambia in a British court for the full amount, which by then had accumulated to $55m. Sheehan won the case and Zambia had to pay $15m to Sheehan's British Virgin Isles-registered company. In 2009 a British court awarded $20m to vulture funds suing Liberia. Cases involving some other countries are pending. The primary reason why vulture funds succeed in court cases is because of the inclusion of a standard *pari passu* clause in many sovereign debt agreements. This means that all creditors must be treated equally and if there is not enough money to go around, all creditors have to receive a pro-rata share of what is available and debtors are forbidden to pay off one creditor in full while others are unpaid (Fukuda 2008:2).

The activities of vulture funds have stirred up anger among a number of NGOs such as Jubilee Debt Campaign, Oxfam and Christian Aid, in addition to the World Bank and IMF (Palast *et al* 2012; Haperskij 2010; Lapziger 2007). The IMF and World Bank both agree that vulture funds significantly endanger the gains provided by debt relief to HIPCs, altogether 41 countries, most of which are in Africa. According to Leipziger, Vice President at the World Bank in charge of Poverty Reduction and Economic Management "the Bank has already delivered more than US$40 billion in debt relief to 30 of these countries under Heavily Indebted Poor Counties (HIPC) Initiative and the parallel Multilateral Debt Reduction Initiative (MDRI); and many other multilateral and bilateral creditors are also playing their part. Thanks to this, countries like Ghana can provide micro-credit to farmers, build classrooms for children, and fund water sanitation projects for the poor." However, the activities of vulture funds threaten to undermine such efforts.

Vulture funds have not been lying low, as they have stubbornly defended themselves and they have their supporters whether in the British Parliament or in the US Congress. Vulture funds claim that they are providing a service to developed countries. There is so much corruption in developing countries, according to them, whose assets have been stolen by their rulers. Thus by suing the poor countries the funds hope to gain access to these hidden assets. By pressuring these poor countries to pay up their debts, vulture funds are carrying out the dirty work the rich countries do not want to be seen doing. The activities of the vulture funds do negatively affect current and previous leaders responsible for the debt as well as future ones who had nothing to do with the debt at all (Haperskij 2010:2).

NGOs are making concerted efforts to have activities of vulture funds banned because they limit debt relief and saddle national economies with huge debt loads. Money saved from debt cancellation ends up in the pockets of vulture funds' owners. Poor countries are forced to spend their very scarce resources on litigations which further compound their economic problems. The rich countries will have to step in by way of legislation to protect poor countries from this notorious pillaging by vulture capitals rather than create some means by which capital is transferred from poor to rich countries.

9

Taming the Triumphalist Juggernaut

What I mean by taming the triumphalist juggernaut is simply lessening the unnecessary effects of globalisation that we have discussed in previous chapters, making it (globalisation) work for every society, including developing countries; and this can only be done by leveling the playing field of international trade for every participant, and completely reforming the World Bank and IMF so that they do not continue to conceive their fundamental role as agents of rich and powerful countries and their multinational corporations. In short, the current international economic order must be reconfigured for the benefit of all.

As I have done throughout this book, I will again turn to various available reports from diverse sources, to re-emphasise the need for changes in the current international economic order so that globalisation can work to the benefit of all participants, thus making it possible to achieve the MDGs, certainly not by 2015 for Africa, but hopefully sometime in the future. Until there is a restructuring or reconfiguration of the present economic order, it will be difficult for poor countries to seriously wage a successful war against poverty.

As stated in Chapter 1, globalisation is a triumphalist juggernaut devastating everything along its path. Kofi Annan, former UN Secretary-General, once expressed his defiance for globalisation. He said that arguing against globalisation is like arguing against the laws of gravity. But that does not mean that we should accept a law that only allows heavyweights to survive" (quoted by Hoberman 2006). The benefits of globalisation, according to its proponents, include higher living standards, faster growth and new opportunities. The problem is that these benefits have eluded poor countries. Reading through the numerous World Bank, IMF and various UN conference reports, one is amazed by the rhetoric of rich nations promising that their goal is to eradicate poverty in the world. Their practices as opposed to their rhetoric prompted Kofi Annan (2000) to state that while there is a lot for the poor countries to do to help themselves, the "rich countries have an indispensable role to play. For them, to preach the virtues of open markets to developing countries is mere hypocrisy if they do not open their own markets to those countries' products, or if they continue flooding the world markets with subsidised food exports, making it impossible for farmers in poor countries to compete. Nor can they expect developing countries to listen to their pleas to respect the global environment, unless they are ready to alter their own irresponsible patterns of production and consumption." Nobody can accuse Kofi Annan of globaphobia, that is, that globalisation can never work for the poor and that integration into global markets will obviously lead to more poverty and inequality. Certainly, Annan does not advocate globaphilia, that is, that increased integration through trade and openness automatically means more rapid growth and poverty production (Watkins 2002). The important thing here is that Annan is advocating that globalisation be made to benefit poor countries, because as at present it is the heavyweight countries that have monopolised the benefits of globalisation.

In 2007, Joseph E. Stiglitz outlined some of the problems he saw with globalisation, having worked as an insider, both in the cabinet of President Clinton and in the World Bank. The title of his lecture was "Making Globalisation Work for Developing Countries." According to Stiglitz, globalisation has brought about failures in development, such as decline in growth in Latin America, associated with benefits among upper income groups, growing poverty, unemployment and crime. In Africa it was a decline in per capita income. There has been growing inequality between countries; and instead of convergence as predicated by standard economic theory, there has been convergence, as well as growing inequality within most countries. Stiglitz argues that "unfair trade treaties have exacerbated problems in developing countries;" that problems have been "compounded by asymmetric liberalisation," and that "Africa has neither resources nor education to take advantage of new opportunities."

Stiglitz further states that international trade "regime is unfair" to developing countries. For example, the Uruguay Round Agenda focused on the interests of rich powerful countries. They focused on "services ...but not unskilled labour intensive services ...subsidies ...but not agricultural subsidies" and "intellectual property rights. Most of projected benefits accrued to rich countries – the rich countries getting 70 percent of gains while the 48 LDCs "actually left worse off." He contradicts Thomas L. Friedman's 2005 book *The World is Flat* because given that a great number of people in the world continue to live in abject penury, the "level playing field" claimed by Freidman is an absolute myth.

Stiglitz complains about global governance as "undemocratic." According to him, "the voice of developing countries is not heard" and even when it is heard, "it is not listened to." Global governance is dominated by the North and by special interests. Thus rules are "made by advanced nations for advanced nations... for their interests, or for special interests within them." Problems of global governance are highlighted by the problems at the World Bank and IMF. The IMF has engaged in a series of policies that have failed to offer relief and have even exacerbated economic problems in developing countries, as we have stated repeatedly. The IMF insists on cutting spending or tax increases and this has often tended to make economic downturns worse. The Fund's prescription for higher interest rates can bankrupt companies that are not ready for sharply higher debt service costs. Its persistent belief in opening up financial markets can allow better-funded foreign banks to drive local banks out of business, as already noted before.

In its report on international trade, Oxfam (2002:5), states that there is a "paradox at the heart of international trade." This trade is one of the most powerful forces linking our lives, much the same way it is a "source of unprecedented wealth." What is baffling is that millions of the world's poorest people are being left behind. Increased prosperity is accompanied by "mass poverty and the widening of already obscene inequalities between rich and poor." There is no doubt that world trade has "the potential to act as a powerful motor for the reduction of poverty, as well as economic growth, but that potential is being lost." The problem is not that international trade is "inherently opposed to the needs and interests of the poor, but that the rules that govern it are rigged in favour of the rich".

The very countries that in their rhetoric promise poor countries assistance in conquering the problem of poverty through the agency of their governments use "their trade policy to conduct what amounts to robbery against the world's poor. When developing countries export to rich country markets, they face tariff barriers that are four times higher than those encountered by rich countries. Those barriers cost them $100bn a year - twice as much as they receive in aid." The harsh reality of rich nations' policies is "inflicting enormous suffering on the world's poor." And, when rich countries "lock poor countries out of their markets," what they do is "close the door to an escape route from poverty" (ibid.).

In the same vein, Benjamin William Mkapa, President of Tanzania states that "Africa as a whole is the continent that has lost more than it gained from the accelerated pace of globalisation" (2004:1). The outcomes of globalisation have been "unbalanced" and these "imbalances are ethically unacceptable and politically unsustainable." Globalisation is falling far short of its potential, and while wealth is being created too many countries and people are not participating in its benefits. Unfortunately, those who are not having a fair share of the benefits of globalisation are the ones having an "unfair share of the risks" (ibid.).

The current process of globalisation has turned Africa and other poor countries of the world into pot-lids of global economy. Millions of people continue "to subsist precariously on the margins of the global economy." Even in those countries that are economically successful, there are still people and communities that continue to suffer adverse effects of globalisation and this has generated anger, frustration, insecurity and a spike in cross-border crime.

The current external environment has not been quite supportive of Africa's desire to develop through trade. Since Africa is quite heavily dependent on commodities, it remains at the mercy of the vagaries of global commodity markets and elements, in addition to "the greed of the value-adding and trading multinational corporations" (p.7). The solution then is to process agricultural commodities. Unfortunately, the escalating tariff regimes in rich countries make this solution quite disadvantageous; African countries "are penalised for trying to break away from the bondage of unprocessed commodities" (ibid.). Mkapa then illustrates by using cocoa as an example. "Unprocessed cocoa attracts only 0.5 percent tariff in the EU, and zero tariff in both the USA and Japan. Semi-processed cocoa is charged 9.7 percent in Japan. If Africans try to sell final cocoa products, they are charged a punitive 30.6 percent tariff in the EU, 15.3 percent in the USA and 21.7 percent in Japan" (ibid.). In addition to this are the staggering subsidies of over \$300bn each year that the Organisation for Economic Cooperation and Development (OECD) countries pump into their farming sector. This poses a monumental problem for African countries whose competitive advantage lies in the peasant dominated agricultural sector. These countries undermine Africa's ability to sell their processed agricultural products to them, and they even make matters worse by dumping subsidised agricultural products from their countries into the continent of Africa (see Offiong 2001). These practices do not in any way suggest that the rich countries really want to see poor countries catapult themselves out of poverty. As stated repeatedly, the current international economic order must be restructured to benefit all that participate in it.

Even the UNDP (2007:12) agrees that the "process of globalisation and interdependence is potentially a powerful and dynamic force that can contribute to growth, poverty reduction and sustainable development" but the process has not been "fair and equitable." The benefits of globalisation have not reached poor countries both for domestic and international reasons. Internally, poor countries continue to grapple with daunting structural constraints, some of which have been inherited from their colonial past. Others include extreme poverty, inadequate financial resources, inadequate physical and social infrastructure, unavailability of skilled human resources and weak institutional and other capacities, as well as the challenge of HIV/AIDS, malaria and tuberculosis, altogether inhibit domestic growth and also jeopardise sustainable development in many LDCs (p.13). Externally, the present phase of globalisation has been "driven by the industrial economies' need for market and investment opportunities abroad, facilitated by the modern technological revolution" (ibid.). The result has been a "playing field which is very uneven." Thus at both the domestic and external level, something has to be done, and this must be treated as an urgent necessity, if the course of current globalisation process is to be changed and make its benefits even.

Before ending this discussion on making the benefits of globalisation even, let me proceed to still add the voice of UNCTAD to this matter. In its "The Least Developed Countries Report 2004," UNCTAD argues that "in conditions of mass poverty such as found in the LDCs, poverty reduction requires sustained economic growth of a type that substantially increases average household incomes and consumption" (p. ii). Sustained poverty reduction cannot rely on welfare transfers although these may be used "to alleviate instances of the most extreme misery." What defeats conditions of mass poverty in the LDCs is "the efficient development and utilisation of productive capacities in a way in which the working-age population becomes more and more fully and productively employed" (ibid.).

International trade is the means by which the LDCs can overcome poverty. This is because "exports and imports facilitate a process of sustained growth, the development of productive capacities and expansion of employment opportunities and sustainable livelihoods" (ibid.). As it is common in most LDCs, the primary sector, especially agriculture, dominates production and employment in the economy, and productive capacities are very weakly developed. In this kind of situation, "exports enable the acquisition, through importation, of goods which are necessary for economic growth and poverty reduction, but which are not produced domestically". Among such goods are food, manufactured consumer goods, fuel and raw materials, machinery and equipment and means of transport, and intermediate inputs and spare parts. Exports bring about the transformation of underutilised natural resources and surplus labour into imports which can support growth.

Although international trade is claimed to play "a powerful role in poverty reduction in the LDCs," the report finds that in reality, the positive role of trade in poverty reduction is actually realised in very few countries. The report explains this disappointment in terms of "a lack of export dynamism in many LDCs" . Closely related to this is "export structure, and in particular commodity dependence". Many non-oil commodity-exporting LDCs are caught in what is referred to as "an international poverty trap in which external trade and financial relations are reinforcing, rather than serving to break, the domestic vicious circles that perpetuate poverty" (ibid.). The problem is that the non-oil commodity-exporting LDCs generally depend on a narrow range of low-productivity, low-value-added and quite weakly competitive primary commodities serving declining or sluggish global markets. A weak export performance has been found to be associated with the build-up of external debt and the "emergence of an aid/debt service system in which aid disbursements have increasingly been allocated, either implicitly or explicitly, to ensure that official debts are serviced" (ibid.); such countries have been marginalised in world trade.

It is the view of the UNCTAD that international trade does not work for poverty reduction if export performance is weak. Even when the LDCs have increased their overall export growth rate (and this has already happened), their better export performance "rarely translates into sustained and substantial poverty reduction. *The relationship between trade and poverty is thus asymmetrical. Although LDCs with declining exports are almost certain to have a rising incidence of poverty, increasing exports do not necessarily lead to poverty reduction"* (ibid; emphasis in original).

In terms of policy option, UNCTAD's recommendation of "unilateral trade liberalisation" in order to increase the "openness" of LDCs' national economies is not a good option. Why? Because the LDCs have since late 1980s been engaging in extensive trade liberalisation, and that in many LDCs there is not much of "trade liberalisation agenda left to implement." And secondly, "the emerging post-liberal trends ... do not indicate that substantial and sustained poverty reduction will occur. On balance, future poverty reduction prospects seem to have worsened" (ibid.). So the LDCs of the world, most of which are in SSA, do not benefit from international trade. It seems that the asymmetrical nature of the international trade must be changed along with other general changes to make international trade in particular, and globalisation in general, benefit all of humanity. This leads us to the issue of reforming the IMF and World Bank. Until these twin international financial institutions are reformed, poor countries will not benefit from globalisation. These two institutions have often adopted detrimental policies to poor countries.

Reforming the IMF and World Bank

We have had a lot to say about the World Bank and IMF in this book and we have contended all along that without reforming the two international financial institutions, not much will be gained from globalisation by poor countries. And this the West, the sponsors of the two financial institutions, must be willing to at least modify the role of the two banks. Many of the policies of the two institutions have proved to be inimical to the interests of poor countries. In his "remarks" at the France-Africa Summit in Yaounde, Cameroon on January 19, 2001 Stanley Fischer, First Deputy Managing Director of IMF stated that "promoting growth and reducing poverty are best achieved by embracing the global economy, improving policies and strengthening institutions...that is what the IMF believes." Fischer disagrees with "pessimists" who claim that Africa is "predestined to endure low growth, in part because it is tropical and suffers from systemic diseases such as malaria; because the quality of its soil is poor; and because many of its countries are landlocked." He refuses to share this pessimism. Things will go well as long as African and other countries "adopt prudent, market-based economic policies, seeking integration into the world economy, and thus conducive to growth and poverty reduction – many of them with IMF and World Bank advice and support." Closer integration, trade liberalisation and more and more dependence on and control by the two international institutions are the solution to African poverty. Above all, they must "play by the rules of the international system." But we have made it abundantly clear that those that benefit from globalisation have not been playing by the rules.

The IMF and World Bank pressure national leaders to place the interests of international financial investors above the needs of their own citizens. By doing this the financial institutions "have short-circuited the accountability at the heart of self-governance, thereby corrupting the democratic process" (Global Exchange 2001:2). This subordination of social needs to the interests of financial markets has consequently made it difficult for national governments to ensure that their nationals receive food, health care, and education. The two financial institutions have engaged in a form of economic "development" that makes paramount the concerns of wealthy lenders and multinational corporations in the industrialised North while neglecting the needs of the poor countries of the world. The two institutions, according to Global Exchange, "work as a kind of international loan shark, exerting enormous influence over the economies of more than 60 countries" (p.2). As discussed previously, in order to get loans, international assistance, and debt relief, these poor countries must agree to conditions imposed by the financial institutions. In their guise of promoting free trade, market liberalisation, and financial stability, they have imposed cuts in health care, education and other social services. This practice has worsened poverty and inequality. All these criticisms call for some changes in the global arena in order for globalisation to serve all countries.

Indeed, a radical reform of the IMF and World Bank is absolutely essential. As observed by Eurodad Report (2006:4), the two financial institutions "need to totally-re-think their current approach to development finance policy conditionality." The efforts by the two institutions to "streamline" development finance conditionality have not worked. This is because institutional guidelines meant to "reduce the number and scope of conditions imposed are not being implemented properly, and are not sufficient to protect developing countries from the negative impact of onerous conditionality".

The two institutions must make a radical cut in the number of binding and non-binding conditions. The Eurodad Report specifically calls on the World Bank to "stop its tendency to micro-manage reform in poor countries." The two institutions should immediately cease to impose "controversial economic policy conditions which push privatisation and trade liberalisation related reforms, even if these are contained in nationally owned poverty reduction papers". Should conditions be imposed, they should "focus only on fundamental fiduciary concerns which enhance developing countries citizens' ability to hold their governments to account, rather than developing countries accountability to the Bank and Fund". Finally, Eurodad calls on the Bank and Fund to "stop all forms of 'cross conditionality'".

Oxfam International (2006) agrees with Eurodad that the World Bank should stop attaching any economic conditions to its aid. It asks the Bank to move to "out-come-based conditionality, linking aid to a few mutually agreed poverty reduction targets, based on the Millennium Development Goals or national poverty targets." Oxfam further asks the Bank to make sure that "all country analytical work as driven by recipient governments' agendas, is made public, and examines a wide range of policy options, assessing each in the light of its poverty impact".

As for the IMF, Oxfam advises that in those countries where micro-economic stability is still an issue, it (IMF) should limit its "quantitative targets (e.g., fiscal deficit, sector wage bill and inflation targets) to a minimum." It should ensure they are backed up by independent analysis and broad agreement that this is the best option to poverty reduction. And finally, "analysis should be based around different economic scenarios and should be vocal about the need for increased aid volume and predictability" (ibid.).

Oxfam also has something for donors as well. Donors are called upon to invest at least 50 percent of their aid in long-term (i.e., five years and more), predictable budget and sector support. They are to move using "outcome-based conditionality, linking aid to a few mutually agreed MDGs or national poverty reduction targets. They are to ensure that "aid and debt cancellation are formally de-linked from IMF and World Bank programmes and rather based on the implementation of mutually agreed poverty reduction goals coordinated across the major donors. Finally, donors are to assist "Southern governments in developing their own capacity to analyse policy-reform options".

As for developing-country governments, they are to ensure "transparent and accountable budget and expenditure processes and involve parliaments and civil society in all national decision-making and setting of poverty reduction goals." Further, they are to increase "capacity to collect poverty data and analyse the impact of different policy options on poor people" (p.5). In sum, all must recognise the need for a new approach. The focus should be on poverty reduction in national economic development programmes. Aid agencies should recognise the need to align their assistance with these national strategies.

In this new realisation three things are basic. The first is that there must be open policy formulation; that is, policies must be more transparent, country-driven and the international financial institutions and other donors simply play an active but supportive role. The process must be participatory, which means that each understanding of the specific nature and causes of poverty in the respective country. There must be consultation with civil society since the poor themselves are often favourably placed to identify priorities for action. And finally, there must be accountability. There must be public consultations to improve monitoring and accountability. Developing countries must strenuously fight to eliminate or at least reduce waste, corruption, and ineffective, control of public expenditure; these have been critical problems (Ahmed 2002:2). Imagine the staggering amounts of illegal financial transfers from poor countries to wealthy countries. Imagine what such humongous amounts would have accomplished in their countries of origin if they were properly used!

We have had reasons on several occasions in these pages to refer to the positions of globaphobes and globaphiles – that is, those who contend that globalisation can never work for the poor and that integration into global markets will certainly lead to more poverty and inequality on one hand, and those who hold that increased integration through trade and openness is an almost automatic passport to more rapid growth and reduction in poverty, on the other. These are extremes. The argument is that openness is associated with higher growth and that increased trade is not associated with a tendency to increased inequality. In other words, "the poor share in growth in proportion to their existing share of national income" (Watkins 2002:1).

In reality, studies have shown that countries such as China, Thailand, and Vietnam have been "premier globalisers." They do have a strong record on economic growth and poverty reduction. However, they have liberalised imports slowly and still have relatively restrictive trade barriers. On the other hand, countries such as Brazil, Haiti, Mexico, Peru and Zambia that have been "world-beaters when it comes to import liberalisation" have weak record on growth and poverty reduction. Evidence shows that "many first-rate globalisers have fifth-rate records on poverty reduction" (Watkins 2002:4). What appears to have gone wrong here was the fact that "export liberalisation and promotion were pursued both in advance of, and far more aggressively than, import liberalisation".

It seems globalisation will work for poor countries only when rich countries practice what they preach – when they match their rhetoric with concrete action. Take the case of openness. This is "a crucial doctrine," as Watkins refers to it.

The rich North through their finance ministers are the most ardent proponents of this doctrine, especially when directing policy advice to poor countries. The sad fact is that "when it comes to their home economies, the principles of free trade are honored more in the breach than in the observance. The underlying ethos is 'do as we say, not as we do,' which is not a constructive basis for more inclusive globalisation" (p.6). In the final analysis, the globaphobes and globaphiles must sink their differences and all, including governments, international financial institutions, and civil society must come together to devise means to make globalisation work as a force for poverty reduction and social justice. Nothing can be achieved until the North is ready to make globalisation work for the poor as well; and this must include tackling the issue of subsidies by the North. The shady practices predominant in global economy bring us to the concern for meeting the MDGs targeted at 2015.

Millennium Development Goals
The World Bank has been issuing what it calls "Global Monitoring Report" to alert the world of the status of the progress of poverty reduction toward the targeted date of 2015. In the way things are, the MDGs pledged by the 189 UN member countries are in great jeopardy. MDGs are an international agenda for fighting and cutting the rate of poverty in order to improve human lives. MDGs aim to halve, between 1990 and 2015, the proportion of people living in severe poverty and hunger, achieving universal primary education, promoting gender equality, improving maternal health, combating HIV/AIDS, malaria and other diseases,

ensuring environmental sustainability, and developing a global partnership for development.

Thus the MDGs synthesise, in a single package, many of the most important commitments made separately at the various international conferences and summits of the 1990s. They recognise explicitly the interdependence between growth, poverty reduction and sustainable development. Furthermore, they acknowledge that development depends on the foundations of democratic governance, the rule of law, respect for human rights and peace and, of course, security. The MDGs are based on time-bound and measurable targets followed by indicators for monitoring progress. The MDGs bring together the responsibilities of developing countries with those of developed countries "founded on a global partnership..." (UNDP 2009:2).

Half way (2008) to the target date of 2015, progress was reported regarding the 91 percent reduction in measles deaths in Africa and new inroads against malaria. On the whole, the progress was judged too slow while hoping that "specific and accelerated investment in the poor countries can still deliver the MDGs on schedule" (Sachs 2008). Sachs argues that the usual standard prescriptions for growth, which include rule of law, security, corruption held in check and open or free trade, are not enough to overcome extreme poverty and diseases. The effort must also include "targeted public investments in agriculture, health, education and infrastructure." These "are needed to provide the basis for productive private-sector activity" (ibid.). Sachs continues that public investments in roads, power and port facilities could quite vividly increase the profitability of agricultural exports in SSA. Such investments do complement preconditions for profitable private-sector investments, not replace them.

As it stands, poor countries cannot afford the public investments by themselves. Some additional $72bn a year of donor financing is needed to accomplish this feat. Although this is a large sum of money, the amount is however "fully compatible with the donor countries' past pledges to Africa" (ibid.). This amount is about 0.2 percent of the donors' gross national product. The donors are Europe, the US, Canada and Japan with a combined income of $37tn a year.

The major G8 countries had promised to double aid to Africa between 2004 and 2010, but they never increased it. The US had the lowest ratio of aid to GNP, at 0.16 percent in 2007; its aid to Africa was actually 0.04 percent of GNP (ibid.). The failure of the donor countries to honour their pledge constitutes the limiting factor in achieving the MDGs in the continent. The implication here is that as long as Africa depends on aid for its development and fight against poverty, it may never get out of its present predicament. The rich countries have their own domestic problems to take care of. Besides, there is a lot of local politics associated with aid and politicians have to be very careful of how they handle it.

Between 1990 and 2005 the rate of severe poverty in developing countries decreased from 42 percent of the population to 25 percent (World Bank 2009). This rate was influenced by China whose poverty rate dropped from 60 percent to 16 percent. As of 2005, all developing countries were on their way to meeting their poverty reduction goal, or had already exceeded it, except for Sub-Saharan African countries. Sadly, however, the soaring food prices in 2007, and the economic down-turn in 2008-2009, brought about by the greed of American Wall Street, significantly impeded the progress toward reducing poverty; it may have reversed the progress in some cases. The approaches for achieving poverty reduction include promoting economic growth, cancellation of debt, financial aid, investing in human capital, and providing microcredit programmes that give loans to poor people; but we have repeatedly pointed out that they do not work well, largely because of the asymmetry of the international economic system. The core countries of the global economic system use their economic and political prowess to preach one thing and practice a completely different thing.

In April 2011 the World Bank and IMF released another *Global Monitoring Report 2011,* subtitled *Improving the Odds of Achieving the MDGs.* This report reviews the evolution of the MDGs towards their achievement deadline set for 2015. It analyses the diverse efforts and achievements in improving human development across developing countries in general but with special focus on Africa. The absolute number of poor in Africa has increased from 296 million in 1990 to over 388 million in 2011.

According to this report, two-thirds of developing countries are on track or close to meeting MDGs. It is the view of the World Bank and IMF that developing countries will likely achieve the MDGs for gender parity in primary and secondary education and for access to safe drinking water, and will be quite close on hunger and on primary education completion. Progress has been too slow regarding health-related outcomes such as child and maternal mortality and access to sanitation; the world is likely to miss these by 2015. This is not good news.

On the basis of current economic projections, the world is on track to reduce by half the number of people still living in extreme poverty. The number of people living on less than $1.25 a day is projected to be 883 million in 2015, compared with 1.4bn in 2005 and 1.8bn in 1990. But as earlier pointed out, much of the decline reflects rapid growth in China and India. The news is not good for many African countries as they have been lagging behind: 17 countries are far from halving extreme poverty, even as the aggregate goals will be reached.

In sum, global progress toward the various targets continues to be mixed, and country performance remains predictably diverse. Regarding developing countries that are off track, the top half are, on average, within 10 percent of the on-track trajectory. Those countries close to the target may still miss 2015 deadline, but they could still achieve the targets soon after. They will, however, need to put in place improved policies and accelerate growth to pre-crisis levels. Those countries with slower growth and poorer institutions are farthest behind. Many of the countries that are far from the target are "fragile states," reinforcing the great need for the international community including the African Development Bank to increase support to these countries.

Finally, it is my view that an important impediment to meeting the MDGs is the movement of illicit funds from developing countries. As we earlier discussed, GFI estimates that developing countries collectively lose an estimated $1tn in illicit financial flows, including through corruption, trade in smuggled goods, and criminal activities such as drug trafficking and counterfeiting. According to a UNDP commissioned paper authored by Dev Kar (2011), about 65 percent of illicit financial flows from LDCs are through trade mispricing, when imports are overpriced and exports underpriced on customs documents. There is need to reform how countries manage customs and tax revenues as well as strengthen anti-corruption and oversight measures.

According to UNDP-commissioned paper, customs and tax in the LDCs should be accompanied with robust legal institutions and regulatory systems to fight one of the nemesis of Africa – corruption. Watchdogs should be empowered to provide adequate oversight over the operations of the financial system including the customs authorities, multinational companies, as well as collection of taxes. There must be political will to execute these recommendations both domestically and internationally, where the system funds end up. UNDP should intensify the effort with both developed and LDCs to enhance their anti-corruption capacities, with the longer term aim of making more resources available for important sectors such as education, health care, and other public investments.

The Rich Controls the Key to Change

After all that has been said up to this point, it is the rich countries that hold the key to change. They must be willing to play the Robin Hood. They must be willing to tell the World Bank and IMF to change their ways, because the two banks do their bidding. The policies of these two institutions are inimical to the interest of developing countries. The institutions are there to enhance the rapacious exploitation of capitalism by forcing poor countries to open their economies to foreign corporations, promoting export production at the disastrous expense of local consumption, encouraging the exploitation of cheap labour as a means of attracting foreign investment, and encouraging the degradation of natural resources as the poor countries sell their natural forests and minerals to earn money to pay back huge loans owed to the sponsors of international financial institutions.

Take, for instance, the heads of the World Bank and IMF. Through an unwritten convention, the US has held the presidency of the World Bank while Western Europe has controlled the headship of the IMF since after World War 11. The World Bank board of directors chooses the president through a system of weighted voting in which the US has 16 percent, the EU states altogether 29 percent, and Japan 9 percent, making a total of 54 percent; the rest of the world has 46 percent, ensuring that for eternity the status quo cannot be changed. The US will always produce the World Bank president while Europe will always choose the head of IMF. In 2012 three candidates vied for the presidency of the World Bank: Jim Yong Kim nominated by the US, Jose Antonio Ocampo nominated by Mexico, and Ngozi Okonjo-Iweala nominated by Nigeria. Of the three, the Nigerian nominee supported by African Union and some others was the best qualified. Mr. Ocampo, to his credit, dropped out so that the Third World could present one candidate in the person of Okonjo-Iweala. This did not help in any way as the US and its Western allies picked the American candidate. One can see how undemocratic the system is; the voice of developing countries is not part of the decision-making process. It is time for the organisation to redefine its purpose in an era in which emerging countries are growing in economic muscle. It is time for leaders of the World Bank and IMF to commit to transforming the institutions into multilateral institutions that truly reflect the vision of all its participants, including the governance structure that reflects current economic and political reality. However, as things stand right now both the IMF and World Bank will continue to cater to the interests of their sponsors, the West, US and Japan. Nations of the North aim to create conditions for their multinational corporations to make money and they have the two financial institutions to do their bidding. So reducing global poverty is at best secondary in their agenda.

Mooney, Knox and Schacht (2011:222) have noted that putting an end to or reducing poverty "begins with the recognition that doing so is a worthy ideal and an attainable goal." Just imagine "a world where everyone had comfortable shelter, plentiful food, clean water and sanitation, adequate medical care, and education". Imagine further that this imaginary world were achieved and that absolute poverty were effectively eliminated, and then further imagine what would be the effects on social problems such as crime, drug abuse, family problems (like domestic violence, child abuse, and divorce), health problems, prejudice and racism, international conflict and inter ethnic or fratricidal conflicts such as have devastated Nigeria, the Congo, Rwanda, Liberia and other African countries? As noted by the World Bank (2005), given the current global situation dominated by conflict and terrorism, we might be delighted that "reducing poverty and the hopelessness that comes with human deprivation is perhaps the most effective way of promoting long-term peace and security" (also cited in Mooney, Knox and Schacht 2011:222). It is impossible to even dream about such a utopian world when rules of international trade are designed to benefit the rich and the powerful nations to the detriment of the poor and powerless ones. But one can hope that cooler heads will prevail some day and the necessary changes will be made in the global economy to accommodate the less privileged countries to also benefit from the blessings of globalisation. With those changes, the juggernaut would have been tamed.

Thinking Aloud

In its report, *Sub-Saharan Africa: From Crisis to Sustainable Growth,* the World Bank (1989:xii) noted that "a central theme (of the report) is that although sound macro-economic policies and an efficient infrastructure are essential to provide an *enabling environment* for the productive use of resources, they alone are not sufficient to transform the structures of African economies. At the same time major efforts are needed to *build African capacities* – to produce a better trained, more healthy population and to greatly strengthen the institutional framework within which development can take place. This is why the report strongly supports the call for a human-centered development strategy..." The World Bank then calls for "increased aid" and that "external finance must be matched by improved policies.' However, "in the long-term, dependency on aid and technical assistance must be reduced."

But from all that we know, the SAPs engineered and executed by the World Bank and IMF do not encourage human-centered development. Much of the foreign aid is drying up; and even the little that goes to Africa is not always properly used and as a matter of policy, strings are attached. There is also the problem of commodity prices for African products. There is no natural or economic law that stipulates that prices of African commodities must be pecked at a very low level. There are growing regional economic organisations in the world the impact of which is not favourable to Africa. Rather than governments not becoming involved, they are increasingly becoming more and more involved in an international political economy which is becoming more and more mercantalistic. While these governments get involved in positions of strength, African countries are powerless and must practice hat in hand Uncle Tomism. Africa does not even have consultants who can stand toe to toe with their foreign counterparts. They are completely outwitted at negotiations, leaving Africa a huge loser.

Donors, including the World Bank, as admitted by Mr. Edward Jaycox, the Bank's Vice President for Africa, "have done disservice to Africa by imposing foreign consultants" on Africa. This practice, Mr. Jaycox believes, is a "systematic destructive force ... undermining the development of capacity in Africa." African governments share in the responsibility for the "amazing brain drain" by inefficiently utilising their own expensively trained professional talent. And yet, with their "world class problems," African countries need world-class economic managers. The continent has been locked in a "vicious cycle" of decreasing local capacity to manage the proliferation of aid projects and donor countries on their aid. What is apparent here is that after more than 30 years of expensive technical cooperation (TC) Africa's institutions remain weak and its dependence on foreign aid and foreign assistance has intensified (Bentsi-Enchill, June 1993:13).

It is time for Africa to produce qualified Africans to help generate economic reform strategies and policy papers. The World Bank, IMF or any other institution should not be writing plans for African countries. While World Bank funding and practical collaboration in such work may be in order, the Bank-funded projects must be run by African ministries and not by project management units based in Washington, DC, and the use of resident expatriate consultants should be significantly curtailed. They are very expensive. Although most African countries are "not capable yet of putting together plans which will solve their problems," Bank methods are also not working. Jaycox, already mentioned above, admits that "the idea that we provide this from 8,000 or 10,000 miles away is ridiculous." Indeed, Africa should have enough economic planners and managers. If they do not, immediate plans should be undertaken to train them in order to break the expatriate grip. Aid "co-management" is a known practice by the Nordic countries; donors should limit their "often incoherent involvement in African policy-making processes and public sector management." Africans must take charge of the assault on the vicious cycle of over-expenditure on foreign expertise and under-spending on building local institutions and mobilising national expertise. In the final analysis, African governments and institutions must wake up from their slumber to take "control of the whole process themselves, own it, and manage it with seriousness and commitment".

Collective decision-making is essential in these trying times. African leaders should collectively take decisions "to turn the situation around through strategic planning and simple hard work" (Mokgethi, December 1993-March 1994:41). As proposed by Ndegwa and Reginald Green, African leaders should convene an extraordinary summit to formulate a strategy for "collective survival through self-reliance programmes." This strategy would thoroughly blend democratisation and social justice at national levels with more realistic programmes for regional cooperation. This "imperative political and economic agenda" would supplant the "waiting disease" that has afflicted African nations since the onset of SAPs. Most countries simply wait for the World Bank and IMF support, for donors to convene meetings on aid, and for others to take new "initiatives" on the continent's external debt.

Since the continent is already neck-deep in SAPs, it should pursue their positive aspects, and mobilise for progress on the two vital issues of mass poverty and external debt. There is urgent need for African countries to build poverty-reduction measures into all development policies and programmes. Africa has little or no influence on terms of trade, but Africans can act to improve domestic resource allocation, improve service delivery and enable those in poverty particularly small farmers, to produce more.

Those SAPs policies as financial and monetary prudence, greater reliance on market mechanisms and support for private sector growth, trade tariffs that reduce over-protection and promote exports, and "good governance" should be pursued. The World Bank and IMF should go beyond their exclusive focus on ensuring changes in domestic policies of African countries. These two powerful financial institutions should exert their influence to encourage bilateral donors to contribute to African recovery in such non-aid areas as trade and debt. African countries on their part should convene an international conference on their external debt, under World Bank auspices. They should use the occasion to make a strong case for debt relief. A collective stand would be necessary because individually they are powerless. (Ndegwa and Green, ibid.)

Africa's marginalisation should be a challenge to Africans. It should provide both the stimulant and motivation for the continent to take action on its own development agenda. To begin with, the developed countries are preoccupied with their own domestic and regional problems; the international economic system will continue to remain inequitable and work "in favour of the rich and the powerful countries (or at least against the weak and poor).´ Since Africa's case is that of how to survive in a hostile political and economic environment, there should be a national political agenda which should include outright democratisation process that promotes social justice by eliminating ethnic and religious chauvinism, localism, nepotism and corruption, and by giving priority concern to gender issues. Every national government should strive to eliminate every form of patrimonialism, patronage system and clientelism. To promote genuine decentralisation, the development of NGOs and community participation should be encouraged (ibid.)

In the area of "political change" of regional cooperation, Africa should not seek to import common market models. It should, instead, emphasise the need for a process and framework that creates "vested interests in each country," while "avoiding an overbearing central secretariat." There should be a form of production sharing and a process of agricultural modernisation that involves collaboration between countries.

The advice by the World Bank that infrastructure should be built according to demand "should be completely disregarded," because coordinated development of infrastructure would provide the facilities required to attract the regionally-oriented private investment crucial to economic recovery and growth (Mokgethi, December 1993-March 1994:41).

Furthermore, solutions to the demoralising debt burden require a collective approach, since the creditors' insistence on a case-by-case approach significantly weakens the negotiating position of individual debtor countries. Probably an initiative by African countries to summon an international conference on their debt burden could encourage the World Bank to insist on realistic ceilings for present and future debt service.

There should also be a regional action for environmental protection and national programmes should not be postponed while waiting for some international actions. There should also be incentives instead of coercion as the path to "a mass base for eco-friendly measures" (ibid.) External roadblocks lie in the route of regional cooperation and therefore collective action is crucial to survival and development. Continued reliance on foreign aid assistance will continue to confound the dependency status of the continent. One does not call for abrogation of aid, because Africa deserves reparations for centuries of exploitation. But there is no free aid. Reliance on aid further consummates African dependency. Therefore, Africa should turn to "effective strategic planning, priority selection and sequencing" that are crucial to hastening the end of external dependence. All those in leadership responsibilities, from grassroots to national levels, must be decisive, knowing that survival and progress depend on themselves. Self-reliance is the word. Africa must stop behaving like a child, expecting gratis from others. Africa must bring itself up from the economic ruins that it assisted the rich and powerful countries to push her into. Only Africa can save itself.

Having said these, we must be realistic that not much can change without the cooperation of the rich and powerful countries. Africa and the Third World in general are very weak economically and politically. They are therefore unable to force the rich and powerful ones to make some concessions to them. While some Third World countries in Asia and Latin America may move out of the periphery to semi-periphery, and even to the core, almost all countries in the Sub-Saharan region remain excellent candidates for perpetual membership in the periphery. I do not want to be an apostle of terrible pessimism. It is possible that the Third World countries will one day recapture the momentum of the 1970s which would force a restructuring of the current international economic order to the advantage of the poor countries. The Third World countries have their self interests to protect and this is why it may be very difficult to act as a bloc. But the inequity and asymmetry of the current global system should spur them to act as a group and demand and get changes in the global economy to their favour.

Profit motive is the driving force of capitalism and the *raison de'tre* of businesses is profit maximisation. From the point of view of most Third World people, who have been at the receiving end of capitalist practices, Western capitalism has always been rapacious, exploitative and ruthless, not benevolent. Simply put, Western capitalists need not be consciously invidious, exploitative or ruthless (as they were during colonialism) in order for them to hurt Third World countries. By their controlling economic power and expertise in the art, Third World countries face an insurmountable competitive disadvantage which amounts to a super-ordinate-subordinate relationship. Intentionally or not, exploitation is an inherent characteristic of such a relationship.

Normally, people who benefit from the status quo are resistant to change. Thus the call by the Third World and the Willy Brandt Commission in the 1970s and 1980s for a new international economic order met with very stiff opposition from President Ronald Reagan and Prime Minister Margaret Thatcher, and other western leaders. The position has not changed. The only alternative left is the conflict route, which could spell global economic anarchy. Hungry people cannot be peaceful people.

But conflict may not really solve anything. We can only hope that the globalisation of the international economy will lead to a truly **economic interdependence** (*not dependence of some countries on others as it is now the case*) among all nations and that this will lead to more cooperation rather than conflict. In a truly **interdependent** economy of the twenty-first century, the rich capitalist nations must not continue to see global development as a zero sum game. Rather, they should realise that a more equitable international economic order demanded by the Third World since the 1970s is a necessity. For, in a globally interdependent economy, the development of each nation is inextricably tied to the development of all others, because they share a common destiny. A more equitable international economic order coupled with internal reforms in Third World countries would minimise poverty and therefore hunger and associated ills.

Bibliography

Adams, P. (1992). "The World Bank and the IMF in Sub-Saharan Africa: Undermining Development and Developmental Sustainability." *Journal of International Affairs.*

Addison, Tony (2006). "Debt relief: The development and poverty impact." *Swedish Economic Policy Review.* Vol. 13. pp.205-230.

Adedeji, Adebayo (1990). "Economic Progress: What Africa Needs." *Transafrica Forum,* Summer 1990.

Adedeji, Adebayo and Timothy M. Shaws (eds.)(1985). "Intra-African Economic Cooperation in   Light of the Final Act of Lagos." *Economic Crisis in Africa: African Perspectives on Development Problems and Potentials* Boulder: Lynne Rienner.

Adigun, Omodele (2012). "Borrowing Spree: Will Nigeria ever get out of debt trap?" *Daily Sun.* April 23.

AEFJN (2011). "Western Cotton Subsidies Endanger African Farmers." Africa/Europe Faith and Justice Network. _____ Online version retrieved 1-10-12.

AfricaFocus (2011). "Africa:Capital Flight Hits Continent Hard." 17 December. Africafocus@igc.org

AfricaFocus Bulletin. (2011). "Africa: Capital Flight Updates." 17 December. Africafocus@igc.org

Africa Grantmakers Affinity Group: Iroko Education Project. (2011a). "Some Basic Facts About Education in Africa." Washington, DC. _____ 2011b. "Education Facts and Figures." Tides Centre. Washington, DC.

Africa Recovery, June 1993.

Africa Recovery, December 1992-March 1993.

Africa Recovery, August 1998.

African Development Bank Report, 1993.

Ahmad, Z. M. (1986). "The Rural Women's World: Overworked and Underpaid." *Third World Affairs.* London: Third World Foundation.

Ahmed, Masood (2000). "Making Globalisation Work for the Poor." *The Independent*, London. Originally published by the IMF.

Ake, Claude (1995). "The New World Order: The View from Africa" in Hans-Henrick and G. Sovensen (eds.). *Whose World Order: Uneven Globalisation and End of Cold War.* London: West View Press.

Akeredolu-Ale, E. O. (1975). *The Underdevelopment of Indigenous Entrepreneurship in Nigeria.* Ibadan: Ibadan University Press.

Akinboye, S. O. (2008). "Globalisation and the Challenge for Nigeria's Development in the 21st Century." International Consortium for the Advancement of Academic Publication. Vol. 7. Issue 1. Pp. 1-12.

Akonor, Kwame (2008). "Foreign Aid to Africa: A Hollow Hope?" *International Law and Politics.* Vol. 40. pp. 1071-1078.

Allen, Will (2004). "Cotton Subsidies and Cotton Problems." Organic Consumers Association. Retrieved 1-10-12.

Amin, S. (1971). *Neo-colonialism in West Africa.* New York: Monthly Press.

Amoda, Moyibi. (1972). "The Relationship of History, Thought and Action with Respect to the Nigerian Situation." Joseph Okpaku (ed.), *Nigeria: Dilemma of Nationhood.* New York: The Third Press.

Anderson, Charles. (1976). *The Sociology of Survival.* Homewood: Ill.: The Dorsey Press.

_____ (1971). *Toward a New Sociology: A Critical View.*
Homewood, Ill.: The Dorsey Press.

Annan, Kofi (2000). "Making Globalisation Work for the
Poor." *The Independent,* London. 12 December.

Antrobus, Kate (2010). "Abolishing agricultural subsidies in
Western countries: the self-interested case." July 21.
Online. Retrieved June 1, 2011.

Arndt, H. W. (1987). *Economic Development: The History of
An Idea.* Chicago: University of Chicago Press.

Ayaji, Ibrahim (1994). "Abacha is a Complete Failure."
Tempo, Vol. 3, No. 18. Nov 3

Babalola, J. B., Lungwangwa, G. and Adeyinka, A. A. (1999).
"Education Under Structural Adjustment Pragramme
in Nigeria and Zambia." *MCGILL Journal of Education.*
Vol. 34, No. 1. pp. 79-98.

Bacchetta, M. and Jansen, M. (eds.) (2011). *Making
Globalisation Socially Sustainable.* WTO and ILO.
Geneva and Switzerland.

Baker, Raymond W. (2005). *Capitalism's Achilles Heels: Dirty
Money and How to Renew the Free-Market System.*
New Jersey. John Wiley and Sons.

Baran, Paul. (1957). *The Political Economy of Growth.*
New York:Monthly Review Press.

Bauer, P. T. (1963). *West African Trade.* New York: A M.Kelley.

Behrman, Jack N. and Wilson E. Schmidt (1957). *Industrial
Economics.* New York: RinBehart and Co.

Bentsi-Enchill, Nii. December 1993-March 1994. "Devaluation
Hits the African Franc Zone." *Africa Recovery.*

_____ (1993). "Breaking the Expatriate Grip on Africa:
UNDP and World Bank Call for Reforms to Technical
Cooperation." *Africa Recovery.* June

Birdsall, Nancy. 1999. "Globalisation and the Developing
Countries: The Inequality Risk." Carnegie Endowment

for International Peace. Remarks at Overseas Development Council Conference, "Making Globalisation Work", International Trade Center, Washington, DC. March 18.

Bloom, L. (1985). "Cultural Fragmentation and Mental Distress: A Psycho-Ethnographic Perspective." *Psycopathologie Africaine,* 20:79-96.

Blunstein, P. (1998). "Annus Panicus for the IMF." *Washington Post.* October 4

Bohan, P. T. (2012). "Vulture Capitalism." *The Evolution of Mediocrity.* Online. March 23. Retrieved 4-12-12.

Bohannan, Paul and Philip Curtin. (1988). *Africa and Africans.* Prospects Heights, Illinois: Waveland Press.

Boone, Catherine (1990). "Status and Ruling Class in Post-Colonial Africa: The Enduring Considerations of Power." Paper read at the 33rd Annual Meeting of the African Studies Association, Baltimore, November1-4.

Bosshard, Peter (2008). "China's Environmental Footprint in Africa." Global Policy Forum. May 29.

Boswell, Terry (1989). "Colonial Empires and the Capitalist World-Economy: A Time Series Analysis of Colonialisation, 1640-1960." *American Sociological Review.* 54:180-196.

Boughton, J. (1994). "IMF Since 1979: Revolutions in the World Economy." *IMF Survey,* Vol. 23, No.14.

Boutros-Ghali, Boutros. (1996). "Global Leadership After the Cold War." *Foreign Affairs,* March/April pp.86-98. Also excerpted in UNCTAD *Bulletin* of January-March, 1996, pp.3-4.

Boyce, James K. and Ndikumana Leonce (2011). "African Debt: Funny Money and Stolen Lives." September 28. Online. Retrieved 1-24-2012.

http://africanarguments.org

Bradshaw, Y. W. and Wallace, M. 1996. *Global Inequalities.* Thousand Oaks, CA: Pine Forge Press. Globalisation Work", International Trade Center, Washington, DC. March 18.

Bloom, L. (1985). "Cultural Fragmentation and Mental Distress: A Psycho-Ethnographic Perspective." *Psycopathologie Africaine,* 20:79-96.

Blunstein, P. (1998). "Annus Panicus for the IMF." *Washington Post.* October 4

Bohan, P. T. (2012). "Vulture Capitalism." *The Evolution of Mediocrity.* Online. March 23. Retrieved 4-12-12.

Bohannan, Paul and Philip Curtin. (1988). *Africa and Africans.* Prospects Heights, Illinois: Waveland Press.

Boone, Catherine (1990). "Status and Ruling Class in Post-Colonial Africa: The Enduring Considerations of Power." Paper read at the 33rd Annual Meeting of the African Studies Association, Baltimore, November1-4.

Bosshard, Peter (2008). "China's Environmental Footprint in Africa." Global Policy Forum. May 29.

Boswell, Terry (1989). "Colonial Empires and the Capitalist World-Economy: A Time Series Analysis of Colonialisation, 1640-1960." *American Sociological Review.* 54:180-196.

Boughton, J. (1994). "IMF Since 1979: Revolutions in the World Economy." *IMF Survey*, Vol. 23, No.14.

Boutros-Ghali, Boutros. (1996). "Global Leadership After the Cold War." *Foreign Affairs*, March/April pp.86-98. Also excerpted in UNCTAD *Bulletin* of January-March, 1996, pp.3-4.

Boyce, James K. and Ndikumana Leonce (2011). "African Debt: Funny Money and Stolen Lives." September 28. Online. Retrieved 1-24-2012. http://africanarguments.org

Bradshaw, Y. W. and Wallace, M. 1996. *Global Inequalities.* Thousand Oaks, CA: Pine Forge Press.

Brinkerhoff, David B., White, Lynn K. and Ortega, Suzanne T. (1999). *Essentials of Sociology.* New York:Wadsworth.

Brown, Michael Barrat, and Pauline Tiffen (1992). *Short Changed: Africa in World Trade.* London: Pluto Press.

Brown, Oli (2008). From Feast to Famine: After Seven Relatively Good Years, What now for Commodity Producers in the Developing World?" International Institute for Sustainable Development, Manitoba, Canada. December.

Brunelli, Biana (2007). "Structural Adjustment Programmes and the Delivery of Health Care in the Third World." Pell Scholars and Senior Theses. Paper 16. Salve Regina Univ. http://escholar.salve.edu/pell_theses16

Bryjak, George J. and Michael P. Soroka. *Sociology: Cultural Diversity in A Changing World.* Boston: Sllyn and Bacon.

Bunwaree, Sheila. 2002. "Globalisation: A Political Perspective," in *Globalisation and Africa: Final Report.* Swiss Agency for Development and Cooperation, September 5-6, Basel, Switzerland.

Callaghy, Thomas R. (1993). "Vision and Politics in the Transformation of the Global Political Economy: Lessons from the Second and Third Worlds." Robert O. Slater *et al* (eds.), *Global Transformation and the Third World.* Boulder: Lynne Rienner. pp.131-160.

Chaliand, Gerard. (n.d.) "Third World: Definitions and Descriptions." *Third World Traveler.* Online.

Retrieved 11-29-11.

Chazan, N. *et al.* (1988). *Politics and Society in Contemporary Africa.* Boulder: Lynne Rienner.

Chiakwelu, Emeka (2009). "Nigeria's payment of foreign debt: The largest transfer of wealth in modern time." Afripol Organisation. www.Afripol.org

Cockerham, William (1995). *The Global Society.* New York: McGraw-Hill.

Cockcroft, James D. *et al.* (1972). *Dependence and Underdevelopment: Latin America's Political Economy.* New York: Anchor Books.

Coleman, James (1986). "Social Theory, Social Research, and a Theory of Action." *American Journal of Sociology.* 91:1309-1335.

_____ (1958). *Nigeria: Background to Nationalism.* Berkeley: UCLA Press.

Clower, R. W. *et al.* (1966). *Growth Without Development: An Economic Survey of Liberia.* Evanston, Illinois: Northwestern University Press.

Colgan, Ann-Louis (2002). "Hazardous to Health: The World Bank and IMF in Africa." *Africa Action.* April 18.

Collins, Carol (1998). "Jubilee 2000 Debt Relief Campaign Targets G-8 Leaders." *Africa Recovery.* August.

Collins, Randall and Makowski, Michael (1993). *The Discovery of Society.* New York: McGraw-Hill.

Collier, P. (1988). "Oil Shocks and Food Security in Nigeria." *International Labour Review*, Vol. 127.

Common Crisis North-South: Co-operation for World Recovery, The Brandt Commission Report. (1983). Cambridge, Mass: MIT Press.

Congressional Record: Proceedings and Debates of the 104th
    Congress, Second Session. Washington, D.C. Thursday
    July 25, 1966, Vol. 142, No.111.
Cooper, Frederick (2002). *Africa Since 1940: The Past of the
    Present.* Cambridge: Cambridge University Press.
Crowder, Michael (1968). *West Africa Under Colonial Rule.*
    Evanston, Illinois: Northwestern University Press.
Curtin, Phillip D. 1971. *Imperialism.* New York: Harper and
    Row.
Davidson, Basil (1992). *The Black Man's Burden: Africa and
    Curse of the Nation-State.* New York: Times Books.
_____ (1971/1967). *Which Way Africa?* Baltimore:
    Penguin Books.
Dede, Brownson N. (1993). "Problems of Security and African
    Development." Paper read at Panel of High-level
    Personalities on African Development, organised by the
    UN, New York.
DFID. (2004). "Rethinking Tropical Agricultural Commodities."
    UK DFID in collaboration with the Overseas
    Development Institute (ODI). London. August.
DeLancy, Virginia (1993). "Economies of Africa." April Gordon
    and Donald Gordon (eds.), *Understanding Contemporary
    Africa.* Boulder: Lynne Rienner.
Dollar, David and Kraay, Aart (2002). "Growth is Good for the
    Poor." *Journal of Economic Growth.* Kluwer Academic
    Publishers, The Netherlands. Vol. 7. pp.195-2
Durning , A. B. (1989a). *Action at the Grassroots: Fighting
    Poverty and Environmental Decline.* World-Watch
    Papers 88. Washington, D.C.: World-Watch Institute.
_____ (1989b). *Poverty and the Environment: Reversing
    the Downward Spiral.* World-Watch Paper 92.
    Washington, D.C.: World-Watch Institute.

Edem, Ukpong (1993). "Ike Nwachukwu Orders 6DC-9
    Aircraft." *African News Weekly.* April 16. Asheville, NC.
Edwards, Sebasti (2002). "Review of Joseph E. Stiglitz's
    Globalisation and Its Discontents." W.W. Norton, New
    York and London. National Bureau of Economic
    Research, Cambridge, USA. 9 September.
Ehrlic, Paul R. and John R. Holdren (1988). *The Cassandra
    Conference.* College Station, TX: Texas A&M Univ. Press.
El-Ojeili, Chamsy and Hayden, Patrick (2006). *Critical
    Theories of Globalisation.* NY: Palgrave Macmillan.
Evans, P. B. and Stephens, D. J. (1988). "Development and the
    World Economy." N. J. Smelser (ed.), *Handbook of
    Sociology.* Newbury Park, CA: Sage. pp. 739-773.
Fact Sheet on Debt for Africa 2008. UN. February 8.
Fairtrade Foundation (2010). "The Great Cotton Stitch-Up."
    Report of Fairtrade Foundation. Nov 10
    www.fairtrade.org.uk
Fanon, Frantz (1966). *The Wretched of the Earth.* New York:
    Grove Press.
FAO (2009). "The State of Agricultural Commodity Markets."
    Food and Agriculture Organisation of the UN, N. Y.
Feagin, Joe R. and Feagin, Clairece B. (1996). *Racial and
    Ethnic Relations.* New Jersey: Prentice Hall.
Feldman, P. and Lawrence, D. (1975). "Social and Economic
    Implications of the Large-scale Introduction of New
    Varieties of Food-grains." *Africa Report.* Geneva:
    UNRISD.
Ferguson, Ian F. (2008). "World Trade Organisation
    Negotiations: The Doha Development Agenda."
    Congressional Research Service Report for Congress.
    Washington, DC. January 18.
Fischer, Stanley (2001). "The Challenge of Globalisation in
    Africa." Speech delivered at the France-Africa Summit,

Yaounde, Cameroon. January. Stanley then was First Deputy Managing Director of IMF.

Fleshman, Michael (2006). "Trade talks: Where is the development?" *Africa Renewal*. United Nations Department of Public Information. Vol. 20, No.1. April.

Food4Africa (2012). "Facts on Poverty in Africa." http://www.food4africa.org/index.asp?pgid=42. Jan.

Fordham, Paul (1968). *The Geography of African Affairs.* Baltimore: Penguin.

Frank, A. G. (1969). *Latin America: Underdevelopment or Revolution?* New York: Monthly Review Press.

_____ (1967). *Capitalism and Underdevelopment in Latin America*. Monthly Review Press.

Freund, Bill (1984). *The Making of Contemporary Africa.* Bloomington: Indiana University Press.

Fukuda, Kenneth (2008). "What is a Vulture Fund?" Univ. of Iowa Center for International Finance and Development. May. Online. Retrieved 4-9-12.

Fukuyama, Francis (1992). *The End of History and the Last Man*. London: Hamish Hamilton.

Gamst, F. C. (1974). *Peasants in Complex Society*. New York: Holt, Rinehart and Winston.

Gans, H. (1996). "Positive Functions of the Undeserving Poor: Uses of the Underclass in America," in J. Levin and A. Arluke (eds.), *Snapshots and Portraits of Society.* Thousand Oaks, CA: Pine Forge Press.

_____ (1971). "The Uses of Poverty: The Poor Pay for All." *Social Policy*. Summer. Pp. 20-24.

Garten, Jeffrey E. (2006). "Rebel with Authority." Book Review of Joseph E. Stiglitz's *Making Globalisation Work*. W. W. Norton and Co., Inc. News Week. Sept 5.

Gascoigne, Clark (2011). "Trade Mispricing Fuels Massive Outflows from Southeast Asian Nation." GFI, Washington, DC. December.

_____ (12-15-11). "Despite Global Financial Crisis, Illicit Financial Outflows from Developing World Remain High." Center for Intern. Policy. Washington, DC.

George, Susan (1992). *The Debt Boomerang: How Third World Debt Harms Us All.* Boulder: Westview Press.

GFI. (2011). "Despite Global Financial Crisis Outflows from Developing World Remain High, Finds New Report." Press Release. December 15

Ghai, Dharan (1991). "Introduction." Ghai, Dharam (ed.). *The IMF and the South: The Social Crisis and Adjustment.* New Jersey: Zed Books.

_____ and Radwan, S. (1983). *Agrarian Policies and Rural Poverty in Africa.* Geneva: ILO.

_____ and C. H. Alcantara (1991). "The Crisis of the 1980s in Africa, Latin America and the Carribean: An Overview." Dharam Ghai (ed.). *The IMF and the South: The Social Impact of Crisis and Adjustment.* New Jersey: Zed Books.

Global Exchange (2001). "How the International Monetary Fund and the World Bank Undermine Democracy and Erode Human Rights: Five Case Studies." San Francisco. September.

Global Financial Integrity (GFI). (2011a). "Illicit Financial Flows from Developing Countries over the Decade Ending 2009." GFI, Washington, DC. December.

Gold Coast Weekly Review. July 20, 1955.

Goode, Erich (1997). *Deviant Behaviour.* N.J.: Prentice Hall.

Gordon, April A. (1992). "Women and Development." In April A. Gordon and Donald L. Gordon (eds.), *Understanding Contemporary Africa.* Boulder: Lynne Rienner.

Gordon, Donald L. (1992). "African Politics." April A. Gordon
and Donald L. Gordon (eds.), *Understanding
Contemporary Africa.* Boulder: Lynne Rienner.

Green, R. H. and Seidman, Ann (1968): *Unity or Poverty: The
Politics of Pan Africanism.* Baltimore: Penguin.

Griffin, K. (1974). *The Political Economy of Agrarian Change.*
London: Macmillan.

Hagen, Everett E. (1962). *On the Theory of Social Change.*
Homewood, Illinois: Dorsey Press.

Hammer, J. (1994). "A Generation of Failure." *Newsweek. Aug. 1*

Hanson, Stephanie (2008). "The African Growth and
Opportunity Act." Council on Foreign Relations,
Washington, DC. December 5.

Haperskij, Evgenij (2010). "Edge on International Finance:
The Fabulous Life of Ravenous Vulture Funds." The
Cutting Edge. Online. May 24th. Retrieved 4-9-12.

Harden, Blaine (1990). *Africa: Dispatches from a Fragile
Continent.* New York: Norton.

_____ (1990). "End of the Line." *The Washington Post.* June 3

Harrington, Michael (1962). *The Other America: Poverty in
the United States.* New York: Macmillan.

Harrison, L. E. (1985). *Underdevelopment is a State of Mind:
The Latin American Case.* Cambridge, MA: The Center
for International Affairs, Harvard University.

Harrison, P. (1987). *Inside the Third World.* NY: Penguin Books.

Harsch, Ernest (1994). "Building Africa's Economic Capacity."
Africa Recovery. April-Sept.

_____ (1998). "Africa Tenses for Asian Aftershocks." *Africa
Recovery.* November.

Harvey, D. (1989). *The Condition of Postmodernity.* Cambridge:
Basil Blackwell.

Helmuth, John W. (1989). "World Hunger Amidst Plenty." *USA Today,* Vol. 117, No. 2526. March.

Henriot, Peter J. (1998). "Globalisation: Implications for Africa." Online. 12 January.

Henrique, F. and Enzo Faletto (1979). *Dependency and Development in Latin America.* Translated by Marjory M. Urquidi. Berkeley: University of California Press.

Hoberman, John (2006). "The World is Tilted." *The Austin American Statesman.* October 25. Online. Stateman.com.

Hobson, John A. (1971/1902). *Imperialism.* Ann Arbor: University of Michigan Press.

Hodges, Tony (1993). *Angola to 2000 - Prospects for Recovery.* London, Economist Intelligence Unit Research Report.

Hollingshead, Ann (2010a). "The Implied Tax Revenue Loss from Trade Mispricing." GFI. Washington, DC. Feb.

_____ (2010). "Privately Held, Non-resident Deposits in Secrecy Jurisdictions." Global Financial Integrity. Washington, DC. March.

Holm, Hans-henrik and Sorensen, George (1995). "Introduction: What has changed?" In Holm and Sorensen, *Whose World Order: Uneven Globalisation and the End of the Cold War.* Boulder: Westview.

Human Development Report (HDR) (2007). United Nations Development Programme. November.

Hyden, G. (1986). "Enabling Rural Development: Insiders and Outsiders." *Third World Affairs.* London: Third World Foundation.

IMF and World Bank (2007. "Stolen Asset Recovery (StAR) Initiative: Challenges, Opportunities and Action Plan. NY.

IMF. (1993). *Economic Adjustment in Low-Income Countries- Experience under the Enhanced Structural Adjustment Facility.* Washington, D.C. Sept

Inkels, Alex and Smith, David H. (1974). *Becoming Modern: Individual Change in Six Developing Countries.* Cambridge, MA: Harvard University Press.

Internâtional Fund for Agricultural Development (1993). *The State of World Rural Poverty. Washington, D.C.*

Irving, Jacqueline. (1998). "Uncertain Prospects for LDC Growth." *Africa Recovery.* November.

Islam, Shada (1993/1994). "Europe Toughens Terms for ACP Countries." *Africa Recovery.* Dec.1993-March 1994).

Jallow, M. K. (2010). "Foreign Aid and Underdevelopment in Africa." Probe Intern. Canada. April. Modern Ghana.co.

Jega, Attahiru (1993). "Professional Associations and Structural Adjustment." Adebayo O. Olukoshi (ed.), *The Politics of Structural Adjustment in Nigeria.* Portsmouth: Heinemann Educational Books.

Joidka, Simran (2010). "Globalisation: The juggernaut will roll on." The Tribune, Chandigarch, India. Online. Nov. 8.

July, Robert W. (1992). *A History of the African People.* Prospect Heights, Illinois: Waveland Press.

Kar, Dev and Freitas, Sarah (2011). "Illicit Financial Flows from Developing Countries over the Decade Ending 2009." Global Financial Integrity. Washington, DC. December.

Kar, Dev, Cartwright-Smith, Devon and Hollingshead, Ann. (2010). "The Absorption of Illicit Financial Flows from Developing Countries: 2002-2006." Global Financial Integrity. Washington, DC. May.

Kar, Dev and Cartwright-Smith (2008a). "Illicit Financial Flows from Developing Countries: 2002-2006 – Executive Report." Global Finan. Integrity. Wash DC.

_____ (2008b). "Illicit Financial Flows from Developing Countries: 2002-2006." Full Report. Global Financial Integrity. Wash, DC. Dec.

_____ (2008c). "Illicit Financial Flows from Africa: Hidden Resources for Development." Global Financial Integrity. Washington, DC. December.

Karmarck, A. M. (1967). *Economics of African Development.* New York: Frederick Praeger.

Kasfir, Nelson (1983). "Designs and Dilemmas: An Overview." Phillip Mawhood (ed.). *Local Government in the Third World: The Experience of Tropical Africa.* Chichester: John Wiley and Sons.

Kates, Jennifer and Carbaugh, Alicia (2006). HIV/AIDS Policy Fact Sheet: The HIV/AIDS Epidemic in Sub-Saharan Africa." Online. Retrieved 4/19/12. www.kff.org

Kay, John (2001). *Financial Times. London.* November 14.

Kendall, Diana (1998). *Sociology.* New York: Wadsworth.

Kevin, Watkins (2002). "Making Globalisation Work for the Poor." *Finance and Development – A quarterly magazine of the IMF.* Volume 39, No. 1. March.

Khor, M. and Raman, M. (2006). "Globalisation, Liberalisation, Protectionism: Impacts on Poor Rural Producers in Developing Countries." Third World Network (TWN). IFAD.

Knapp, P. (1994). *One World - Many Worlds: Contemporary Sociological Theory.* New York: Harper Collins.

Kornblum, William (1998). *Sociology: The Central Questions.* New York: Harper Collins.

Kovach, H. and Lansman, Y. (2006). "World Bank and IMF Conditionality: A Development Injustice." Eurodad Report. June.

Kusi, N. K. (1991). "Ghana: Can the Adjustment Reforms Be Sustained?" *Africa Development.* Vol. 16, 3-4, pp. 181-206.

Laishley, Roy (1994). "Faster Growth But No Economic Turnaround?" *Africa Recovery.* April-September

_____ (1993-1994a). "World Bank says Adjustment Works." *Africa Recovery.* December-March

_____ (1993- 1994b). "Africa's Debt Burden Continues to Grow." *Africa Recovery.* December - March.

Lancaster, Carol (1990). "Reform or Else?" *Africa Report.* July - August.

Lappe, F. M. and Collins, J. (1994). "Why Can't People Feed Themselves?" *Annual Edition: Anthropology.* Guilford, CT: The Duskin Publishing Group.

_____ (1986). *World Hunger: Twelve Myths.* New York: Grove Press.

_____ and David Kingsley (1981). *Aid as Obstacle: Twenty Questions About Foreign Policy and the Hungry.* San Francisco: Institute for Food and Development Policy.

Leipziger, Danny (2007). "Let's Stop Vulture Funds from Preying on the Poor." Online. June.

_____ http://www.dannyleipziger.com/documents/ LetsStopVultureFund.pdf

Lemarchand, R. (1988). "The State, the Parallel Economy and the Changing Structure of Patronage Systems." Donald Rothchild and Naomi Chazan (eds.), *The Precious Balance: State and Society in Africa.* Boulder:Westview

Lerche, Charles O. (1998). "The Conflicts of Globalisation." International Journal of Peace Studies. Vol. 3. January.

Lerner, Daniel (1958). *The Passing of Traditional Society.* New York: Free Press.

Leslie, Winsome J. (1987). *The World Bank and Structural Transformation in Developing Countries: The Case of Zaire.* Boulder: Lynne Rienner.

Lewellen, Ted C. (1995). *Dependency and Development: An Introduction to the Third World.* Westport: Bergin and Garvey.

LeVine, R.A. (1966). *Dreams and Deeds.*

Chicago: Univ. of Chicago Press.

Lewis, Oscar (1966). "The Culture of Poverty." *Scientific American,* Vol. 115, pp. 19-25.

Lipset, M. (1963). *The First Nation.* New York: Basic Books.

Lipton, M. (1983). *Poverty, Undernutrition and Hunger.* Staff Working Paper 597. Washington, D.C: World Bank.

Lodge, G. C. and E. F. Vogel (1987). *Ideology and National Competitiveness.* Boston: Harvard Business School Press.

Lone, Salim (1993-1994). "Adjustment Report Skirts Questions of Poverty, Sustainability." *Africa Recovery.* December - March.

Louis, W. Roger (1963). *Rwanda-Burundi: 1884-1919.* Oxford: Clarendon Press.

Macionis, John J. (1994). *Sociology: The Basics.* Englewood Cliffs: Prentice Hall.

MacGaffrey, Janet (1988). "Economic Disengagement and Class Formation in Zaire."

Madden, Peter (1993). "Brussels Beef Carve-up: EC Beef Dumping in West Africa." *Viewpoint* No.3, Christian Aid, London. April.

Madunagu, E. (1999). "Globalisation and Its Victims." *The Guardian*, Lagos, Nigeria. July 26.

Maizels, Alfred (1994). "The International Primary Commodity Markets: Key Policy Issues for Developing Countries." UNCTAD *Bulletin,* April.

Makwana, R. (2006). "Poverty and Inequality." Share The Resources. January 6. Online. Retrieved on 1-5-12. _____ _____www.stwr.org.

Marshall, Monty G. and Cole, Benjamin R. (2011). "Global Report 2011: Conflict Governance and State Fragility." Center for Systemic Peace, Vienna, VA, USA. _____ _____www.systemicpeace.org.

Masland, T. (1997). "Goodbye, Mobutu?" *Newsweek.* April 21.

Mayer, Scott. 2012. "Vulture Capitalism." *American Thinkers.* ___
_____www.politiseeds.com

McClelland, D. (1963). "Motivational Patterns in Southeast
Asia with Special Reference to the Chinese Case."
Journal of Social Issues. XX1/1.
_____ (1961). *The Achieving Society.*
New York: Van Nostrand Reinhard.

McGiffen, S. (2002a). "Review of Globalisation Unmasked."
Spectrezine magazine.
_____ (2006b). *Globalisation.* UK: Pocket Essentials.

McGrew, A. (1996). "A Global Society?" Stuart Hall *et al.* (eds.)
Modernity: An Introduction to Modern Societies.
Cambridge, Mass: Blackwell Publishers. pp. 467-503.

McMichael, P. (1996). *Development and Social Change: A
Global Perspective.* Thousand Oaks, CA: Pine Forge

Miers, S. (2003). *Slavery in the Twentieth Century: The
Evolution of a Global Problem.* Walnut Creek, CA.:
AltaMira

Mills, C. Wright (1956). *The Power Elite.* New York: OUP

Mittelman, J. H. (2002). "Making Globalisation Work for the
Have Nots." *International Journal on World Peace.*
Vol. 19, No.2. Pp.3-25. June.

Mkapa, B. W. (2004). Statement by the President of
Tanzania and Co-Chair, World Commission on the
Social Dimension of Globalisation, presenting the
Commission's Report to the Third Ordinary Session
of the Assembly of the African Union, Addis Ababa,
Ethiopia, 6 July 2004.

Mokgethi, Shala (1993-1994). "Africans must take charge."
Africa Recovery. December-March.

Molina-Gallart, Nuria (2009). "Bail-out or blow—out? IMF policy advice and conditions for low-income countries at a time of crisis". Eurodad Report.

Mooney, L. A., Knox, D. and Schacht, C. (2011). *Understanding Social Problems.* Belmont, CA. Wadsworth.

Moore, W. (1963). *Social Change.* New Jersey: Prentice Hall.

Mosley, P. and Weeks, J. (1993). "Has Recovery Begun? Africa's Adjustment in the 1980s Revisited." *World Development.* 21:10. pp. 1583-1606.

Moyo, Ambrose (1992). "Religion in Africa." April A. and Donald L. Gordon (eds.), *Understanding Contemporary Africa.* Boulder: Lynne Rienner.

Murray, Victor A. (1967). *The School in the Bush.* New York: Barnes and Noble.

Mutethia, James. (2000). "Africa and Globalisation." *The Guardian*, Lagos, Nigeria. August 15.

Mutume, Gumisai (2003). "African Cotton Farmers Battling to Survive." *Africa Recovery.* United Nations Department of Public Information. Vol. 17, No.1. May

Muyale-Maneji, Fridah (2010). "The Effects of Globalisation on Culture in Africa in the eyes of an African Woman." *ECHOES.* World Council of Churches.

Naiman, R. and Watkins, N. (1999). "A Survey of the Impacts of IMF Structural Adjustment in Africa: Growth, Social Spending, and Debt Relief." Center for Economic and Policy Research. Washington, DC.

Ndebbio, J. and Ekpo, A. H. (1989). *Employment Potentials and Strategic Policy Options in Nigeria's Rural Sector.* Lagos: Spectrum Books.

Ndikumana, L. and Boyce, J. K. (2011). *Africa's Odious Debts: How Foreign Loans and Capital Bled a Continent.* London: Zed Books.

Newman, D. M. 1997. *Sociology: Exploring the Architecture of Everyday Life.*Thousand Oaks, CA: Pine Forge Press.

Nkrumah, Kwame (1973). *Revolutionary Path.*
New York: International Publishers.

_____ (1970). *Africa Must Unite.* NY: International Pub.

Noble, Kenneth B. (1989). "Wheat Rift Splits Nigerians and U.S." *New York Times.* December 31.

Noonan, P. (1993-1994). "Continuing Crisis in African Education." *Africa Recovery.* December-March.

North-South- A Programme for Survival: The Report of the Independent Commission on International Development Issues under the Chairmanship of Willy Brandt. (1980). Cambridge, Mass: The MIT Press.

Nsouli, S. M and Gall, F. Le (2001). "Globalisation and Africa: Overview of the Main Issues." *Finance and Development Quarterly Magazine of the IMF.* Dec.

Nwabuikwu, Paul *et al.* (1989). "Confronting the Economy." *The African Guardian.* June 19

Nwosu, O. (1994). "Economists Re-open Debates on SAP." *The Guardian.* Lagos, Nigeria. March 8

Nye, J. (2002). *The Paradox of American Power: Why the World's Only Superpower Can't Go It Alone.* NY:OUP

Obadina, Tunde (1998). *Africa Recovery.* December.

O'Connor, James (1971). "The Meaning of Economic Imperialism," in K. T. Fan and Donald C. Hodges (eds.), *Readings in U.S. Imperialism.* Boston: Porter Sargent.

Offiong, Daniel A. (2008a). *Secret Cults in Nigeria's Tertiary Institutions.* Lagos: Apex Books Limited.

_____ (2008b). *An Introduction to the Ibibio of Nigeria.* Lagos: Apex Books Limited.

_____ (1983). *Organised Labour and Political Development in Nigeria.* Calabar: Centaur Press.

_____ (1980). *Imperialism and Dependency: Obstacles to African Development*. Enugu, Nigeria: Fourth Dimension Publishers. Reissued by Howard University Press in 1982.

Ogan, Amma. (1993-1994). "Struggle for Child Health in Africa." *Africa Recovery*. December-March.

Ogunkola, E. O., Bankole, A. S. and Adewuyi, A. (2008). "China-Nigeria Economic Relations." Trade Policy Research and Training Prog. (TPRTP). Univ. of Ibadan, Nigeria.

Ogunmefun, Remi (2005). "Legalities in repudiating Nigeria's foreign debt." *This Day*. Lagos, Nigeria. Online.

Oliver, Roland and J. D. Fage. (1975). *A Short History of Africa*. Baltimore: Penguin Books.

Oman, Charles W. (1994). *Globalisation and Regionalisation: The Challenge for Developing Countries*. Paris: Development Centre.

Organisation for Economic Cooperation and Development. (1985). *Twenty-Five Years of Development Cooperation: A Review*. Paris.

Oxfam (2006). "Kicking the Habit: How the World Bank and the IMF are still addicted to Attaching Economic Policy Conditions to Aid." November.

_____ (2002a). *Cultivating Poverty: The Impact of US Cotton Subsidies on Africa*. Oxfam Publication.

_____ (2002b). "Rigged Rules and Double Standards: Trade, Globalisation, and the Fight against Poverty." Online. Retrieved January 5, 2012. www.marketradefair.com

Oxfam (1993). *Africa, Make or Break Action for Recovery*. Oxford: Oxfam Print Series.

Ould-Mey, Mohameden (1996). *Global Restructuring and Peripheral States: The Carrot and the Stick in Mauritania*. Boston Way: Rowman and Littlefield.

Page, Sheila and Hewitt, Adrian (2001). "World Commodity Prices: Still a Problem for Developing Countries?" Overseas Development Institute. London.

Palast, G., O'Kane, M, and Madlena, C. (2012). "Call to shield poor countries from 'vulture debts." OneWorld South Asia. Online. April 9. Retrieved 4-9-12. oneworld.net.

Palley, T. (2006). "Thinking Outside the Box about Trade, Development and Poverty Reduction." Washington, D.C. Foreign Policy Focus. January 17.

Pamberg, Mai (1983). *The Struggle for Africa.* London: Zed.

Parsons, A. W. (2008). "World Bank Poverty Figures: What Do They Mean?" Share The World's Resources.

London, 15th September. info@stwr.org

Parsons, T. (1964). "Levels of Organisation and the Mediation of Social Interaction." *Sociological Inquiry,* 34: 207-220.

_____ (1951). *The Social System.* New York: Macmillan.

Perkins, John (2004). *Confessions of an Economic Hit Man.* San Francisco: Berrett-Koehler Publishers.

Petras, J. and Veltmeyer, H. (2002). *Globalisation Unmasked: Imperialism in the 21st Century.* London: Zed Books.

Polanyi, K. (1944). *The Great Transformation: The Political and Economic Origins of Our Times.* Boston: Beacon Press.

Polaski, S. (2006). "Winners and Losers: Impact of the Doha Round on Developing Countries." Carnegie Endowment Report. Washington, DC. March.

Polgren, L. and French, H. W. (2007). "In Africa, China is Both Benefactor and Competitor." *New York Times.* Aug. 20.

Population Reference Bureau (1993). World Population Data Sheet. Washington, DC.

Portes, A. (1993). "On the Sociology of National Development: Theories and Issues, " in M. A. Seligson and J. T. Passe-

Smith (eds.), *Development and Underdevelopment.*
    Boulder: Lynne Rienner.
Ramsey, B. (2006). "Making Globalisation Work: Nobel
    winner's fresh view on globalisation." Review of Joseph
    E. Stiglitz's *Making Globalisation Work.*
    W. W. Norton and Co., Inc. October 13.
Randel, J. (1996). *Understanding Development: Theory and
    Practice in the Third World. Boulder: Lynne Rienner.*
Rasheed, Sadig and Dele Olowu (eds.) (1993). *Ethics and
    Accountability in African Public Services.*
    Nairobi: African Academy of Sciences.
Ritzer, George (1996). *Modern Sociological Theory.*
    New York: McGraw-Hill.
Rodney, Walter (1972). *How Europe Underdeveloped Africa.*
    London: Bogle-L'Ouverture Publications.
Rodrik, Dani (2002). "Globalisation for whom? Time to change
    the rules – and focus on poor workers.'
    Harvard magazine. Online. July-August.
Rostow, Walt Whitman (1960). *The Stages of Economic Growth:
    A Non-Communist Manifesto.* Cambridge: Cambridge
    University Press.Vol. 15, No.1. January. pp. 75-94.
Ruccio, David F. (2003). "Globalisation and Imperialism."
    Rethinking Marxism.
Ruggles, Patricia (1989). "Short and Long Term Poverty in the
    United States: Measuring the American Underclass."
    Washington, DC: Urban Institute.
Ryan, William (1971). *Blaming the Victim.*
    New York: Vintage Books.
Sachs, Jeffrey D. (2008). "Millennium Goals at the Midpoint:
    Overdue investments from rich nations could still
    transform Africa by 2015." *Scientific America.* August.
Said, Edward (1978). *Orientalism.* New York: Random House.

Sandbrook, Richard (1993). *The Politics of Africa's Economic Recovery.* Cambridge: Cambridge University Press.

_____ (1991). "Economic Crisis, Structural Adjustment and the State in Sub-Saharan Africa." In Dharam Ghai (ed.), *The IMF and the South: The Social Impact of Crisis and Adjustment.* New Jersey: Zed Books.

_____ (1985). *The Politics of Africa's Economic Stagnation.* London: Cambridge University Press.

Sanger, David E. (1997). "The Stock of 'Asian Values' Drops." *New York Times.* November 23

Sanusi, J. (1986). *"The Origins and Nature of African Debt Crisis."* Mimeo. Benin City, Nigeria.

Schnepf, Randy (2009). "Brazil's WTO Case Against the U.S. Cotton Programme: A Brief Review." Congressional Research Service Report for Congress. March 17. _____www.crs.gov

Scholte, Jan Aart (2000). *Globalisation: A Critical Introduction.* London. Macmillan Press.

Seligson, Mitchell A. (2008). "The Dual Gaps: An Overview of Theory and Research," in Seligson, Mitchell A. and Passe-Smith, John T. (eds.), *Development and Underdevelopment: The Political Economy of Global Inequality.* Boulder Co.: Lynne Reinner.

SDC Workshop on Globalisation and Africa Final Report. September 5-6, 2002.

Shafacddin, S. M. (1994). "The Impact of Trade Liberalisation on Export and GDP Growth in Least Developed Countries." UNCTAD *Bulletin.* July-August/September-October

Shagwan, Jagdish and Panagariya, Arvind (2000). *Financial Times of London.* June 29.

Shah, Anup (2010). "Poverty Facts and Stats." Global Issues.
      September. http://www.globalissues.org/article/26/
      povert-facts-and-stats

Shannon, Thomas Richard (1989). *World System Perspective.*
      Boulder: Westview.

Simensen, J. (2011). "Africa: The cause of underdevelopment
      and the challenges of globalisation." Online. May 2.

Skocpol, Theda (1977). "Wallerstein's World Capitalist
      System: A Theoretical and Historical Critique."
      American Journal of Sociology, Vol. 82, pp. 1075-1091.

Slater, R. O. , Schutz, B. M., and Dorr, S. R. (1993). *Global
      Transformation and the Third World.*
      Boulder: Lynne Rienner.

Silvard, Ruth Leger (1988). *World Military and Social
      Expenditures, 1987-88.* Washington, DC: World
      Priorities.

Smith, Patrick (1993-1994). "Aid Conditionality is 'Swamping'
Africa." *Africa Recovery.* December-March.

_____ (1998). *"African Debt Hopes Disappointed.*
      Africa Recovery. November.

South. January 1990; February 1989; September 1985.

Stone, John (1985). *Racial Conflict in Contemporary Society.*
      MA: Harvard University Press.

South Centre (2005). "Commodity Dependence and
      International Commodity Prices." Towards Human
      Resilience: Sustaining MDGs Progress in an Age of
      Economic Uncertainty.

Stiglitz, Joseph (2007). "Making Globalisation Work for
      Developing Countries." Sir Winston Scott Memorial
      Lecture. Central Bank of Barbados.

Streeten, Paul (2001). "Integration, Independence, and
      Globalisation." *Finance Development* (IMF). Vol. 38,
      No.2. June.

Sutcliffe, Robert (2001). "100 Ways of Seeing an Unequal
World. London: Zed Books.

Swingewood, Alan (1993). *A Short History of Sociological
Thought.* New York: Martin Press.

*Transnationals: Quarterly Newsletter of the United Nations
Centre on Transnational Corporations.* July 1993;
Oct. 1992; July 1991; Dec. 1991; and July 1989.

Tupy, Marrian L. (2005). "Poverty that Defies Aid." CATO
Institute. Washington, DC. June 2. cato.org

Tugehat, Christopher (1971). *The Multinationals.*
London: Eyre and Spottiswoode.

Turnbull, Colin (1968). *The Lonely Africa.*
New York: Clarendon.

Tyehimba, Ras (2006). "Globalisation is as old as
Colonialism." *Rasta Times.* May 28.

Ubani, Obinna Ebere (1992). "The Impact of Economic
Austerity and the Structural Adjustment Programme
(EA & SAP) on the Financing of Nigerian Universities,
1976-1990." An unpublished dissertation, Clark
Atlanta University.

Ungar, Sanford J. (1989). *Africa: The People and Politics of
Emerging Continent.* New York: Simon and Schuster.

Ukpong, Ebebe A. (1989). "Training the Small-Scale Farmers:
The Human Resources Approach to Self-Reliance."
Paper presented at the 8th Annual Conference of the
Professors World Peace Academy of Nigeria, Lagos.

UN. (2005). The Report of the World Social Situation 2005:
The Inequality Predicament. UN Publications.

UN Department of Public Information (2005). Press Release
SOC14681. New York. August.

UN. (2003). "Economic Development in Africa: Trade
Performance and Commodity Dependence." United

Nations Conference on Trade and Development,
Geneva.

UNAIDS (2011). "World AIDS Day Report." Online. _____
_____communications@unaids.org

UCSF (2011). "HIV In Site: Sub-Saharan Africa." University of
California, San Francisco.

UNCTAD (2004). "The Least Developed Countries Report:
Linking International Trade with Poverty Reduction."
New York and Geneva.

UNCTAD *Bulletin.* July-August 1993.

UN Economic Commission for Africa (1989). *African
Alternative Framework to Structural Adjustment
Programmes for Socio-Economic Recovery and
Transformation (AAF-SAP).* New York /Addis Ababa.

UNDP (2011). "Discussion Paper, Illicit Financial Flows from
the Least Developed Countries: 1990 – 2008.
New York. May.

UNDP (2009). "About the MDGs: Basics." New York.

United Nations Conference on Trade and Development
(UNCTAD) (1999). Handbook of Trade and
Development Statistics 1996/1997: United Nations.

UNDP Human Development Report (2005). UN Publications.

UNDP (2007). "Making Globalisation Work for the Least
Developed Countries." Istanbul Declaration on Least
Developed Countries: Time for Action.

UNESCO (1993). *World Education Report.*

United Nations (1993). "African Debt Crisis: A Continuing
Impediment to Development." New York.

UN. (1993). *World Investment Report 1993: Transnational
Corporations and Integrated International Production.*
UN Publication (WIR93), New York.

Ukim, Utibe (1994). "In the Boondocks: Prospects for Economic Recovery are Bleak – says the Central Bank of Nigeria." *Newswatch.* November 14, Lagos, Nigeria.

USAID. (2011). "HIV/AIDS Health Profile: Sub-Saharan Africa." Online. http://www.usaid.gov/our Retrieved 4/19/12.

US Senate Permanent Subcommittee on Investigations (2010). "Keeping Foreign Corruption out of the United States. Four Case Histories." Washington, DC. Feb.

U.S. Committee for Refugees (1993). *World Refugee Survey.* Washington, DC.

U.S. Congress (1989). *Structural Adjustment in Africa: Insights from the Experiences of Ghana and Senegal.* Report of a Staff Study Mission to Great Britain, Ghana, Senegal, Cote d' Ivoire, and France, 29 November-20 December 1988. Submitted to the Committee on Foreign Affairs, U.S. House of Representatives.

U.S. Dept of State (1991). *Dispatch,* Vol. 2, No. 37. Sept 16

U.S. Department of State *Bulletin*, August 1980, no. 2041; 6 June, 1977, no. 1980; and 8 Dec. 1975, no. 1902.

Vakhrushev, Vasily (1973). *Neocolonialism: Methods and Manoeuvres.* Moscow: Progress Publishers.

Valenzuela, J. S. and Arturo V. (1978). "Modernisation and Dependency: Alternative Perspectives in the Study of Latin American Underdevelopment." *Comparative Politics,* Vol. 10, pp.543-557.

Waldman, P. (1997). "Crisis Management: 'Asian Values' Concept is ripe for Revision as Economies Falter; the 'Guardian' Status Quo Faces Societal Challenges; Money Spigot is closing, clearing the air in Thailand." *The Wall Street Journal.* Nov 28.

Wall, Tim. (1993-1994). "Ambiguous IMF Review of ESAF Experience." *Africa Recovery.* Dec - March.

Wallbank, T. W., Taylor, A.M., and Bailkey, N.M. (1962). *Civilisation: Past and Present.* Chicago: Scott, Foresman & Co.

Wallerstein, I. (1992). "America and the World: Today, Yesterday and Tomorrow." *Theory and Society,* Vol. 21, pp. 1-28.

_____ (1989). *The Second Era of Great Expansion of the Capitalist World-System, 1730-1840.* New York: Academic Press.

_____ (1986). "Marxism as Utopia: Evolving Ideologies." *American Journal of Sociology, Vol. 91, pp. 1295-1308.*

_____ (1984). *The Politics of World Economy: The States, the Movements, and the Civilisations.* Cambridge: Cambridge University Press.

_____ (1983). "Crises: The World Economy, the Movements, and the Ideologies" in Albert Bergesen (ed.), *Crises in the World-System.* Beverly Hills, CA: Sage. pp. 21-36.

_____ (1980). *The Modern World-System 11: Mercantilism and the Consolidation of the European World-Economy, 1600-1750.* New York: Academic Press.

_____ (1979). *The Capitalist World-Economy.* New York: Cambridge University Press.

_____ (1975). "The Present State of the Debate on World Inequality." Reprinted in M. A. Seligson and John T. Passe-Smith. 1993. *Development and Underdevelopment.* Boulder: Lynne Rienner.

_____ (1974). *The Modern World System: Capitalist Agriculture and the Origins of the European World-Economy in the Sixteenth Century.* New York: Academic Press.

Veltmeyer, Henry (2001). "Development and Globalisation as Imperialism." *Canadian Journal of Development Studies.* Vol. XXV1, No. 1. pp.89-106.

Weber, Max (1958). *The Protestant Ethic and the Spirit of Capitalism.* New York: Scriners.

Weeks, John (2011). "John Weeks Reviews: Africa's Odious Debts" - by Leonce Ndikumana and James K. Boyce. African Arguments. London. October 5.

Weiissman, R. (2012). "The Summers of our Discontent." CounterPunch. Pretolia, California. March 21. Online. Retrieved 3-22-12. counterpunch@counterpunch.org

Wikipedia, the Free Encyclopedia 2010. "Structural Adjustment." Online. Retrieved 4-22—2010.

Woddis, Jack (1961). *Africa: The Lion Awakes. London: Lawrence and Wishart.*

_____ (1967). *Introduction to Neo-Colonialism.* London: Lawrence and Wishart.

Wolf, Eric R. (1982). *Europe and the People Without History.* Berkeley: University of California Press.

World Bank and IMF(2011). "Global Monitoring Report: Improving the Odds of Achieving MDGs Heterogeneity, Gaps and Challenges: Overview." Wash, DC. April 16.

World Bank (2009). "Global Monitoring Report 2009." Washington, DC.

_____ (2005). "Global Monitoring Report 2005." Wash, DC.

_____ (2003). *World Development Report.* New York: OUP.

_____ (1996). *El Salvador: Meeting the Challenge of Globalisation.* Washington, DC.

_____ (1990). *World Development Report.* Wash, DC.

_____ (1989). *Sub-Saharan Africa: From Crisis to Sustainable Growth.* Washington, DC.

_____ (1994). *Learning from the Past, Embracing the Future.* New York. July 19.

_____ (1994). *World Development Report.*

_____ (1992). "Adjustment Lending and Mobilisation of Private and Public Resources for Growth." New York.

_____ (1992). "Adjustment Lending and Economic Performance in Sub-Saharan Africa in the 1980s: A Comparative Performance with other Low-income Countries." World Bank Paper WPS 1000. New York.

_____ (1990). *Islamic Republic of Mauritania Structural Adjustment Programme: Completion Report.* Washington, DC.

Worsely, Peter (1967). *The Third World.* Chicago: The University of Chicago Press.

Yansane, Aguibou Y. (1980). *Decolonisation and Dependency: Problems of Development of African Societies.* Westport, Connecticut: Greenwood Press.

_____ (1967). *Introduction to Neo-Colonialism.* London: Lawrence and Wishart.

Wolf, Eric R. (1982). *Europe and the People Without History.* Berkeley: University of California Press.

World Bank and IMF(2011). "Global Monitoring Report: Improving the Odds of Achieving MDGs Heterogeneity, Gaps and Challenges: Overview." Wash, DC. April 16.

World Bank (2009). "Global Monitoring Report 2009." Washington, DC.

_____ (2005). "Global Monitoring Report 2005." Wash, DC.

_____ (2003). *World Development Report.* New York: OUP.

_____ (1996). *El Salvador: Meeting the Challenge of Globalisation.* Washington, DC.

_____ (1990). *World Development Report.* Wash, DC.

_____ (1989). *Sub-Saharan Africa: From Crisis to Sustainable Growth.* Washington, DC.

_____ (1994). *Learning from the Past, Embracing the Future.* New York. July 19.

_____ (1994). *World Development Report.*

_____ (1992). "Adjustment Lending and Mobilisation of Private and Public Resources for Growth." New York.

_____ (1992). "Adjustment Lending and Economic Performance in Sub-Saharan Africa in the 1980s: A Comparative Performance with other Low-income Countries." World Bank Paper WPS 1000. New York.

_____ (1990). *Islamic Republic of Mauritania Structural Adjustment Programme: Completion Report.* Washington, DC.

Worsely, Peter (1967). *The Third World.* Chicago: The University of Chicago Press.

Yansane, Aguibou Y. (1980). *Decolonisation and Dependency: Problems of Development of African Societies.* Westport, Connecticut: Greenwood Press.

Index

Abdusalami Abubakar, 163
Academic Staff Union of Universities, 182
Action Aid, 74
AEFJN, 107
Africa's odious debts, 120, 121, 122
Africa Recovery, 134, 135, 140, 159, 168, 177, 192
AGOA, 110, 112, 113
AIDS, 188, 189, 190
Atiku Abubakar, 239, 240
Angola case history, 240

Barack Obama, 80
Benjamin Mkapa, 253
Boutrous, Boutrous-Ghali, 124, 205
British Parliament, 43, 247
Bunwaree, 1, 2

Canadian Council of Churches, 188
CFA Franc, 170, 171

China, 9, 115, 118
Central Intelligence Agency, 89
Cotton, 4, 104, 111
Cotton subsidies, 103

Debt relief, 136
Dependency
- *neo-dependency,* 142
-*new dependency,* 142
-*post neo-dependency,* 142
DFID, 65
Direct Foreign Investment, 2, 4, 117, 126, 232
Double Standards Index, 97

Economic Commission for Africa, 211
Economic interdependence, 16
Fairtrade, 106
Food and Agricultural Organisation, 64
Frantz Fanon, *v*
Functional alternatives, 90

G-8 summit, 153

Gatekeeper states, *40*
GATT, *69, 167*
GFI, *219, 225*
Global Exchange, *195, 196*
Globalisation, *5, 6, 7, 8, 11, 14, 18, 19, 22, 49*
Globaphiles, *96, 262*
Globaphobes, *96, 262*

Hawala, *222*
Hazardous wastes, *82, 83*
HIPCS, *132,139, 149*
Hot money method, *221*
Human Development
    Report, *26, 92*

IDRC, *185*
IFAD, *57, 58, 101*
International
Development
Association, *138*

Jennifer Douglas, *239*
Joseph Stiglitz, *22, 23, 101, 250, 257*

Karl Marx, *vi*
Koffi Annan, *250*

Legal flight capital, *221*

Liberalisation, *19, 39, 101, 163*
Lome Convention, *70*
London Club, *122, 123*

Madunagu, *5*
Millennium
    Development
    Goals, *v, 1, 149, 227, 260, 263, 266*
Mohammed Farah
    Aideed, *81*
Modernisation, *5*

OECD, *69, 72*
Official   Development
Assistancce, *5, 7, 72, 219*
Okonjo-Iweala, Ngozi, *124, 269*
Omar Bongo, *238, 239*
Organisation of
    Petroluem
    Exporting
    Countries, *30*
Over-development, *77*
Oxfam, *94, 95, 106, 107, 110, 197*

Paris Club, *122, 123, 129, 163*
Politically Exposed

Persons, *236*
Poverty - *absolute, 51*
   - *extreme, 51*
   - *relative, 51*
Privatisation, *39, 163*

Robin Hood, *v, 44, 108*

Sahara desert, *33*
Slave trade, *34*
Stolen Asset Recovery
   Initiative, *242*
Structural Adjustment
   Facility, *172*
Structural Adjustment
   Programmes, *46,
   147, 151, 152, 157,
   162, 202*
Sub-Saharan Africa, *7,
   50, 54*
Swiss Agency for
   Development and
   Cooperation, *3*

Teodoro, Nguema
   Obiang, *237, 238*
The Heritage
   Foundation, *47*
The Treasure Island, *v*
Third World Network,
   100
Toronto Economic

Summit, *129*
Trade misinvoicing, *223*
Trade mispricing, *227,
   230, 231, 235, 267*
Transnationals, *82, 83,
   143*
Transnational
   corporations, *95,
   144*
Triumphalist
   Juggernaut, *7, 248*

UNECA, *150*
UNCTAD, *66, 166, 176*
Underdevelopment, *77*
UNDP, *92*
UNICEF, *50, 138, 139*
United Nations, *vi*
UNODC, *243*

Vulture capitalism, *243,
   244*
Vulture funds, *243, 244,
   246*
World Health
   Organsation, *61,
   64*
World Bank, *39, 46, 54,
   72, 89, 204*
World Development
   Series, *154*
World Education

Report, *178*
World Social Situation
    Report, *27, 28, 93*
World Trade
    Organisation,   *9,*
    10, 48, 94